I0235062

FALLEN SPARROWS: THE INTERNATIONAL BRIGADES IN THE SPANISH CIVIL WAR

FALLEN SPARROWS:
THE INTERNATIONAL BRIGADES IN THE SPANISH CIVIL WAR

Michael Jackson

American Philosophical Society
Independence Square • Philadelphia

MEMOIRS OF THE
AMERICAN PHILOSOPHICAL SOCIETY

*Held at Philadelphia
For Promoting Useful Knowledge
Volume 212*

Library of Congress Catalog Card Number 94–71672
International Standard Book Number 0-87169-212-0
US ISSN 0065-9738

Dedicated to KVB:
then, now, always.

Are not two sparrows sold for a farthing? And one of them shall not fall to the ground without your Father.

Matthew 10, 29

Contents

Tables

Illustrations

Cover: These Internationals have seen action. They are smiling for the camera, but their faces suggest this is a souvenir for friends and relatives who may never see them again. Look at the two standing on the right or the man with the cap on kneeling. There is irony and detachment. The man on the left bending forward looks sad. It is reproduced in *The Spanish Civil War: A History in Pictures* (New York: Norton, 1986) on page 141.

Figure 1. Inverse Pyramid of Literature on the International Brigades, p. 28.

Figure 2. War as glamor, a single handsome and youthful individual strikes an idealized pose. The man is Juan Modesto (a Republican military leader of early note). This picture was widely published in Spain and abroad. Its image of the dramatic individual would have been known to many in the International Brigades, and so perhaps set a standard for them. It is reproduced in Hugh Tomes, *The Spanish Civil War* (Rev ed) (New York: Harper, 1977), p. 464.

Figure 3. This is perhaps the most famous picture from a war that generated many famous pictures. It has a title, 'Muerte en accieón' (Death in Action). We can be confident it was staged. It is by Robert Capa. The man does not look like an International Brigader from his uniform, but his image was well known to many of them. It appeared in *Life.*

Figure 4. A man carries a wounded comrade up a mountain road. Another Robert Capa picture from *Life* and it, too, looks staged. I reproduced it from Tomas Salvador, *La Guerra de España en sus Fotografias* (Barcelona: Ediciones Madrid, 1966), p. 222.

Figure 5. Defeat and retreat in the snow after the brutal battle at Teruel in the bitter cold of February 1938. These are Republicans climbing out of the valley, an escape only possible because the bad weather limited the Nationalist air force. It is reproduced from Vincente Rójo, *España Heroica* (3d ed) (Barcelona: Ariel, 1975 [1942]), p. 96.

Figure 6. A group of severely wounded Internationals awaiting repatriation. The one-armed man is placed carefully in the center to show his loss. It is reproduced in *The Spanish Civil War: A History in Pictures* (New York: Norton, 1986) on page 90, 173.

Figure 7. Marching through the streets of Madrid. These men are not armed or uniformed. The small number of spectators show no enthusiasm (at upper left or across the street on the right). This must have been a memorable occasion for the marchers, giving what was probably a full-throated rendition of the 'Internationale.' It is reproduced from Hugh Tomes *et al., La Guerra Civil Española* (Madrid: Ediciones Urbion, 1980), Volume II, p. 365.

Figure 8. This is an action photograph that looks less staged than most. The closer man has an arm patch which looks like the Saint George Cross (which would make him English). It is clearer in the photograph than the photocopy. The other man has on a helmet that looks French from this angle. Reproduced from Ricardo de la Cierva, *Historia ilustrada de la guerra civil España* (Madrid: Danae, 1970), p. 27.

Figures 2 - 8 begin after page 66

Preface

On my first sabbatical leave, I took a reading vacation for the first four weeks, perusing what I liked. One of my subjects was the Spanish Civil War. It had loomed large in the literature I read during my formative, undergraduate years. The plays, novels, stories, and poetry of Ernest Hemingway, André Malraux, and George Orwell, among others, were dark with the shadow of the Spanish Civil War. Consequently, it also figured in the minds of the teachers whom I admired. It had long been a subject about which I wanted to know more.

When my reading vacation began, I knew that the Spanish Civil War was a good story and an important event. I also knew that something called the International Brigades existed. I was also vaguely aware that Stalinism was relevant. When the time came, I read a shelf of books, starting with that redoubtable classic *The Spanish Civil War* by Hugh Thomas.

Even the most general books devoted a chapter to the International Brigades. The many brief and superficial accounts stimulated me to pursue books on them. These I found to be in short supply. Further, I found that they often re-told the same basic story, leaving many basic facts unreported. Finally, I found that there were few scholarly works on the International Brigades, though those that exist are very valuable.

I emerged from this avocational study of the International Brigades with many questions. How many foreigners went to Spain? Who were they? Why did they go? How did they get along with Spaniards? What were the relationships among the foreigners, especially those of different national and political stripes? And many more.

Other projects took priority, but I sometimes found myself in circumstances where I could pursue questions about the International Brigades. No one else had answered them, and, indeed, it seemed that many people did not think them important. If they were to be answered I would have to do it myself. I found myself with a new project. So powerful was the call, that I also found my other scholarly pursuits in the political theory of justice were influenced by my impressions of the world the International Brigaders lived in and made for themselves.

I had read Hannah Arendt's *The Human Condition* in graduate school, to the regret of my supervisor, and I saw something of the hero she imagined in the men of the International Brigades. They were as weak, querulous, and unattractive as the antique heroes that her typewriter conjured from ancient Greece, but like those heroes the men of the International Brigades had recognized the moment to act, and had acted. It was now the responsibility of observers, especially those of us who are paid to do so, to reflect upon their action.

Mine may not be the most important questions to ask about the International Brigades, but they are pertinent. Not all of my questions have been answered in these pages. But some of them have been and I have shown how the answers arrived. Where an answer cannot be given with confidence I have detailed the problem and drawn a heavily qualified conclusion. Many of even the most basic questions, like how many foreign volunteers served in the International Brigades, cannot be documented. There are both conceptual and empirical difficulties in the question, and these are explained in the text, but there is also a larger constraint that needs to be explained.

Studying the International Brigades is sometimes as tedious and tendentious as detective work. A shred of evidence sustains a house of inferences; alternatively a rank of assumptions must be paraded before a fragment of evidence can be seen. It is not one of those Agatha Christie mysteries where there is someone who knows all the answers, but refuses to tell, or has gone into hiding, or destroyed the vital evidence. Rather it is that other kind of mystery where no one really knows the answers to the naive questions posed. Moreover, as I discovered with further investigation, most of those involved did not want to know these simple things. Too much was at stake, many of them must have thought, to be tied down to facts and figures, or to take the time to probe the human reality. Better to shape the truth through slogans and stereotypes, and to inflate or deflate facts as opportune. Ignorance freed and fed the imagination.

No one can overcome the deficiencies in the historical record, and I fear I have made my own mistakes. In some cases, I have had enough sense not even to try. Where I have tried and failed, my hope was to treat the elusive and illusory record with attention and respect.

I came to this study without a personal stake. Though I have since met some International Brigaders, I knew none when I started this work. Nor did I come to it with an ideological conviction that the defenders of the Spanish Republic had a monopoly on virtue. While my investigations have concentrated on the Republican side of the Spanish Civil War, I realized that their Nationalist opponents were flesh of their flesh, and not the monsters portrayed in the propaganda of the time, which has been too long perpetuated. If there are those who have seen the Spanish Civil War from the Nationalist perspective among the readers of this book, perhaps they might also see that their enemies in the International Brigades were but mortals, too.

Many acknowledgments are due. The most important is first: a sabbatical leave from the University of Sydney made this study possible. Tenure as a visiting fellow at the Hoover Institution in Stanford, California, provided the initial opportunity to do research on the subject. Additional investigations were conducted in the New York City Public Library, the International Institute for Social History in Amsterdam, the Zentralbibliothek Zürich, the British Museum, the Bibliothèque Nationale in Paris, Brandeis University Library, the Library of Congress, and the Toronto Public Library. Much progress was made while a visiting fellow at the Netherlands Institute for Advanced Study. The manuscript was completed while I was Merril Endowment Visiting Professor at Utah State University. Librarians at these institutions and others, most especially at the University of Sydney, contributed much to this study. I thank them one and all. With pleasure, I acknowledge the counsel, assistance, and encouragement of my colleagues Fred Teiwes, John Ravenhill, Graeme Gill, Terry Irving, Judith Keene, Michael Hogan and Bob Miller. The opportunity to present a paper at a conference sponsored by Siena College first forced me to organize some material in writing. I am grateful to Thomas O. Kelly and his colleagues for their efforts in organizing all of the World War II conferences, but particularly this one. Liz Kirby and Lyn Fisher tracked down many strange requests, while Lynne Thomson and John Robinson made computers work for and not against me. Shereen Mathews effectively keyed in the main body of the text from a cryptic and confused typescript when the transition to the new technology was made. Debbie Gessaman wielded a firm blue pencil on the manuscript. Rebecca Simmonds supported the project in many ways, mostly by moral support, but also by securing the hardware.

Most important, though, were the International Brigaders themselves. Their books, letters, diaries, and memoirs produced the odd feeling that somehow I had friends among them. That feeling kept the project going even when there was much competition for attention on the agenda.

CHAPTER 1

Introduction

Invisible, man-killing gun-fire pinned Harold Smith to the iron-hard Spanish earth at Brunete in the searing heat of July 1937. Later he said he had thought to himself:

> The unanswerable logic that had brought him across the sea to Spain did not appear at this moment. The slogans . . . were not on his lips . . . . There was no conscious decision but he knew he would not turn back. His decision had been made before.[1]

He had earlier made a personal declaration of war in going to Spain to fight in the International Brigades. So did thousands of others.

The International Brigades emerged during the Spanish Civil War. They were made up of men who went to Spain to fight in the civil war for the Spanish Republic. Though estimates vary greatly, by the time the civil war ended about 36,000 foreigners had served in the International Brigades, 32,000 of them men in the ranks.

There were many resident foreigners and visitors in Republican Spain when the civil war began, and some of them were the first foreigners to contribute to the Republic's defense. Others rushed to Spain at the start of the conflict. For a year and a half men were actively recruited from around the world to serve in Spain. Most of those foreigners who fought for the Republic served in the International Brigades.

The first occasion when these foreigners attracted attention was during the defense of Madrid in November 1936. They paraded through the city streets, armed and uniformed, to take up important positions in the University City on the outskirts, where they bore the brunt of the fighting. When the Nationalist attack dwindled in the winter of 1936-1937, much publicity credited the International Brigades with saving Madrid.

Five brigades were designated "International." During the rigors and confusion of the campaign, military units appear and disappear. This was as true of the International Brigades as of any other armed force. Where possible they were kept together in groups with a common language, but given the number of languages this was not possible for the Balkans, the Dutch, and Scandinavians. Besides the five brigades called International, there were also three other formations of International volunteers in the infantry. Table (1) offers a summary of the organization of the International Brigades.

The 150th Brigade consisted of two battalions, the norm being four, and one of them was transferred to the 13th International Brigade. The 129th International Brigade was an effort to re-group those from central Europe and the Balkans. It comprised Czechoslovakians, Bulgarians, Yugoslavians, and Albanians. These men are least known in Western Europe; some have published books but these have not been translated into Western European languages. Quite probably, few of them survived the Spanish Civil War. Perhaps one result of changes in Eastern Europe in the 1990s will be opportunities for some of their history to reach wider audiences.

By and large the International Brigades served together as a single force. When Republican Spain was divided by the successful Nationalist drive to the Mediterranean in 1938, however, the International Brigades were also divided.

Table 1.
Summary of the Organization of the International Brigades

Brigade	Date Formed	Main Language
11th	October 1936	German
12th	November 1936	Italian
13th	December 1936	French
14th	December 1936	French
15th	February 1937	English
150th	July 1937	Hungarian
129th	July 1937	Balkan
86th	Contained an international battalion.	

Source: Hugh Thomas, *The Spanish Civil War*, pp. 968-969.

The first International Brigade consisted mainly of Germans, but even from the start there were English, Italians, and others present. Italians quickly increased in number and constituted a second brigade. Two brigades were French-speaking and the language of the last was English; other international units were made up of central Europeans, Poles, Czechs, Slovaks, Hungarians, and others. The International Brigades existed between November 1936 and March 1938 when the League of Nations supervised their repatriation.

While they were under arms the International Brigades were deployed by the Republican general staff. Apart from the defense of Madrid, they participated in every offensive until disbanded, usually as the first units to assault the enemy, the shock troops. The original plan for the Republican offensive at the Ebro River had called for withholding the International Brigades so that the Republic could claim to be fighting its own battle, but when the offensive stalled the Internationals had to be sent in. After the repatriation, the ranks of the International Brigades filled with Spaniards as the Republic prepared for the apocalypse. But many foreign volunteers still remained in Spain, some in International Brigades while others were scattered in smaller units.

The men of the International Brigades were recruited from Europe, North America, and elsewhere by the Communist International, the Comintern, and its front and allied organizations. The Comintern turned its powerful propaganda forces toward the Spanish conflict, drawing it to attention and rendering it a powerful drama. Those moved by this drama found that it was possible to go to Spain to contribute materially, and many did. The Comintern organized their journeys, paying fares for those who had to travel by ship or train, providing hotel accommodations at a rendezvous such as Paris, and arranging for the frontier crossing by hiring guides or bribing guards or a prudent combination of the two.

The International Brigades established a headquarters in Albacete, a remote town about 150 miles from Madrid. When recruitment increased, foreign volunteers were channeled there. Those who entered Spain of their own volition were directed there by Spanish authorities. Those who entered under the auspices of the Comintern were taken directly there.

André Marty, a French Communist, whose party could spare him for foreign service, ran the base at Albacete. His military fame was as a naval mutineer in World War I. At Albacete he seems to have been a law unto himself. The foreigners who collected at Albacete were anxious for the fight, but they often waited there for weeks, occasionally subjected to ideological harangues on the perfidy of the enemy—who often seemed to be Trotsky, not the fascism that moved so many of the volunteers, nor the Spanish Nationalists. When a sufficient number of men had arrived at Albacete, they were formed into units and dispatched to the International Brigades in the lines. At times of crisis small groups of newly arrived volunteers were herded into trucks and driven straight into a battle.

Convenience of communication and command required that the basic units speak the same language. In time, each of the brigades had a dominant language, as indicated above, though there were many occasions when the languages were mixed, with confusion the result. Communication in Spanish with the Republican army was always difficult. First there was the language barrier. Second, many Spaniards distrusted the foreign intrusion.

Many of the men who made their way to Spain to take part in the International Brigades were confirmed Stalinists for whom bourgeois democracy was a hollow shell. Their primary enemy was fascism, and they were the hammers of communism's world revolution. Since bourgeois democrats also opposed fascism, a temporary alliance was possible. Fearing a confrontation with fascism, Soviet leaders moved to a Popular Front policy that concentrated on the common enemy of fascism. The antagonism of Communists for Socialists, democrats, and liberals was not diluted, but veiled.

On this point communist theory and the interest of the Soviet Union departed. Stalin supposed that if a European conflict was to come, far better for it to be in distant Spain than closer to the Soviet Union. When the civil war began, the prospect of supplying Republican Spain with moral and material support sufficed to shift attention to Iberia. At the end of the civil war when all of the Republicans but the most die-hard Communists wanted to cease hostilities, one suspects that Stalin's view was that the continuation of the civil war served the interest of the Soviet Union. Viewed from the Kremlin a long, terrible war confined to Iberia might bring Germany and Italy into collision with England and France, leaving the Soviet Union on the sidelines, free to chart its own course. World revolution would have to wait.

Accordingly, the Comintern in Paris was charged with promoting interest in the Spanish Civil War. To do so, its powerful propaganda machine was set in motion. It produced striking posters, photographs, and slogans. Meanwhile, individuals had already suggested an international column as a vehicle for propaganda. These suggestions were stimulated by the observation that some foreigners were already taking part in the Republican struggle, while others were going to Spain to do so.

There were many foreigners in Spain, both Nationalist and Republican. The foreigners in Republican Spain were not all in the designated International Brigades. On this point, more will be said later.

Italian Socialists, German and French Communists, Belgian and Welsh miners presented themselves to the Republic. Republican officials were disinclined to accept the services offered, until it became clear that Soviet good will and aid depended in part on doing so.

* * *

This book is an attempt to peel off some of the layers of myth that have obscured the International Brigades. These myths concern factual questions of their number, nation, class, age, and political affiliations; others concern the meaning of their commitment. The truth is that the International Brigades were both more complex and simpler than portrayed in propaganda, myth, or history: more complex because the men in the ranks were far more varied than any ideology can accommodate and simpler because they had the universal experience of war. The significance of the International Brigades lies less in the ideological convictions that recruited (some of) them than in the labor of their endurance once there. In one part, the goal of this book is iconoclastic; to expose some of the mythology. Another goal is interpretative, to draw out some of the significance of the International Brigaders. In this it is no more original than were the experiences of the men of the International Brigades.

What follows is an extended reflection upon the acts and experiences of these men of the International Brigades. Chapter Two provides a brief overview of the Spanish Civil War, while Chapter Three locates the volunteers in the moral environment of the 1930s. Such an interpretation can be no better than the information on the nature and character of the men. Consequently, Chapter Four examines the motivations of the foreign volunteers, through their own testimony and what we know of their circumstances and of the history of the times. Two themes are pursued. The first is that the volunteers were marginal men produced by economic and political upheavals of the time. The second, related, theme is that they reacted, as others did in different ways, to the moral incoherence of their world, as explained in Chapter Three. Volunteers each made a personal declaration of war in going to Spain, taking the sovereign's right to declare war.

The subjective information of Chapter Four tells something of the men's minds, though that knowledge must be founded on an understanding of their objective characteristics as well. Chapter Five surveys the most obvious yet elusive objective aspect of the International Brigades, that is, how many international volunteers were there? Conceptual, empirical, and political problems exist in estimating their number. No less difficult is establishing their social identity in Chapter Six, starting with their nationalities. Incomplete evidence on their ages and class background is also examined, together with their political affiliations. It is apparent from the outset that our knowledge of these men is none too sound. Since no single source is authoritative, many sources have to be evaluated to arrive at the best estimates. If the arrival is without surprise, the trip is instructive.

Once knowledge of the volunteers has been clarified, Chapter Seven examines the justifications given at the time for founding the International Brigades. R. Dan Richardson has convincingly argued that the Comintern, acting on instructions from the Kremlin, pressured the Republican government to accept the idea.[2] He has also explained that many key individuals in the Comintern and the Kremlin, as well as others within Republican Spain, saw advantages in a Comintern army. A ready-made weapon at hand without local loyalties might be needed to strike one's enemies, especially those ostensibly on the same side. This had appeal. Neither the Republican government nor the Comintern could broadcast these private, internecine reasons for forming the International Brigades. Instead, several other public justifications were explicitly and implicitly promoted. Among them were three that have been at the center of many myths about the International Brigades, so effective was the Comintern propaganda. These three must be treated separately to get beyond myth to more of the reality of the International Brigades. Even historians committed to debunking the myths of the International Brigades sometimes accept the truth of some of these public justifications with little or no examination, as though they were descriptions of what happened. Word has become deed in the mythology of the International Brigades.

The **first** justification was that the volunteers would be veterans who would fight until replaced by a new popular army to defend the Republic. The **second** was that these veteran volunteers would serve as a model of martial discipline to that new army. The **third** was that they would also be moral exemplars of commitment to the anti-Fascist cause, which was the rallying cry of Socialists, Communists, liberals, and democrats in Spain and around the world. As we shall see, the first two justifications fail, but the third remains, though it must be considerably revised.

Chapter Eight concludes by re-evaluating the moral meaning of the foreign volunteers, emphasizing that it was political dying. The conclusion is based on the testimony and experiences of the men themselves. Once in Spain, once the firing began, once the skin began to tear, once the bones began to break, the overwhelming fact was that they were soldiers, not that they had an ideology or had volunteered. Their experiences under fire were those of the universal soldier. Chapter Nine is a short epilogue.

The bibliography is not exhaustive. Fifty nations were represented in the ranks of the International Brigades, almost as many as participated in the Berlin Olympics in 1936. The men in the ranks spoke 20 languages or more; one veteran noted 18 languages alone within one of the International Brigades, probably not counting Spanish. No wonder Verle Johnson referred to the Tower of Babel in the title of his book about the International Brigades. Surviving veterans have doubtlessly written of their experiences in every major European language and more. Insofar as their stories inspired the historians of their nations, an historical literature on the International Brigades has been written in each of these languages. Most of that secondary literature has been published in English, French, Spanish, Italian, and German. The research for this study concentrated on these languages as listed above. A few Russian, Dutch, and other sources were also examined.

The propensity to write of their experiences does not seem to have fallen evenly across all nationalities. Despite the large number of French-speaking volunteers, they have published little primary literature, while Italian, English, and German survivors left more first-hand accounts. This variation in national literature is partly a result of the nature and experiences of the International Brigades, as will be shown.

If the preceding paragraphs outline what is included in this study, what is excluded must also be stated. There are three important parts of the story of the International Brigades that have already been fully treated. First is the organization of the International Brigades. The role of the Comintern in recruiting the International Brigades and in providing the officer corps is readily available. For the purposes at hand, as individuals these cadres come within the ambit of this study. They were ordered to Spain in an inner-party conscription by the Comintern (to be officers), they were not volunteers, though some had volunteered before receiving their orders. Their number can only be estimated, not extracted from quantitative information about the International Brigades. Moreover, some of these cadres left written accounts that must be used because no source can be dismissed out of hand when a paucity of information exists.

Second is a description of the military campaigns of the International Brigades. These are readily available in the general accounts of the military conflict. Many come "to the reading of History, with an affection much like that of the People in Rome, who came to the Spectacle of the Gladiators, with no more delight to behold their blood, than their Skill in Fencing," as Thomas Hobbes once admitted.[3] It is still commonplace for undergraduate courses in world politics to be dominated by men attracted by the guns and rockets they perceive in international politics. Perhaps this study will seem less easy to read shorn of the romantic element otherwise inevitably produced by a narrative history of the combat of the International Brigades, but the result will be a slightly cooler and clearer perspective on what the foreign volunteers did and how little is known of them. If anywhere, truth lies at the margins, often in the shadows. Understanding is like developing photographs; the raw material is there on the negative. The developer must choose the appropriate quality and size paper and then mix in a blend of chemicals gradually to reveal the latent image. Those who use the International Brigades to prove some point add a distinctive blend of chemicals that enhance part of the picture while distorting the whole composition.

The third and final omission is the international diplomacy that finally led the Republican government to make a gesture by withdrawing the foreign volunteers of the International Brigades, hoping to use world opinion to pressure the Nationalists to reciprocate by sending home their German and Italian allies. Though these intrigues decided the fate of the spear carriers in the ranks of the International Brigades, it is unlikely that any consideration of their best interests informed the deliberations. By that time, the soldiers in the ranks of International Brigades were truly pawns in the game. The international context of the Spanish Civil War only provides a backdrop to this study.

ENDNOTES

1. Harold Smith, "Action at Brunete," *The Heart of Spain*, ed. Alvah Bessie (New York: Veterans of the Abraham Lincoln Brigade, 1952), 187.
2. R. Dan Richardson, *Comintern Army: The International Brigades and the Spanish Civil War* (Lexington: University Press of Kentucky, 1952).
3. Thomas Hobbes, *Hobbes's Thucydides*, ed. Richard Schlatter (New Brunswick: Rutgers University Press, 1975), 8.

CHAPTER 2

The Beginning

Nowhere do events
correspond less to man's
expectations than in war.
Livy, History of Rome

At 4:20 P.M. of 17 July 1936, parts of the Spanish Army rebelled against the constitutional government of the Spanish Republic, unwittingly bringing about the Spanish Civil War. This chapter briefly traces the background to the Spanish Civil War and discusses the emergence of the International Brigades, along with first impressions of some of them.

1. The Uprising

After centuries of monarchy, Spain experienced an uncertain period of autocratic rule from 13 September 1923 to 14 April 1931 when the Second Republic was proclaimed. A Center-Right coalition won an election in which few understood or were committed to the democratic process. In turn, this government lost a popular election to a government of the left on 16 February 1936. Understanding of and commitment to democracy had not greatly increased. The world economic depression, together with the competition of the great powers, added to the crisis atmosphere in Madrid and throughout Spain. The night of 17–18 July became "La noche de los generales" (The night of the generals), a[1] night that lasted three years. In the first 24 hours of the rebellion, the greatest problem for all concerned must have been information. Both the rebels and the government scrambled to ascertain the scope of the uprising. Such an event had long been rumored. Spain then had no king who could uphold the constitution while remaining aloof, as Juan Carlos has done in the face of another restive Spanish Army.

The telephone was crucial as the rebels and the government contacted one military installation after another demanding that the garrison declare itself for the rebellion or for the government. Inside most garrisons, opinion divided between those who wanted to join the insurgents, those who opposed them, and the prudent who wanted to wait and see. Despite the outcome, those who wanted to wait and see may well have been in a majority. Nonetheless, many military garrisons declared for the rebellion. However, some of these were overwhelmed by leftist militants. Militants ended the émeute at the Montaña barracks in Madrid in a blood bath that was grotesque at the time, but events soon surpassed this horror many times over. Elsewhere, officers of different persuasions shot it out, if not individually then in small groups. Sometimes the men under their command looked on, or at other times they took part. Many in the army swung to the rebellious officers in the first two days, but enough of the army remained uncommitted if not enthusiastically loyal to convince the government to retain its position. The sanguine realized that many such storms had been weathered in the past.

No doubt the rebels had hoped instantly to win complete support from the whole army and much of the civilian population, forcing the government to resign or even to flee in disgrace. It would have been over in 48 hours with little or no bloodshed. For its part, the government must have hoped, once the rebellion occurred, that a steadfast refusal to capitulate would cause this latest example in a long line of loosely organized military malcontents to break up. Both sides must have expected the matter would be over in days when the other collapsed. Each underestimated the tenacity of the other this time.

The division of opinion between the rebels and the Republic was too even to make either side the winner. Each was too weak to deliver a decisive blow. Though it was claimed at the time, and repeatedly claimed since, that all or most of the army swung to the rebels, scant evidence supports such a conclusion, an example of the propaganda of the time becoming history for many people.[2]

Time was needed to marshal and mobilize strength. Though lines of communication for both the rebels and the government were unreliable, serious military operations began quickly. In this, the rebels had one great advantage over the government—they had a target, Madrid. General Emilio Mola, a leader of the plot, moved from the north to within 40 miles of the capital. Meanwhile, General Francisco

Franco, another of the key participants, launched an attack on Madrid from the south. At the outset, many people must have supposed that this would be a repetition of the aborted military uprising of August 1932, or at worst a recurrence of the days of street fighting in October 1934. Informed of the military uprising, the president of the Republic dismissed the subject by saying "I'm going to bed."[3]

Franco had earlier been commander of the Army of Africa in Spanish Morocco where the Spanish had long been in conflict with native tribes while cooperating and competing with the French in the Protectorate. He was a very experienced and widely respected field commander. Much of the Army of Africa consisted of Moors recruited from North Africa, and of a foreign legion, called the Tercio, recruited from Europe and the Americas, as well as Spain. Franco had begun his combat career in the Tercio. Since neither the Moors nor the legionnaires were thought to have any loyalty to the Republic and were thought willing mercenaries in search of booty, they figured prominently in the rebels' plans. Much of the small Army of Africa was speedily transported across the Straits of Gibraltar by aircraft of the German air force. While military bases around Spain fought out their own civil wars before siding with the rebels or the government, Franco returned from exile in the Canary Islands, resumed command of the Army of Africa, and set out for Madrid. The chief architect of the plot, General Mola, planned to decapitate the Republic symbolically by seizing Madrid and, if possible, functionally by seizing the Republican government. The aim was a campaign of a few weeks at most. Communication, supply, and organization of the rebel army were all *ad hoc*. There were diversions, like the relief of the Alcazar in Toledo, which were politically and symbolically important but delayed strategic gains. The weather and terrain were factors. Supply was difficult only where it was not impossible. The pace slowed. Discipline was difficult to maintain. Most of all, Franco's caution meant that the vanguard of the rebel army took three months to arrive before Madrid although it had encountered no serious military obstacle in its progress. As Franco approached, the Republican government promptly fled, as if according to the script, but the rebels found that Madrid was not ready to capitulate. Evidently, the rebel generals had their own ambitions, for there was little strategic cooperation among them. As colleagues often are, they were rivals. Indeed, another two years would pass before the rebels, who by then called themselves the Nationalists, would enter exhausted and depleted Madrid in triumph, a bare six months before the start of World War II. Like much of the Spanish Civil War, the surrender of Madrid was perceived by many participants and observers as a battle between

Communists and anti–Communists. In the last act, the Communists were those who wished to continue the struggle at all costs, destroying Madrid while saving it, while the anti-Communists were those who thought the war was over. Ultimately, Madrid's surrender ended the night of the generals. By that time, the Republican government had once again fled, this time to exile in France.

From the onset, the Spanish Civil War was interpreted abroad in the context of the wider European politics of 1936. It was seen as a struggle of democracy (the Republic) against fascism (the rebels) or as the struggle of the Christian West (the Nationalists) against Bolshevist East (the Republic), but there is no doubt that it sprang from deep-seated, uniquely Spanish matters. However, once the civil war began, foreign intervention, in both word and deed, made the conflict international. Beyond Iberia the civil war embodied and symbolized the conflict between fascism and democracy that ran across the face of Europe. This interpretation still dominates the popular consciousness of the Spanish Civil War outside Spain, though scholars since Gerald Brenan's 1943 *The Spanish Labyrinth* have argued for its Spanish nature.[4] Apologists for the Republic ignore that the most ardent defenders of the Republic were not naive democrats but case-hardened Spanish Stalinists for whom democracy was a bourgeois fiction, an expedient, and nothing more. That only one of the four sizable factions within the rebel coalition had a vague similarity to German nazism or Italian fascism is equally neglected. This was the Falange, a group with which Franco never identified.

The Republican government, elected in February 1936, was a coalition of bourgeois liberal parties with a very slight electoral margin. The cabinet consisted exclusively of liberal Republicans of various persuasions. Socialists and Communists did not participate in the Popular Front government of the Republic because it was bourgeois, yet the Socialists had more popular support and the Communists better organization than the governing parties; thus, the Republican government had the responsibility of governing without the legitimacy to do so. In the interest of maintaining the allegiance of the bourgeoisie to the Republic, the government tempered revolutionary demands from the Socialists and Communists. This satisfied no one. If anything, the Spanish Socialist party exceeded the Communist party in its criticisms of the Republican government, calling for a social revolution. Unions struck; capitalists considered flight; members of the bourgeoisie watched; army officers plotted. Few enthusiastically supported the government of the day.

The government retreated into its offices and into the legislative chambers, the *Cortes*. As Spain became increasingly volatile, the government all but abdicated. Slogans proliferated. Each and every faction held political rallies. Violent clashes occurred. Individuals disappeared, went into hiding, or were abducted. Immediately prior to the uprising, Republican police arrested and murdered Calvo Sotelo, a leading opposition politician. In all the world's turmoil at the time, this is the only instance of an opposition politician being killed by the government police in an electoral democracy. Conservative forces, fearing that the Republican government was about to acquiesce in the radical demands of the Socialists and Communists, organized ever more intensely. More army officers dreamed of the historic mission of the army to impose order. Political militants organized party militias to enforce party decisions, first on party members, and then on others. Ministries failed to open and all parties issued declarations. In all, there was a great deal of politics but precious little government. Observing the introduction of democracy in the Soviet Union and Eastern Europe in the 1990s has reminded us that voting is a pointless ritual if there is no moral commitment to accept the outcome and no cultural appreciation of the role of the opposition that loses the election.

Perceiving the Republican government to be an empty shell, the generals struck. As if dazed by the explosion of a large flash bulb, the government did not respond. A collapse was the most likely result. But as hours and days passed, the attack on the Republic galvanized the strongest factions on the left. In time the Socialists and Communists supported the government and by September 1936 joined the cabinet. The government enjoyed a new legitimacy. Had the government appeared this united earlier, there might have been no rebellion. Paradoxically, while the rebels gained strength as more military units secured territory for their cause, the Republican government also became politically stronger. The ceaseless agitation of the left had finally produced a revolution, but one from the right, not the left.

Crisis paralyzed Spain, but most of the rest of the world had other problems. The world press had seldom reported Spanish politics before the July uprising. Beyond Iberia, neither journalists nor their readers could assess the strength that the Republican government found. Instead, they saw the confident and often unopposed, if slow, advance on Madrid of the rebel army from all directions but especially from the south and it seemed only a matter of time before Madrid fell. Observers agreed that with the capture of Madrid, the Republican government, wherever it might fly, would have to concede. Without Madrid, the Republican government would have nothing of importance to govern.

When the rebels were reported in Madrid at the end of October 1936, the matter seemed settled. Then on 8 November, while the rebel army was investing the southwest perimeter of Madrid, a contingent of international volunteers paraded down the *Gran Via* in Madrid, taking up positions at the front that ran through the sprawling campus of the University City, then under construction. The rebel offensive stalled. More foreigners arrived. By the start of the winter, the battle for Madrid would clearly be siege not storm. The Republic was spared for the time being. Many supposed the foreign volunteers had saved Madrid, a supposition to be examined in more detail later. By December, one American diplomat in Barcelona reported to Washington the thousands of foreign volunteers in Republican Spain.[5] It was an unexpected development and promised to be on a scale that was unprecedented.

The first foreigners to take up arms for the Republican government were some of those already present in Spain when the military rebellion occurred, exiles from German and Italian fascism. There were others who had come to Spain for the alternative Workers' Olympiad scheduled to open in Barcelona on 19 July.[6] When the fighting started on 17 July, Barcelona in particular and Spain in general had a large resident population of politically committed foreigners who had come to seek refuge under the aegis of the Popular Front government. For more than a crucial half year Spain represented the only united and declared anti-Fascist government in Europe until the Popular Front government won office in France in the middle of 1936. Some of these resident foreigners took part in the Spanish Civil War from the first days, helping to build barricades in Madrid and participating in brief street fighting in Barcelona.

No doubt some of these foreign residents in Spain at the time left, but many stayed, and some fought. Perhaps those who stayed did so because they had no means of travel and, more important, no place to go. German and Italian exiles in France purposefully entered Spain to join the fray, quickly joining those foreigners who stayed. By August, Frenchmen were reported crossing into Spain at Perpignon, coming to the aid of the Republic. In August 1936, Belgians were identified in the fighting at Irún near the French border. Like these Belgians, the early volunteers clubbed together into language groups or individually joined militia units, usually choosing units of their own political persuasion. The international press soon reported groups of French and Polish fighters on the Republican side.

The most famous of the language groups was German. A group of Germans in Barcelona, most of whom were Communists, constituted themselves as a fighting unit in the first weeks of the Spanish

Civil War. Comrades who had been living in France soon joined them. They came to be called the Ernst Thälmann Centura, after the leader of the German Communist party then held by the Gestapo. He was later executed for the crime of opposition. Later when the International Brigades grew, the common practice was for each formation to name itself after a leading political figure or a notable political event of the left. These were names selected from the history of the dominant nationality in each formation. Most of the early volunteers, like the Thälmanns, served on the quiet Aragon front until what became known as the International Brigades formed in the fall of 1936.

2. Madrid in November and December of 1936

Madrid was the prize. To have it was to claim Spain. The best way for General Franco to establish ascendancy would have been to reach Madrid. There was little coordination among the rebel forces in the early stages of the civil war. In addition, two of the key generals died in plane crashes, disrupting the original plan. Rebel gains early in the conflict were not a credit to its arms or organization but the result of its supporters' overthrowing those loyal to the Republic. Meanwhile the Republican government, as if paralyzed, waited for the blow to fall.

While it took no genius to see the rebel's strategy, the Republic was slow to defend Madrid. When Nationalist troops came within 20 miles south of the capital, the Republican Prime Minister preferred not to order preparation of fortifications and trenches, fearing it would panic the populace.[7] Madrid's construction and cement workers were not diverted to defensive work. Instead, as reported, they continued work on municipal housing and the people's underground.[8] Nothing but open country stood between Republican Madrid and the Nationalist army. Central Spain is rugged and inhospitable, all the worse in high summer, making for slow going. Only popular militias resisted the Nationalists and when the Army of Africa crushed these untrained, underarmed, and uncoordinated militias, political orators and writers in Madrid accused them of ideological failings. Evidently, words were bullets in the correct ideology and ideology made the warrior. Belief in the power of the cause also applied to the International Brigades, as will be shown.

Information was hard to gather, but by the end of October it was clear that words alone—even ideologically correct words—would not stem the Nationalist tide. The Madrid garrison was reorganized under a Defense Council on 5 November 1936. With rebel troops within ten miles of Madrid, panic and uncertainty were common. The government itself was reconstituted, and on 6 November when it fled to Valencia on the assumption that Madrid was about to fall, it seemed to be the beginning of the end. The Defense Council asserted an undeclared martial law; many Madrileños felt betrayed by the government. Suspicion and recrimination within the Republican ranks germinated, later to plague the International Brigades. Meanwhile, the Defense Council was desperate for fighting men and even more desperate for material aid. General Franco had already declared the liberation of Madrid. Foreign journalists wrote that the capital would not be defended. Radio Lisbon led the way by purporting to describe Franco's victorious entry into Madrid. Everything seemed over on 7 November when the vanguard of the rebel Army of Africa entered the outskirts of Madrid at the *Casa del Campo*, a park once the exclusive preserve of the royalty but opened to the public by the populist dictator, General Miguel Primo de Rivera, who had been Franco's mentor. The park became the conduit of the Nationalist advance. Franco's force was stretched thin, his flanks exposed, and his lines of communications over-extended, all of this too much for such an experienced officer and such a cautious man to be comfortable; moreover, he had bypassed more than one Republican redoubt in his rear. On 7 November Franco had as few as 3,000 fit men to press into the attack across the river Manzanares and up the high, wooded grounds of the University City.

On 8 November, Nationalist artillery bombarded the incomplete buildings of the University City in Madrid. Franco's army, composed largely of Moors and the Spanish Foreign Legion, advanced. At this desperate moment, the first unit of the International Brigades went into action. For the immediate benefit of the Republic and the lasting fame of the International Brigades, the script could not have been more dramatic. Since the middle of October, foreign volunteers for the Republic had been concentrated at Albacete about 150 miles from Madrid. Battalion-strength contingents of French, German, Italian, and Polish volunteers had been organized. These first men—the Germans—marched to the front, silent in manner and foreign in appearance. Partisans of the Republic had been hoping for Soviet intervention at the eleventh hour, and this first body of foreigners to appear in Madrid, wearing strange uniforms and helmets and, most of all, carrying proper rifles (which were scarce in Madrid) was supposed to be Russian. Cries of "Vivan los rusos!" (Long live the Russians!) went up. Marching men do not always accurately hear cheers along the way. Moreover, since few of these International Brigaders spoke Spanish, the mistaken identification was not easily rectified, especially while under the discipline of the march. Further still, many committed partisans in the ranks may well have been pleased to be thought Russian. At the end of the day, about 2,000 men of the XIth International Brigade were deployed around the University City. Many of them were Communists who accepted iron discipline. Since some were veterans of World War I, they had a strong respect for fortifications. Compared with many of the popular militias of the Republic, they were well equipped, highly disciplined, and experienced; they had few machine guns, but most had helmets and rifles, and they were spoiling for a fight. In two days, the XIIth International Brigade joined them and in the next several days the battle was fought in and around Moncloa, as this part of Madrid is called. The rebel advance stopped, and a stalemate ensued. By 23 November, both sides were exhausted. As many as one-third of the first men of the XIth International Brigade died in battle at University City, a rate of mortality usually taken to measure the ferocity of the fight or the drive of the Internationals. It was a rate of mortality that remained characteristic of the International Brigades. Whether it is proof of fierce fighting or motivation will be questioned later.

These 2,000 Internationals, who materially contributed to the defense of Madrid, had a far greater psychological impact. Ignored by the international community, abandoned by the government, with winter approaching, the arrival of the International Brigaders showed to Madrilińos that they were not alone. "The idea that men came from all over the world to fight for the republic raised the population's morale," remembered one witness many years later when free to speak.[9]

Failing to decapitate the Republic at the end of November, the Nationalists tried a maneuver to cut the lines of communication to Madrid. This move was rebuffed with the aid of the XIIth International Brigade. On 13 December when the Nationalists attacked Boadilla, the town capitulated after a furious fight, but the Nationalist offensive stalled a week later. Their resources and organization were overtaxed. As weather and organization permitted, the Nationalists tried other maneuvers to encircle and engulf Madrid. In the fight for the Coruña Road, only 32 men from the Thälmann Battalion survived the intensity of the struggle.

In January 1937, the XIth and XIIth International Brigades were removed from the line for rest and reorganization. Replacements were also inducted. By then, only about 600 of the original 2,000 men of the XIth International Brigade remained.[10] Each week 600 to 700 new foreign volunteers arrived in Spain. This was the peak of recruitment. During the defense of Madrid in November and

December, two more International Brigades came into being, the XIIIth and XIVth. Although an effort was made to organize these brigades on linguistic lines, they were polyglot at first and later units were transferred from one brigade to another in order to concentrate language groups. Even so, among the 750 men of a battalion of the XIVth International Brigade at Christmas 1936, nine languages were spoken. The XVth International Brigade, constituted on 8 February 1937, contained English-speakers and others.

In all, at least 32,000 men from as many as 50 countries went to Spain voluntarily to fight in the International Brigades. Nearly all of them went in an 18-month period from the middle of 1936 to the end of 1937. Despite the large number of books devoted to the International Brigades, we know very little about the men in the ranks, called "fallen sparrows" in the title of a 1943 American film. Propaganda at the time portrayed them on the one hand as simple paragons of democratic, proletarian virtue and on the other as mindless red zombies. This effective propaganda still colors contemporary perceptions of the International Brigades which have become a legend of this century.

The world press, having written off the Republic, fastened onto these volunteers and gave renewed attention to Spain. Not only were the International Brigaders unexpected and unusual, but they also provided a human interest dimension for readers around the world. English journalists sought out English volunteers. Dutch journalists sought out Dutch volunteers, and so on. Photographic displays were arranged and action pictures staged for consumption around the world. Propagandists in the Republican camp courted world opinion by promoting the foreign volunteers as an international plebiscite in the global struggle of democracy against fascism. In time, many writers were associated with or joined the International Brigades. The stories and books of these individuals focused so much worldwide attention on them, and by implication on the perceived international context of democracy versus fascism, that the uniquely Spanish character of the civil war received little or no attention outside Spain.

Simply declaring themselves bound for Spain involved risks for many of the International Brigade volunteers and going involved losses for all of them. Many governments made getting a passport difficult for those suspected of traveling to Spain to volunteer. Some passports were marked invalid for Spain, and those who ignored that warning could only believe their own citizenship in jeopardy. Governments issued statements reminding citizens that service in a foreign army was grounds for losing one's citizenship. Moreover, the anabasis itself was arduous for all and dangerous for many. Some volunteers supposedly walked across countries in Europe to get to the Iberian peninsula. French guards along the Spanish border were not always friendly or inattentive after the French Popular Front government, for its own reasons, closed the frontier in August 1936. After that, most volunteers had to climb the forbidding Pyrenees in the dead of night, many traversing these difficult slopes in winter, entering Spain thirsty, sore, cold, bruised, stiff, and frightened.

In short, thousands left their homes, compromised their citizenship, and endured hardships on the trek, not following Moses to the promised land, but to take part in someone else's war. If that alone strikes the imagination, there is more. Men who remembered the charnel-house of the Great War, some who had taken part in that war, went readily and willingly to Spain to make war once again. Their adversity had only just begun when they reached the peninsula.

3. The History of the Spanish Civil War

The international dimensions of the Spanish Civil War had two consequences. First, the Spanish origins and character of the civil war were displaced, on one side, by a "democracy versus fascism" thesis that defenders of the Republic used to court world opinion and, on the other side, by a "Catholicism versus Communism" thesis that opponents of the Republic advanced. Second, the role of foreigners in the civil war has been systematically inflated. A large literature has examined the intervention of Germany, Italy, and the Soviet Union, together with the foreign volunteers. The inaction of France and England has been more thoroughly studied in some quarters than the actions of the combatants themselves.

These international interpretations of the Spanish Civil War have pretty much had the field to themselves. The Nationalist victory cut into stone its official interpretation of the war, emphasizing the intervention of the International Brigades and their like to explain why the Republic's defeat took three arduous years. Since Spaniards in Spain found it difficult to do research and to debate fully and freely their findings, Spain has for a long time contributed little to the historiography of its own civil war. The books about the civil war published outside of Spain since 1939 were probably more numerous, and were certainly more varied, than those published in Spain. No doubt, the best books on the Spanish Civil War have been produced outside Spain.[11] Since the passing of the Franco regime, the implicit collective preference in Spain seems to have been publicly to forget the war. Its 50th anniversary in 1986 occasioned no sustained works of reappraisal.[12] But then the great books on the American Civil War emerged only as its centennial approached.

To the uncommitted observer, one of the most surprising things about the history of the International Brigades is how partisan it remains today. During the Spanish Civil War, much propaganda was produced and developed with a new sophistication; if that was only to be expected, what is surprising is the degree to which that kind of material continues to be produced and reproduced these many years later. New books continue to appear by veterans of the International Brigades, all too often repeating the lies, half-truths, and delusions of the 1930s propaganda. The old battles are fought repeatedly. For example, the apparent fact that 50 Australians joined the International Brigades, but only one is known to have journeyed to Franco's side, is intoned even today as though it were a judgment on the merits of the antagonists. In 1981, veterans resorted to litigation to protect the integrity of their version of the past.[13] These books seem to freeze history permanently in the frame of 1938. If these veterans can be forgiven for being unable or unwilling to come to terms with their own past and the burden of their long dead comrades in arms, no such tolerance should be extended to journalists and historians who have credulously repeated the propaganda, the apocrypha, and the hagiography of the past, all in the interest, it seems, of telling a good story.

The truth would be the best story, but if the truth is forever beyond our grasp, then as near to it as possible is a good story. The challenge is to "tell the heavy story right," as Christopher Marlowe once said. Researchers on the Spanish Civil War parade their political commitments, privately if not publicly, as a credential. Failure to express the faith renders the writer, and by extension the writer's research, suspect. Between friends and enemies there is a no-man's land where the heavy story will be found.

If a cache of hitherto hidden documents about the International Brigades were unearthed, it would receive a mixed reception. Since 1939, the Spanish Civil War has risen to become one of the mythic events of our time. Those whose eyes glaze over with boredom at the mention of Belsen have remained ready to debate the Spanish Civil War. People who care nothing for Spain or any Spaniard have cared passionately about the Spanish Civil War for years. In lecture halls and bookstores this war has commanded the attentive and uncritical respect that *The Iliad* must have enjoyed around the camp-fire. Outside Spain, no part of the civil war has received more reverence than the International Brigades. As Anthony Verrier said of Britain's Special Operations Executive's war-time myth, so one might say of the International Brigades: They "bore little resemblance to an organization that remains associated in the popular imagination " struggle against fascism.[14] Lacking reliable information, the myth-makers—be they eternal propagandists for whom the war has never ended, romantics who delight in the story, or wishful thinkers who dream like Walter Mitty about the good cause—have at least kept interest in the subject alive.

Paul Johnson wrote in 1983 that "no episode of the 1930s has been more lied about than this one [the Spanish Civil War]." One powerful example was the distortion of the bombing of Guernica.[15] The Spanish Civil War has been, he adds, buried under a "mountain ... [of] ... mendacity ... for a generation." No one wanted to know the truth and some still do not. As Julian Symons found, "Truths and lies were so inextricably entangled, that the deceivers were also deceived."[16] George Orwell emphasized the mendacity in his 1943 essay "Looking Back on the Spanish Civil War" by asking, "How will the history of the Spanish Civil War be written?" He feared lies might well gain universal acceptance. The pages that follow review many examples that vindicate Johnson and confirm Symons and Orwell.

Because of the participation of foreign volunteers and because of perceptions of the forces involved, the Spanish Civil War has become connected to the larger conflicts of the time. After all, high school history textbooks routinely describe it, with the benefit of unerring hindsight, as the first act of World War II. In so doing, no allowance is made for the Spanish origins and character of the civil war. Consequently, one of the most obvious characteristics of the Spanish Civil War is the degree to which foreigners have expropriated its history. Foreigners' knowledge of the Spanish Civil War rests mainly on the International Brigades and on books by foreigners. Inevitably, the International Brigades and the Spanish Civil War as a whole are interpreted in the European context, not in the parochial Spanish context. In 1983 Spanish historian Angel Viñas said at a public conference that the Spanish Civil War originated in Spanish seeds, and subsequently became international. American veterans vigorously attacked him, claiming that the Spanish Civil War was the first shot of World War II.[17]

This prodigious library on the Spanish Civil War has been estimated at 15,000 or 20,000 volumes.[18] Another writer has asserted without explanation that more fiction has come from the Spanish Civil War than any other twentieth century conflict.[19] Whether either claim be true, an enormous literature exists and it must answer some need.

One indication of the power of myth regarding the International

Brigades is the creation of a formation that never existed, namely the Abraham Lincoln *Brigade*. This alleged brigade figures in the title of the organization of American veterans of the International Brigades: Veterans of the Abraham Lincoln *Brigade*.[20] It is also to be found as the title of volunteer veteran Arthur Landis's history of this alleged brigade.[21] Such is the power of repetition that veterans routinely referred to their service in this fictitious brigade.[22] Myths, political myths especially, are impervious to facts, as Gilbert Cuthbertson has observed.[23] Because an insufficient number of Americans volunteered at any one time to create a brigade of three or four battalions, a George Washington and a Lincoln Battalion were created, which merged under the latter name after devastating casualties. (Note that the American units were not named after figures from the left, like Joe Hill or Emma Goldman.) The Americans served in the XVth International Brigade with the other English speakers from England, Scotland, Wales, Ireland, Australia, New Zealand, and Canada. Occasionally mention is also made of the Eugene V. Debs Column of American Socialist volunteers named after the Socialist leader and frequent presidential candidate, but it never existed, not even under another name, even though a photograph shows recruits signing up for it.[24] This photograph is still presented as evidence that the American volunteers were not limited to Communists, but extended so far as to include Socialists. No doubt, following directions from the Kremlin, the Comintern staged the photograph to emphasize the broad popular front; its aim was to convince viewers that the International Brigades were not instruments of the Communist party.

Another indication of the short distance between myth and reality is Judith Cook's 1979 claim that actor Errol Flynn was so sympathetic to the Republican cause that he visited Spain.[25] In truth, the nearest he got to Spain was attending a private screening of *Spanish Earth* in 1938, a film Ernest Hemingway produced.[26] Of course the broader question is what possible meaning Flynn's sympathies might have.

Furthermore, historian-volunteer John Gerassi asserted in 1986 that in August 1936 thousands of Americans "applied to the Spanish embassy in Washington for combat visas."[27] How could he know that? Was such a surge reported in the *New York Times*? What is his evidence? Gerassi cites Soviet propaganda. Saying it is so makes it so all too often in the case of the International Brigades and the Spanish Civil War.

Skeptical readers who doubt that the ideological battle continues might look at *Spanish Front: Writers on the Civil War*, edited by Valentine Cunningham. In this preface, the editor writes that

> Nationalist clerics were bumped off, to be sure, but peasants and soldiers were taught to read by the Republic's teams of adult-educators and reading matter was widely disseminated in the Republic's powerful drive for popular literacy.[28]

In this passage the editor mocks the ritual slaughter of priests and nuns with the gangster film slang "bumped off" and labels the fact too well known to be excited about by adding "to be sure." Finally, the editor shifts the focus from bloody churches to chalk-boards with reference to the "powerful drive" to spread literacy, as if reading and writing were only possible after a good bloodletting—*engagé* intellectualism at its worst.

This same editor assures us that the Spanish Civil War lives on because it is a lived text, the participants' text; and "it is as text that Spain exists . . . for most of us, the belated readers of their textmaking labours." If this passage means that the Spanish Civil War continues to seem important because of the stories of the individuals who took part in it, that is an even more significant point than Cunningham may realize. These are profoundly political stories, as will be argued throughout these pages. In passing, note that none of the writers included in *Spanish Front* is Spanish.

The time has long passed when efforts should be made to recover, as if from a deep-sea crevice, some fragments of the truth of the International Brigades by stripping off the incrustations and piecing together the shards to enlarge understanding of the phenomenon.

ENDNOTES

1. Juan Simeon Vidarte, *Todos Fuimos Culpables: Testimonio de un Socialista Español* (Barcelona: Ediciones Grijalbo, 1978), 1: 259.
2. See Michael Alpert, *El Ejército Republicano en la Guerra Civil* (Barcelona: Ruédo Iberico, 1977), 23–37.
3. Leo Palacio, *1936: La Maldonne Espagnole: Où la Guerre d'Espagne comme Répétition Générale du Deuxième Conflit Mondial* (Paris: Editions Privat, 1986), 13.
4. Gerald Brenan, *Spanish Labyrinth* (Cambridge: Cambridge University Press, 1943).
5. James W. Cortada, ed., *A City in War* (Wilmington: Scholarly Resources, 1985), 49.
6. Ibid., 27.
7. Randolfo Pacciardi, *Il Battaglione Garibaldi* (Lugano: Nuove edizioni di Capolago, 1938), 17–18.
8. "Spain," *The Economist*, 10 October 1936, p. 62.
9. Fraser, 264.
10. Gustav Szinda, *Die XI Brigade* (Berlin: Verlag des Ministeriums für National Verteidigung, 1956).
11. The obvious example is the leading work on the subject, Hugh Thomas, *The Spanish Civil War*, 3rd ed. (Harmondsworth: Penguin, 1977). Everyone who studies the Spanish Civil War waters at this fount.
12. Sheelagh Ellwood, "Spanish Notes," *Times Literary Supplement*, 9-15 October 1987,

p. 1108. Cf. Juan Luís Cebrian, "La Memoria Historica," *El Pais* (International Edition), 21 July 1986, lead article in an eight-page insertion.

13. Steve Nelson, J. R. Barrett, and R. Ruck, *Steve Nelson: American Radical* (Pittsburgh: University of Pittsburgh Press, 1981), p. 438 n. 5.
14. Anthony Verrier, *Through the Looking Glass* (London: Cape, 1983), 24.
15. Herbert Southworth, *Guernica! Guernica!* (Berkeley: University of California Press, 1977).
16. Julian Symons, *The Thirties: A Dream Revolved* (London: Faber and Faber, 1975), 106–107.
17. Tom Burns, "Abraham Lincoln Brigade Vets Hold a Reunion," *Washington Post*, 5 October 1983.
18. The former figure is given by Paul Preston, *The Spanish Civil War, 1936–1939* (London: Weidenfeld and Nicolson, 1986), 1, and the latter by Alberto Fernandez, "Judicos en la Guerra de España," *Tiempo Historia*, September 1975, p. 4.
19. James Cortada, "Literature," *Historical Dictionary of the Spanish Civil War* (Westport, Conn.: Greenwood, 1981), 300.
20. Note the publisher of the following work, Alvah Bessie, ed., *The Heart of Spain* (New York: Veterans of the Abraham Lincoln Brigade, 1952).
21. Arthur Landis, *The Abraham Lincoln Brigade* (New York: The Citadel Press, 1967).
22. John Tisa, *Recalling the Good Fight* (South Hadley, Mass.: Bergin & Garvey, 1985), 6.
23. Gilbert M. Cuthbertson, *Political Myth and Epic* (East Lansing: Michigan State University Press, 1975), 156–157.
24. Allen Guttmann, *The Wound in the Heart* (Glencoe, Ill.: The Free Press, 1962), pp. 101–102.
25. Judith Cook, *Apprentices of Freedom* (London: Quartet, 1979), 25.
26. Guttmann, 131.
27. John Gerassi, *The Premature Anti-Fascists: North American Volunteers in the Spanish Civil War 1936–1939* (New York: Praeger, 1986), 13.
28. Valentine Cunningham, "Preface," *Spanish Front: Writers on the Civil War* (Oxford: Oxford University Press, 1986), xxii.

CHAPTER 3

A Morally Incoherent World

Whereon the pillars of this earth are founded, toward which the conscience of the world is tending-a wind is rising and the rivers flow.

Thomas Wolfe

1. The 1930s: Then and Now

The 1930s featured a good deal of self-conscious myth making.[1] New technologies of film and radio created new opportunities. Though the Spanish Civil War was certainly not unique, it has become the sort of international myth of which history is all too readily made. Why is there no comparable mythology for any of the other wars of the period: the Russo-Finnish War, the Italian invasion of Abyssinia, the Yugoslav or the Greek civil wars? Each of these conflicts, among others that might be listed, involved forces similar to those mobilized in Spain. The Winter War between Finland and the Soviet Union was noteworthy for the thousands of foreign volunteers who went to Finland's aid, something all-but-forgotten outside Finland, a perfect contrast with the Spanish case where outside Spain, the Spanish contribution to their own civil war is equally forgotten.

Each reason ordinarily given to explain the mythic status of the Spanish Civil War has a counterpart in Finland, Abyssinia, Yugoslavia, and Greece, yet Spain was and still is different. Undeniably, the Spanish Civil War was dreadful, a bigger war than the others when measured in duration and destruction. Hugh Thomas estimates the total number of deaths at 500,000, with another 300,000 permanent exiles, and a material destruction of $9,375 million in 1977 American dollars.[2] To explain interest in the war by the enormity of its destruction, however, begs the question. Would the Spanish Civil War have attained this magnitude had it not been for all of the international interest in it in the first place? The six-month eye separating this conflict from World War II, proved to be the calm of the gathering storm that is no peace, as Thomas Hobbes once remarked.[3] No one at the time could know anything of the size of the coming war.

Located *in* Europe and involving forces that figured in the great political tensions that dominated the nations of the continent, the Spanish Civil War refracted the hopes and fears of many Europeans and others. It occasioned much international involvement. The death and destruction were horrible and fascinating to the watching world as a reminder of the Great War and as a precursor of what might come, purveyed by skilled writers, dramatic still photographers like Robert Capa, and compelling news reel films. But superior talents also covered the other, equally deadly conflicts of the time yet failed to inflame the imagination. Though explaining the legend of the Spanish Civil War itself is not the purpose here, it must be drawn into question to dampen some of the central myths of the International Brigades. Outside Spain, the two are inevitably, perhaps inextricably, connected.

The foreign volunteers are the main source of interest in the civil war outside Spain. Millions of people around the world have read Ernest Hemingway's novel *For Whom the Bell Tolls* or André Malraux's *L'Espoir*, both recounting the adventures of foreigners during the Spanish Civil War. The former was made into a major motion picture seen by still more millions. Far fewer have read any historian's account and even fewer a Spanish historian's account.

Books about the International Brigades and indeed books about the Spanish Civil War customarily mention some of the famous names among the men in the International Brigades. Naming the famous is occasionally carried further by naming the children of the famous as though they were enlarged by the reflected, parental renown. With or without progeny, the list is long and varied.[4]

In 1987, Martin Blinkhorn concluded that "... the Republic's near monopoly of foreign volunteer support and intellectual sympathy surely says something about the respective virtues of the two sides of the conflict."[5] This bland assumption is hardly uncommon and will repay closer inspection. Does Blinkhorn mean that the list proves the justice of the cause of the Republic? The list offers no more proof than does the list of famous intellectuals who sang the praises of Stalin's Soviet Union in the 1930s or Mao's China in the 1960's, to show the virtues of those repressive, corrupt regimes. Rather, it may prove the terrible need of some people, even intellectuals, at the time to identify a just cause to which to commit themselves, and it may also prove the credulity of many people, including intellectuals, when they enter the world of political action.[6] The bloodthirsty attitude of comfortable middle-class intellectuals who took an interest in Spain became a brilliant satire in Lionel Trilling's novel *The Middle of the Journey*.[7]

If it serves any purpose at all, the list of the famous demonstrates both the scope and range of the call Spain made. That list will not be repeated here, not because it is too well known to bear repetition, but because the focus of this study is the nameless men in the ranks, not the famous few. "History is still mostly written from the top down, not from the bottom up," as Arthur Schlesinger Jr. has observed.[8] That tendency will be limited here, though it cannot be completely eliminated without losing precious knowledge. Inevitably, references must be made to many of the famous few, particularly those who were writers or later wrote about their experiences in Spain, because their work is one of the principal sources of information about the nature and circumstances of the 32,000 as a whole. However, to list the famous few at the outset as a way of exciting the reader's imagination and interest would only distract attention from the subject at hand. Worse still, such a list might cause the reader to suppose that the International Brigades were entirely composed of these well-known individuals. Or more pernicious still, such a list might imply that famous individuals endowed the cause with virtue. The matter is more complicated because many of the most famous foreigners associated with the Spanish Civil War were not among the 32,000 in the International Brigades. For example, Ernest Hemingway was there as a journalist for the *Toronto Star*, a tireless participant in word, not deed. André Malraux and George Orwell were both participants, but not in the International Brigades.

Not only did these 32,000 men suffer the trials that are any soldier's lot, but they also suffered far more besides due to their peculiar nature and circumstances. As many as half died in Spain by the end of the civil war; there is no telling how many more succumbed to their wounds after they left Spain. Nor is there any reckoning of how many more of them the German Gestapo or the Soviet NKVD later killed mainly because of their Spanish service. Even more difficult are estimates of crippling wounds, onset of chronic disabilities, or mental psychoses subsequently suffered. Still more obscure is the grief of those who loved them.

Save for the famous few, the 32,000 are historically nameless, strangers to the history they made. Few records of their identities were made. The little information collected was far from reliable, and most of that has not survived. Despite all claims, there is little knowledge of even basic questions like how many foreign volunteers there were in the Republican camp. In the mountain of primary and secondary literature on the International Brigades in particular and on the Spanish Civil War in general, established facts describing the foreign volunteers are at a premium. The volunteers chose to go, endured, suffered, and died largely in anonymity. Moreover, that literature shows too little demonstrable interest in questioning and establishing facts to curtail myth. Assertions abound but only infrequently are they buttressed by any more authority than an earlier assertion by a like-minded author. This study will clarify and evaluate our knowledge of the men of the International Brigades.

The literature on the International Brigades forms an inverse pyramid, as illustrated below in Figure 1. At the small base lies the remaining documentary evidence, the card files collected by the national recruiting offices, the residual Republican government files in Salamanca, and the files of the League of Nations in Geneva. Next come the reports of participants and observers made at the time and even more made a good deal later, a sizable literature, followed by the enormous secondary literature, to which this book contributes.

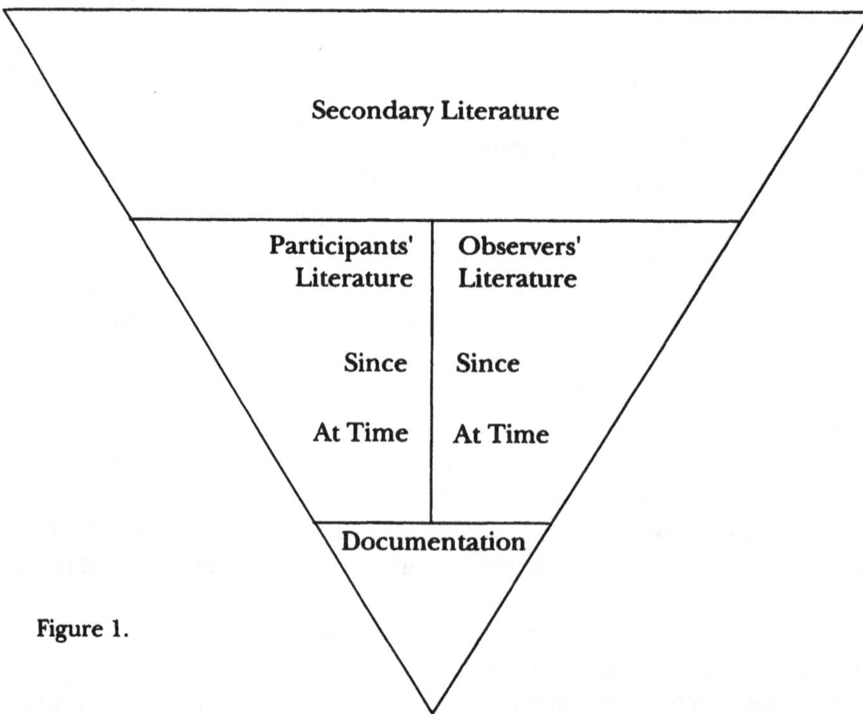

Figure 1.

2. Interpretation

This study aims not only to analyze the International Brigades, but also to reflect on the meaning of their story as literary critics once interpreted the themes of *The Iliad.* If one important question is "Why did these men go to Spain?" then who better to answer than the men themselves. Their answers will receive most careful consideration. As a literary critic cannot defer to the poet's authority, neither can the historian or the moralist defer to the actors. We must canvass other meanings. If the surviving veterans of the International Brigades could not, would not say why they went, their silence would not mean that their acts were meaningless. If we look further than their silences, we must also look further than their words. Autobiographical accounts are one place at which to begin, not the place to end. The philosopher Hannah Arendt has noted that when a man acts in the world, then he no longer owns his action because its nature and meaning exist for everyone to examine. Action is public property. When a hero who saves victims from a fire later says modestly, "Any one would have done it" or "I was only doing my duty," observers may see a different significance to the act, as they may see differently onlookers who failed to help another victim, saying that "it was none of my business." Such interpretations also apply to the International Brigaders.

According to their own testimony, the foreign volunteers were marginal men, produced by the social, economic, and political upheavals of the time. Finding no moral justification for their plight, these men usurped the jealously guarded right of sovereigns to declare war. Each made an individual declaration of war and journeyed to distant Spain to act. If war is the continuation of politics by other means, as Carl von Clausewitz said, then these men were making politics as well as war.[9] This was definitely not a case where, in the words of Herbert Hoover, "Older men declare war. But it is youth that must fight and die." For the young men in the International Brigades this was a voluntary war.

The exiled Republican general Vincente Rójo, more than a little prescient, wrote in 1939 that the Spanish Civil War had ended in deed but not in word.[10] That the conflict remains a polemical subject seems sign enough of its verbal continuation. The start of World War II froze the Spanish Civil War. No subsequent peace offered a period when information could be gathered, at least not for the defeated. No period of normality followed when both participants and observers could gradually adjust to the results. Instead, the Spanish Civil War along with many of its participants and observers was swept aside in the breaking storm. Many Republicans and their sympathizers stubbornly clung to the hope that Franco's regime would be displaced by the war. Franco's Spain might enter the war with the Axis powers, or be occupied by Great Britain to prevent entry. At war's end, irreconcilable Republicans pressed the Allies to turn on so-called Fascist Spain, just as others pressed for an invasion of the Soviet Union. Efforts were also made to indict Nationalist Spain before the International Military Tribunal at Nuremberg. For these exiles the Spanish Civil War was not the harbinger of World War II; rather, World War II was the extension of the Spanish Civil War. In 1939, exiled Republicans in Europe found that their war had not ended at Spain's border, even if they had so wanted. Many of them reciprocated for the International Brigades by volunteering for military and resistance forces battling Germany and Italy, some having little other choice since exiled Republicans bore the mark of Cain to Fascists and their collaborators. Though seldom noted in discussion, no evidence indicates that the victorious Nationalists asked the political police in Occupied Europe to hunt down its former enemies. The hunt for Spanish Republicans and International Brigaders under the German occupation seems to have resulted more from the political police's need to prove its worth by pursuing the regime's real and imagined enemies, than from any Nationalist desire for revenge. It is hardly conceivable that the Gestapo and its analogs would have done favors for so unaccommodating a friendly power as Franco's Spain proved to be.

The same fate was even truer for real or imagined veterans of the International Brigades identified in German-occupied Europe and later in Soviet-dominated Eastern Europe. Some men from the International Brigades began their personal struggle, in 1925 or earlier in Italy or perhaps in 1933 in Germany, not to end until 1945, if then. For a Greek exiled by the Metaxas regime in the 1930s, the end might have been another exile, this time to Bulgaria in 1949, provided he was lucky enough to survive the dictatorship, the Spanish Civil War, World War II, the Greek Civil War, and the vagaries of the Bulgarian regime throughout the Cold War. By comparison Odysseus had it easy. International Brigade veterans from Poland, Hungary, Yugoslavia, and elsewhere would also have known a decade or more of violent conflict. Eastern European survivors who returned to their countries were later suspected of contamination by their experiences in Western Europe, and punished. They were "pre-mature anti-Fascists." That is, they fought fascism before Germany attacked the Soviet Union. Even if they had no intentional, subjective guilt, they were objectively guilty of contamination by Western Europe. That may be a sad fact, but what is worse is that more than one Western European intellectual justified this version of Stalinist justice. The term "pre-mature anti-Fascists" had its origins in the West, but the idea was devised in the East. American, Canadian, and English veterans of the International Brigades were also reviled during the early days of the Cold War for a similar contamination. Here "pre-mature anti-fascism" meant fighting fascism before England and the United States, respectively, entered the war. In each case the real fear was that International Brigaders had been infected by contact with each other and were carriers of dangerous spores. The irony is that there was little, if any, contact among the International Brigaders divided by language. If contamination is a crime, few were guilty, but many were punished.

3. Moral Incoherence

An International veteran named Pietro Nenni reflected that the Brigaders had "lived an *Iliad*."[11] In *The Iliad*, the Greeks believed that only animals are content to fight their own wars; men are like the gods who take part in the wars of others, like Sarpedon from far Lycia who came to Troy to make common cause with the besieged Trojans against the Greek onslaught. Men are unlike the gods, however, in being mortal as Sarpedon was, he whom the gods favored, for he was a rare thing, a prince worthy of being a prince. Sarpedon went to Troy to prove to the Lycians that he did deserve the preferments of a prince. To prove something to those at home also motivated the deracinated men of the International Brigades. When Sarpedon died, Zeus wept a tear of blood.[12] The Greeks are said to have believed that as long as a man's name was remembered, his shade in Hades remained conscious. Sarpedon's name lives on. The war never ends for the fallen, and as long as we the living remember them, the war never ends. Books about wars are like small memorials that nourish the spirits of the dead.

The men of the International Brigades should be remembered for the frangible beings they were. If they remain bloated with myth, they are still pawns in the ideological game of propaganda. Defeat has cast a mantle over them that no victory could have done. The defeated are untouched by future mistakes and compromises. Julian Symons has observed that "those who fought and died in Spain, with the bloom of their illusions untouched, were the lucky ones."[13] A victorious Republic might well have proved unworthy of the sacrifices of the international volunteers, exacting a terrible vengeance on the vanquished, forever sullying the reputation of the International

Brigade volunteers. Volunteers who condemned the Western democracies as oppressive tools of plutocracy in the 1930s might have seen what real oppression was like in a triumphant Republic beholden to Moscow. Bourgeois liberalism would never have looked better.

Lest the continuing ideological struggle be doubted, consider this story. When an International Brigade veteran, a Jew who was interviewed in the United States for a documentary film, expressed fears of the Soviet Union, he was told that his interview would be jettisoned. After all, he was obviously a cold warrior. Only an ideologically correct view of the International Brigades could be documented.[14]

Thucydides concluded more than two millennia ago that the worst war is civil war because it produces a moral anarchy that transforms treachery into courage;[15] cowardice into bravery; deceit into cunning; greed into virtue; savagery into nobility. Not knowing what will happen next, men become indifferent to every constraint, as in a plague. Frenzied violence becomes the order of the day with revenge more important than survival. Family relations weaken before political commitments. War turns the political world upside down; civil war does that and, in addition, turns the moral world inside out. So too in Spain during the Spanish Civil War, but not only in Spain. Stanley Payne sees the Spanish Civil War as the last act of the social revolutions that followed World War I.[16] Hugh Thomas, who refers to the Spanish Civil War as World War II in miniature, writes that it "exceeded in ferocity many wars between nations."[17] That analogy is misleading. Civil wars are inevitably more ferocious than international wars, if anything contingent can be inevitable. The Spanish Civil War, which was not only Spain's civil war, though it most assuredly was that for the Spanish, was Europe's civil war as well. It was not only the last of the social revolutions unleashed by World War I, as Payne argues, but also the greatest and most terrible of these civil wars. This war drew the International Brigaders, and this war killed half of them. Elsewhere, Thucydides reports Pericles' famed funeral speech in which Pericles proclaimed that a man who dies in the defense of Athens becomes wholly Athenian, personal identity submerging in union with the polity.[18] In dying in Spain, the foreign volunteers underwent a kind of naturalization by fire. Dolores Ibarruri, La Pasionaria, a Spanish Communist leader, said as much at a demobilization parade for some International Brigaders when she declared that they would always have a home in Spain, an eternal home in Spanish earth, and history more than residence in Franco's Spain.[19] In Europe's civil war, they became wholly Europeans.

A morally coherent world rewards merit, according to the bucolic wisdom of Hesiod.[20] In such a world, life is secure and the future transparent because they can be predicted on the basis of a moral evaluation of the present. The virtuous will prosper, and the vicious will not. To hope for such a world may be wise but to act as though it exists is not. The people of Melos portrayed by Thucydides made exactly this mistake, confusing prescription with description. They trusted justice in a morally incoherent world, and the Athenians made them pay dearly for their error. If any epoch in our century could be called morally incoherent, it is the 1930s, when the economic, political, and social orders were disintegrating. Moreover, this disintegration was not confined to distant backwaters; it was most visible and most advanced in the richest and most powerful nations.

Individuals often display a courage and self-sacrifice that defies explanation in the rational and pragmatic terms so loved by moral philosophers. Georges Sorel noticed this discrepancy and surmised that these qualities were particularly pronounced in violent popular upheavals, that is, in strikes, *émeutes,* revolutions, and civil wars.[21] Sorel did not abide by Thucydides' explanation of *stasis,* which is the maddened condition that arises when civility breaks down in a civil war. Though *stasis* may well describe the forces at work when social disintegration graphically reveals the world's moral incoherence, *stasis* does not explain the fire in the minds. If Thucydides' grim account of civil war places the experiences of the International Brigaders in Spain in its moral context, it does not suffice to explain their motivations. Sorel goes on to surmise that people are inspired by a vision; they "picture their coming action as a battle in which their cause is certain to triumph." They think "the moral coherence of the world will be restored, if [they] act now." To think in this way and not to act is a catastrophic failure. Individuals have a personal responsibility to act to restore coherence. To conceive of the task as restoration rather than creation assumes that coherence is the natural state while incoherence is unnatural. The assumption that moral coherence is natural adds impetus to the sense of mission and, more importantly though mistakenly, to the sense of power. Following this way of thinking, one arrives too easily, too disastrously at a political teleology in which right is might, where right is defined as restoration of the putative moral coherence that would exist naturally but for the opponents' ill will. As the pages that follow will demonstrate, the men of the International Brigades perceived the moral incoherence of the world; they were inspired by the need for moral coherence, though not united in picturing what that would mean; and they supposed that right made might. They were utopians who could not accept the world as they found it. To be a misfit in such a world is no shame.

They found war a stern teacher that concentrated their minds on circumstances, as Thucydides, an unsuccessful general, had better reason than most to know.

Viewed from Olympus, the world as a whole may not be any more morally coherent today than in 1936, but we seem to have learned to live with it. Even if telecommunication brings more detailed knowledge of the world's injustices, it neither overwhelms nor moves us, since advertisers and programmers are mindful of our limits. Where were the International Brigades of anti-apartheid? The evils of apartheid excited much outraged innocence around the world, especially among the articulate and complacent middle classes for whom the boycott of South African grapes and letters to the editor about the Gleneagles agreement were political acts. The African National Congress, Swapo, and their white South African supporters for whom a letter was in fact, not just in fancy, a momentous political act, fought the battles. That a contemporary International Brigade could be raised for even the most worthy causes seems impossible. Though the world is not morally coherent now, we seem neither to care much, except as a topic of conversation, nor do we seem to have any idea what to do about the world's moral incoherence, though many can explain it in contrived, abstruse theoretical language.

If many of the men of the International Brigades are shown to be misguided pawns in much of what follows, do not lose sight of these facts: they were not content with the word rather than the deed; that they were not complacent; that they did not accept a morally incoherent world; that they thought they knew what to do about it; and that they acted. Because they saw not so much the chaos of the morally incoherent world as the injustice, they decided to act and act they did, entering what Hannah Arendt has called the "political world" where actors leave their marks on history.[22] In traveling to Spain, the volunteers also traveled to another strange and threatening new world, the political world, where they found the further, blacker moral incoherence of civil war that Thucydides had described. But even so they did not descend to frenzied violence like the Athenians at Melos or sullenly retreat to their tents like Achilles at Troy. They accomplished something far more difficult: they endured. This study is but one attempt to retrieve the markings of the men of the International Brigades. It is those markings that must be rescued from the incrustation of myth. How much more noble they were than those intellectuals who tortured logic to justify their own liaisons with nazism or Stalinism.[23]

ENDNOTES

1. See Julian Jackson, *The Popular Front in France: Defending Democracy, 1934–1938* (Cambridge: Cambridge University Press, 1989).
2. Hugh Thomas, *The Spanish Civil War,* 3rd ed. (Harmondsworth: Penguin, 1977), 927 ff.
3. Thomas Hobbes, *Leviathan,* chap. 13.
4. Equally long is the list of fictional characters from the period who counted the Spanish Republic in their resume, e.g., Richard (Rick) Blaine from the 1942 film *Casablanca;* Johnson from John Mulgan, *Man Alone* (Auckland: Longman, 1939); Erridge from Anthony Powell, *Casanova's Chinese Restaurant* (London: Heinemann, 1960); the title character from Thomas Heggen's *Mr. Roberts* (Boston: Houghton Mifflin, 1946); and many more.
5. Martin Blinkhorn, "Darkness and Light," *History Today* 37 (February 1987), 54. A similar remark is in Marjorie Valleau, *The Spanish Civil War in American and European Films* (Ann Arbor: University Microfilms Research Press, 1982), 2.
6. Paul Hollander, *Political Pilgrims* (Oxford: Oxford University Press, 1981), 29–31 and passim.
7. Lionel Trilling, *The Middle of the Journey* (New York: Viking, 1947).
8. Arthur Schlesinger Jr., *New York Times Book Review,* 6 February 1983, p. 3.
9. Carl von Clausewitz, *On War* (Princeton: Princeton University Press, 1976), 87.
10. Vincente Rójo, *España Heroica,* 3rd ed. (Barcelona: Ariel, 1975 [1942]), 177.
11. Pietro Nenni, *Espagne* (Milan: Edizioni del Gallo, 1958), 172.
12. Homer, *The Iliad,* Book 21.
13. Julian Symons, *The Thirties* (London: Faber and Faber, 1975), 111.
14. David Evanier, "How Sammy Klarfeld Became a Vacillating Element in Spain," *Journal of Contemporary Studies,* Summer/Fall 1985, p. 106.
15. Thucydides, *The Peloponnesian War* 3, Chap., 81–82.
16. Stanley G. Payne, *The Franco Regime, 1936–1975* (Madison: University of Wisconsin Press, 1987), 160.
17. Thomas, 926.
18. Thucydides, *The Peloponnesian War* 2.
19. Thomas, 852–853.
20. Henry Tudor, *Political Myth* (London: Macmillan, 1971), 110.
21. Georges Sorel, *Reflection on Violence,* trans. T. Hulme and J. Roth (New York: Collier, 1950 [1906]), 41–42.
22. Hannah Arendt, *The Human Condition* (Chicago: University of Chicago Press, 1958), 155 ff.
23. The most famous case is that of Martin Heidegger, see Victor Farias, *Heidegger and Nazism* (Philadelphia: Temple University Press, 1989 [1987]) and also Richard Wolin, *The Politics of Being: The Political Thought of Martin Heidegger* (New York: Columbia University Press, 1990).

CHAPTER 4

Why Did They Go?

1. Fools or Heroes?

"Dupes" is the word the redoubtable J. Edgar Hoover chose to portray Americans who went to Spain to serve in the International Brigades.[1] By that he meant dastardly Communists had fooled the Americans but they were not Communists themselves.[2] The infamous Senator Joseph McCarthy's committee viewed the American volunteers as innocent victims led to the slaughter. In Hoover's and McCarthy's views, their sufferings and deaths served no larger purpose.[3] Taking these two men seriously for a moment, what were the volunteers fooled by? Hoover refers to fame and fortune, things that they did not find.[4] Who is not fooled by these things from time to time, including Hoover and McCarthy? What is more important, Americans and the other volunteers were also fooled into thinking the fight in the Spanish Republic was a just cause and their own cause. Justice, too, has fooled many of us, and a good thing.

Hoover's conclusion that the International Brigades consisted of foolish Americans and deceitful foreigners contrasts with that of Juan Negrín, an intellectual who was the Republican prime minister toward the end of the war. Though a man of considerable intelligence, Negrín lacked the astounding oratorical force of La Pasionaria, the Communist leader. Nonetheless, he nearly reached her level when he declared Spain the universal frontier between Fascist tyranny and democratic freedom.[5] The International Brigades represented a plebiscite on tyranny and freedom in which some of the world's men had voted with their bodies in joining the International Brigades.[6] Some volunteers must have felt this to an extent. Jason Gurney reflected that it was time to choose against fascism.[7] "Freedom," "tyranny," "the universal," "world opinion": these words are high moral ground. This rhetoric must have accomplished the purpose of boosting morale. When the decision was announced later to withdraw the volunteers, Negrín excelled himself.[8] He went to Geneva to address the Assembly of the League of Nations. Leaving Republican Spain at the time and traveling over Europe was dangerous for Negrín, but the withdrawal was part of a desperate bid to mobilize world opinion to the Republican cause by consciously addressing the world press. His address shows the calumny of his foes and their allies and the foolishness of the Non-Intervention policy adopted by the League of Nations. These statements were directed over the heads of the delegates of the Assembly, who had heard it all before, to world opinion at large. All of this was expected in the circumstances. There is something else as well, not unexpected on the occasion, but surprising all the same. Negrín spoke directly to the foreign volunteers as well as of them.[9] He spoke of the volunteers' bravery and generosity. He said further:

> I wish to testify here to the high moral value of the sacrifice they made, not for trivial and selfish interests, but for the service and defense of the purest ideas of liberty and justice.[10]

The record does not show the response his address received in Geneva, but one hopes that at least this part of his statement received a silent, if not solemn, hearing. Negrín might have used the volunteers only to prove the justice of his cause. That would have been expected, and it had been done often before. In the ceaseless propaganda battle words were bullets and there was no shortage of this ammunition. What is noteworthy is that he used the forum to praise the men in the ranks.

Negrín pledged that those who had fallen would not be forgotten and promised them all eternal affection. In short, he called them heroes. Heady stuff! Moreover, he hoped that one day "their own countries will feel equally proud of them. That will be their best and higher moral reward."[11] This would make them heroes not just to the Spanish of the Republic but also to the world where they originated.

Victims to Hoover and heroes to Negrín, that is the contrast. It is more appropriate to take the Internationals as ordinary men, neither fools nor heroes, but a little of each as the ordinary person is likely to be. The men of the International Brigades are called "sparrows" in a 1943 Hollywood movie called *Fallen Sparrows*, in which John Garfield plays an International Brigade veteran (a performance doubtless held against him by the House Un-American Activities Committee a few years later when he was black-listed as unreliable).[12] The film's title springs from a line of dialogue where a character says in a war many sparrows must fall. Men in the International Brigades were as ordinary as sparrows, neither mythological heroes nor Kremlin zombies but ordinary men, which makes them even more extraordinary. Achilles, too, was an ordinary man, once, before the mythology raised him to the divine. This work is entitled *Fallen Sparrows* partly in reference to this film, but also in the Biblical sense that the fall of even a sparrow is of universal interest.

2. Volunteering

A hero must do heroic things; a fool—foolish things. If only heroes and fools had gone to Spain, they would have caused no surprise. It is the ordinary men who surprise us. Having no duty to Spain, ordinary men might well have stayed at home, if they had one, or found a home, if they hadn't one. These men did neither. No sense of duty, no obedience took them to distant Spain. They were not the passive instruments of a sovereign. The essence of the International Brigaders is that they were volunteers, acting of volition. Those from England and the United States risked the wrath of their governments later, while European exiles provoked unrecorded summary justice. For example, two Germans reportedly were caught, tried, and executed in Germany for trying to reach Spain to join the International Brigades.[13]

Resolve, not obedience, took these men to Spain. In 1938, journalist Herbert Matthews put it this way: "A man (even a communist) is under no compulsion to come from Kalamazoo or Belgrade to give his life for Spain."[14] American Communists, who had earlier volunteered and had been told not to go then, were later ordered to Spain. The exiled Communist parties of Germany and Italy directed their members to volunteer for Spain, and in the circumstances these directives must have had something of the moral force of orders for true believers; however much they seemed like orders, they were appeals, not commands. They were neither the conscription orders by which most armies are raised even in Communist countries nor the appeals based unequivocally on patriotism that can also be used to raise national armies. The process resembled patriotic recruitment, but it was not that. No one would have been more aware of the differences than recruiters who aped appeals of the patriotic call and volunteers who responded.

To make the point another way, perhaps if Republican Spain had called for volunteers no doubt thousands would have volunteered even if Communist parties had not been involved and even if the Comintern had not recruited and transported volunteers. Even with the Comintern busily recruiting for the International Brigades, as many as 5,000 individuals like George Orwell made their *own* way to Spain and carried arms for the Republic outside the ranks of the International Brigades. Moreover, women and men also went to Spain to contribute in non-combatant roles, particularly medicine.[15] The timing of events makes clear that the Communists and the Comintern seized the opportunity events provided, they did not determine them. Foreigners took the Republican side in the fighting of the first days, individuals who already resided in Spain.[16] A German *centura* was already in the line when Tom Wintringham, identified by historians as one key promoter of the idea of the International Brigades, visited Spain. He got the idea of a foreign legion from the object lesson of these Germans.[17] Frenchmen were already identified in the war before Maurice Thorez, another key figure in the creation of International Brigades, played his part.[18] Groups of Italians had already sought leave to enter the battle.[19] The Kremlin did not create the volunteers, it reacted to the opportunity of the moment, as Robert Rosenstone has written.[20] As unlikely as it seems Comintern propaganda chief, Willi Münzenberg, was reputed to have aided volunteers for Spain before Stalin announced the policy.[21]

The recruitment of the International Brigades is usually attributed to the tireless efforts of Communist parties and agents.[22] This explanation seems so important to some analysts that they imply, if not assert, that nearly all the volunteers were Communist, an assertion unencumbered with documentary evidence.[23] This assertion occurs, for example, during Richardson's convincing argument that the International Brigades were raised and served as the Comintern's army in Spain, as an outgrowth of the Popular Front strategy of the Kremlin. Without a doubt, line officers and commissars, and the general staff of the International Brigades, were either Soviet officers, Comintern agents, or the most loyal members of the national sections of the Communist party. Yet the Italian Pacciardi and the Frenchman Putz, and their respective followers, and others, are exceptions within the leadership. To steadfast Communists, the International Brigades existed for the political, propaganda, and party purposes that Richardson details. The men of this elite, however, were not the whole of the International Brigades. Looking at the International Brigades from the top down flattens the profile. At the bottom the spear carriers knew that what the International Brigades did was to fight and die.

The Comintern component of the International Brigades was the elite of officers and commissars that determined much of the course of events, but it may have numbered no more than 2,000 to 3,000 at one time, perhaps 5,000 all told. It is true that far fewer men would have gone to Iberia if the Comintern had not provided the stimulus and the transportation. Equally, no American astronaut would have hurled skyward without the National Aeronautics and Space Administration and its rockets, but knowing this only tells us how and not why they went. At most, the organizational efforts of communism harnessed forces it did not generate.[24] Even if being a Communist meant the same thing to all men from across Europe and the world, a dubious proposition, and if it meant being somehow obedient to Moscow, remember that not all who were Communists went to Spain. Some did and some did not and, perhaps, those who went did not all go for the same reasons.

Republican and National propaganda often agreed that the International Brigades were the product of intention. Nationalists argued that Stalin's intention, manifested through the Comintern and national parties and their front organisations, created the International Brigades. Republican propagandists accepted the thesis of intention but attributed it to individual, proletarian democrats who rushed to the cause. The propagandists on each side admitted that the road twisted but it led from point "A" of intention to point "B" of conclusion in the International Brigades. Convenient though the intentional thesis is, enough has been said in these pages to suggest that it is not accepted. Instead the origin and development of the International Brigades were a result of often chaotic circumstances. Early individual volunteers were the progenitors of the International Brigades, but Stalin's decision to support the idea gave it a powerful sponsor who could act as a catalyst throughout the world. One of the most important elements in the recipe was world opinion. It influenced who volunteered, how actively volunteers were sought, and the efficiency with which arrangements were made to transport men to Spain. Of course, it was not world opinion unalloyed, but world opinion as perceived by the masters of the Comintern, finally, for the greater good of the Soviet Union.

Volunteering is a question of motivation, which falls within the realm of the emotions, of the subjective. This chapter prefaces the objective description of the International Brigaders that will follow with an account of their motivations. The motivation to go to Spain is not the whole of their subjective side, but it is the first in importance for seeing things from their point of view, which is all that subjective means here.

Understanding of the subjective side of things must remain impressionistic, relying on the words of participants and those who observed them, and our own sympathy. Especially for the former but also for the latter, a danger of the loss of perspective must be anticipated. A further problem may be reliance on the words of only some, for a start, the survivors, and there is no means to establish that survivors represent all participants. Moreover, if the writers were probably bourgeois intellectuals, they formed a distinct minority in class terms, though the assumption will be made that their experiences and emotions did not differ from those of the other volunteers. While social class may not be very important to us, it was extremely important to many of them. Finally, the greatest portion of available material comes from volunteers from one nation, the United States. This proliferation may derive from the composition of the Americans, who were more educated, younger, more like students, than others. They came later to both the Spanish Civil War and World War II, so more of them were alive by 1945 and have remained so since to write their stories.

3. The First Volunteers

How did the volunteers see the world? Their own accounts provide the best answers. Several of the men themselves suggested typologies that distinguish kinds of volunteers. Volunteer Jason Gurney listed five types: idealists, political opportunists, ideologues, adventurers, and rogues.[25] Volunteer John Reed said that he saw idealists, Communists, holiday-boozers, and adventurers.[26] Both Gurney and Reed classed themselves as idealists. These two typologies provide important points of reference, but neither is clear nor discriminate enough. Gurney's distinctions among idealists, ideologues, and opportunists are not clear, while Reed's between idealists and Communists is not discriminate. In the case of Gurney's distinction, when does an ideologue shade into an idealist? In Reed's distinction an idealist may be a Communist and vice versa. There were some individuals who combined several analytically distinct motivations, making types of motivation neither mutually exclusive nor jointly exhaustive. Rather than explain the motivation of any particular individual, the point is to canvass the motivations among the men who went, assuming there were many other similarly motivated men who almost went, but did not go for some reason. In sum, there were as many reasons to go to Spain as there were men who went. On the near side of the final analysis, we must settle, if uncomfortably, on a few generalizations.

Motivation was never in doubt to the publicists for the International Brigades. William Rust said in 1939 that "the International Brigades came to Spain as crusaders in the cause of world peace and the advancement of mankind."[27] These are fine and noble sentiments. Perhaps Gurney and Reed had these sentiments in mind when they wrote of idealists. But even an idealist must be asked how these ideals came to be held and how Spain came to galvanize them? In one basic sense at least, all foreign volunteers in Spain, women and men, were idealists. They formed the idea of going to Spain and acted upon it. There is no more profound way to be an idealist than to act upon an idea. In a second sense, too, they were idealists because they had the idea that fighting in Spain contributed to a larger goal, perhaps as grand as those Rust asserted. However, the point ought not to be settled with abstract definitions. Let us turn to men and the deeds. If they are not called idealists, it is not because none of them were what that word means, but that they all were, and in the event it is necessary to try to be more specific.

Europe was full of exiles and refugees in 1936.[28] Among them were Hungarians who had fled the failed revolution led by Béla Kun after World War I and the subsequent reactionary dictatorship of Admiral Horthy, Poles who fled the virulently anti-organized labor military dictatorship established by General Pilsudski in 1926, Greeks fearful of the Metaxas dictatorship that ended a decade of civil strife in April 1936, Romanians on the run from the Fascist-like Iron Guard, Yugoslavs pursued by royalist police, White Russians longing for home,[29] Germans fleeing Nazis, Austrians dispossessed after the shelling of Vienna in 1934, and Italians who had left Mussolini's Italy some time after the March on Rome. In France alone there were 2 1/2 million exiles at the time, more than 5 percent of the native population. Some had been driven into exile while others had exiled themselves, and some had been displaced for more than a decade before the Spanish Civil War started. Others had not yet unpacked their bags. The election of the Popular Front government in Spain made Madrid a political Mecca for these people. As fascism developed and reactionary regimes grew more desperate, Prague to the East and Paris to the West afforded exiles safe havens from which to plan a New World. In these two places, at least, fascism was at bay. The electoral triumph of the Spanish Popular Front looked like a turn in the tide, a defeat of forces perceived as Fascists. Spain must have seemed like a place from which to fight fascism, not just a sanctuary but a fortress.

The 1936 Olympiad was scheduled for Berlin. The Popular Fronts planned a counter-Olympiad to protest German nazism. What better place than the one country that seemed to have spurned fascism, Spain. This magnet drew to Spain militant anti-Fascists and also exiles and refugees.[30] One source asserts that "15,000 participants and spectators ... had gone to Barcelona for the People's Olympiad."[31] Though the number of people who went to Spain because of the election of the Popular Front and the Barcelona Olympics can only be estimated, given the intensity of political mobilization, it must have been many thousands.

Whatever the number of politically active friends of the Republic who arrived in Spain, some spontaneously took the cause of the Republic as their own. The fighting began on 17 July, two days before the Workers' Olympiad was to commence. From that date, foreigners joined the fighting. On 26 July 1936 the *New York Times* identified Frenchmen among the participants in battle.[32] A short time later, Belgians had formed their own fighting unit.[33] After several references to foreigners on the Republican side, the London *Times* reported the parade of anti-Fascist foreign volunteers in November, singling out Germans, Italians, Frenchmen, and Russians.[34] Spanish crowds often cheered parading foreigners as if they were Russians. "Russian" was almost a generic term to refer to foreign allies, and that alone may have influenced the writer of this dispatch. This is a small example of how saying it makes it so in the Spanish Civil War. The reference to Russians may also have referred to Soviet tank crews who were there, but that is not specified. Not until 18 November did the Italian and German governments formally recognize the Franco regime as the government of Spain.[35] On 21 November 1936, the *New York Times* reported that 3,300 foreign volunteers had just crossed the border to join the fight at Madrid.[36]

The rapid deployment of the International Brigades caused one writer to conclude that they must have been planned and organized well before the uprising.[37] Nothing else could explain the speed with which they appeared on the scene. What this observer attributes to planning and organization is better understood as the spontaneity of the volunteers. Those resident foreigners who joined the fighting provided impetus to other individuals, like George Orwell, to go to Spain, and also eventually to Stalin, who ordered the Comintern Executive and its sections to send men to Spain. For all the turmoil of the 1930s, no one could have foreseen something like the Spanish Civil War or prepared a worldwide network of volunteers for it.

4. The Exiles

The first of the types, the exiles, includes the flotsam, jetsam, and lagan of European politics: Hungarians, Poles, Germans, and Italians among others who had become refugees from their own nations by political upheavals. These exiles did not flee Spain, which had afforded them a safe haven, though flight would have been easy to understand. Nor did they stay out of weariness or an underestimation of the magnitude of the crisis. They stayed by choice, not by chance. Staying was more difficult because Spanish Republicans were likely to suspect Italians and Germans of sympathy with the rebels.[38] In the confusion of July 1936, 800 Italian refugees from fascism in Italy were not allowed to land at Barcelona but were shipped back to Italy, an unhappy result for an anti-Fascist exile who had come that far.[39] The matter was confused because not each and every Italian in Spain was an exile. If Spain offered exiles something before the civil war started, it offered even more after the war started. For some, the war made Spain all the more attractive, because they got what they really wanted, a fight. Note how often the word "fight" appears in the titles of books by International Brigaders, usually preceded by an adjective of approval such as "good."

Some exiles were looking for an opportunity to continue the struggle they had lost at home and seized the opportunity to fight; others came from France and elsewhere to join. Members of the Republican government were not altogether eager to welcome the volunteers. None of the personal accounts by volunteers mentions any ceremonial welcome of volunteers by high officials of the Republican government. In contrast, when the International Brigades were mustered out high officials were there to share the limelight. The government's initial ambivalence reflected two things: it wanted arms, not men, and it wanted to win world opinion by emphasizing that its fight was wholly Spanish. Perhaps that ambivalence also stemmed partly from a recognition that the foreigners had not come only to fight Spain's war. The Italian volunteer Emilio Lussu said, "We had a greater need of going to Spain than the Spanish republic had need of us."[40] Another Italian, Randolfo Pacciardi, provided an apt slogan: "The road to Rome is through Madrid."[41] According to the legend, he had spent his exile in France studying military history, awaiting trial by combat.[42] The same sentiment is expressed in the title of Carlo Rossilli's *Oggi in Spagna, Domani in Italia* (Today in Spain,

Tomorrow in Italy), published in France in 1938.[43] Italian exiles were not alone in the desire to join the battle. German Communist Gustav Regler said, "It isn't their [the Spaniards'] war; it's ours."[44] "Doch wir haben die Heimat nicht verloren, Unsere Heimat is heute vor Madrid," was another German sentiment.[45] (We have not lost the homeland; our homeland is before Madrid.)

By renewing on foreign soil the war they lost at home, exiles hoped that a defeat of fascism in Spain would contribute to its defeat in each of their homelands. As one Pole ostensibly stated, "Today you will plant your flag there . . . but you will go [on] with me until you plant it on the Belvedere in Warsaw," a kind of thinking that could only have been encouraged by support of the Nationalist cause by the German Nazi and Italian Fascist governments.[46] The Spanish Nationalists were guilty by association, a distinction that made little difference to the committed looking for their Armageddon. If the Nationalists were not openly Fascist, this was a subterfuge that was only to be expected from Fascists.

In hindsight, the war in Spain was not a struggle between the abstractions of fascism and democracy but a confused conflict of factions in a highly fragmented, volatile society. The Nationalist movement coalesced as broadly as the Popular Front, even if one group within it—the Falange—resembled the German Nazi and Italian Fascist parties. None of the details mattered. An enemy was needed, and in the prevailing demonology its name was fascism. In the fever of the times the Nationalists would have been labeled Fascists by determined anti-Fascists even if the German and Italian governments had kept at a distance. After all, the sedate London *Times* labeled the insurgents Fascists within 24 hours of the uprising.[47] It took the *New York Times* only two weeks to follow suit.[48] By the end of 1936 a *New York Times* editorial compared the International Brigaders to the Europeans who took part in the American War of Independence, but the War Between the States from 1861–1865 might have been a better analogy.[49] Long before going to Spain, George Orwell termed the rebels Fascists.[50] However much fascism was disliked by some people at the time, it was not yet identified with genocide and war crimes on a national scale as it came to be by 1945. In the end, the German and Italian governments did not keep their distance since they too were spoiling for a fight. Whatever the true nature of its origins, the Spanish Civil War became Europe's civil war to exiles, anti-Fascists of all stripes, and probably a good many Spaniards.

Though numbering the exiles in the International Brigades is quite impossible, some indication of size can be given by estimating Germans, Italians, Poles, Hungarians, and some others.[51] In fact, all of the first two nationalities must have been exiles and probably most of the last two. Individuals from other countries may have been legal or moral exiles; there is no way of telling. While none of the four exile nationalities was dominant in the International Brigades, the four together represent a considerable proportion of the total, as shown in Table (2).[52]

Analyzing the figures in Table (2), exiles were more than a quarter to a third of the foreign volunteers in the International Brigades. This would still be true if some Poles and Hungarians were excluded from the calculations because they had not yet left Poland and Hungary when recruited. In short, numerically the exiles were strong.

In addition, exiles were also among the first foreigners, figuring in the earliest, most crucial battles, including the battle at the University City in November 1936.[53] Italians, Poles, and Germans formed their own International Brigades in time, and each group was prominent throughout the war. Germans won the reputation of the best fighters,[54] whether they were fighting for a new home in Spain, as one writer has said, or to return to the old home of Germany.[55] While there is no disputing the importance of Germans in the International Brigades, their reputation was built by the Comintern's anti-Nazi publicity campaign, which would have praised anti-Fascist Germans no matter what they did. When they left Spain, after official demobilization or later, the exiles had no home to take them. They had lost a second home and had become exiles twice over. France was the only place for most of them, offering respite but not rest. Soon, war came

Table 2.
The Exiles as Number and Percent of Whole

	Sources							
	Delperrie de Bayac		Castells		Soviet Army Archives		League of Nations Commission	
	N	%	N	%	N	%	N	%
German	5,000[1]	14.1	4,324	7.2	2,180	6.9	1,749	13.5
Italian	3,100	8.7	5,108	8.6	2,908	9.3	1,553	12.0
Polish	4,000	11.3	5,411	9.1	3,034	9.7	1,560	12.0
Hungarian	—[2]	—	2,148	3.6	510	1.6	279	2.2
Totals	12,100	34.1	16,941	28.5	8,632	27.5	5,141	39.7

[1]Includes Austrians.

[2]Not identified in Delperrie de Bayac.

[3] Percent based on the number stated in each the four sources.

to France, again uprooting them and many found a way to continue their war to death.[56]

5. The Displaced

All kinds of exiles appeared in a time of exiles as social systems, like heavenly bodies under pressure, cast off fragments. Along with political exiles, economic exiles—the displaced—appeared after seven years of the Great Depression. Economic exiles created by the Great Depression were not political exiles in the first instance, if later they adopted radical politics that made them outcasts. This is hard to judge because the only sources available are propaganda publications and observations and confessions of middle-class intellectuals in the International Brigades, an educated guess is the best that can be made.[57]

Rosenstone's examination of a card file of the Lincoln Battalion indicates that almost half of the 1,804 cases examined listed no occupation, covering 834 individuals or 46.2 percent of the total.[58] That a recruit provided an occupation does not mean he was employed at the time of recruitment. Equally, not supplying an occupation does not prove the man was unemployed.

The volumes of propaganda about American volunteers and their own accounts seldom mention a common man, and the same is true for other nationalities.[59] Hywel Francis found that only 18 to 20 percent of the Welsh volunteers were married, far below the norm for men over 30 at the time.[60] Statistically, a common man has a wife, children, a home, a job, and is a member of a community. All these things might have been jeopardized by the Depression, and the family's standard of living might have fallen. If one in three were unemployed at the time, two in three were not. If some families disintegrated under the pressure, not all did. The attempts of the American Communist party to make dead heroes out of the fallen in Spain tell us something about both the preoccupations of the party and those it sent to Spain. Volunteers Dave Doran and Ben Leider were depicted as all-American heroes in propaganda pamphlets. Doran was a second-generation American, reared by a politically radical uncle; he joined the Young Communist League, making it his mission in life.[61] Leider, said to have been Jewish, gave up a brilliant, but unidentified, career to go to Spain.[62] Though he was later identified as a journalist, nothing was said about an established job, home, or family. The suspicion is unavoidable that his journalism was practiced at the *Daily Worker*, the daily newspaper of the Communist party in New York. Occasionally, other equally vague references in similar sources mention men giving up jobs to go to Spain.[63] These references are so rare that they seem contrived to offer a touch of normality; an example is volunteer Leonard Levinson, named by Edwin Rolfe, himself a volunteer, as having left an unspecified government job.[64] In the Depression a government job might well have been a Works Progress Administration job that was neither secure nor a career. Volunteer John Tisa had such a job.[65]

Accounts by those who wrote of their experiences in the International Brigades do nothing to allay the suspicion that there were few common men in the ranks. These writers are usually intellectuals of some kind, as their writing shows, whether that makes them bourgeois or not. They do not seem to have lived the common life described above but were often journalists of a sort, like volunteer Alvah Bessie working for the *Daily Worker* or *New Masses* in New York, or Communist party cadres like volunteers Doran, John Gates, Steve Nelson, and Sandor Voros. This same impression emanates from volunteer William Herrick's *Hermanos!*, which traces the Spanish experiences of a small group of Lincolns. At the end of the day, volunteer Louis Fischer's remark that "these fighters had left peaceful jobs and peaceful countries to die . . . in the struggle against Fascism" did not apply to Americans any more than it applied to the exiles.[66] There is little evidence that any of the Americans or the exiles had much to leave. They were available for recruitment.

The exiles were much more available, ready to strike a blow against fascism, the proven enemy that had exiled them. The translation for the displaced Americans is less obvious. The appeal of the one-struggle thesis, according to which American captains of industry were little different from Hitler, convinced many and led them to join the Communist party. Others feared importation of European fascism to the New World. Robert Rosenstone recalls the growth of indigenous proto-fascism in the United States at the time.[67] Neither publicist nor veterans, however, mention these indigenous movements, perhaps a case of assumed knowledge. Abstract hatred of fascism and capitalism are more likely to be mentioned. In one pamphlet re-issued in 1948, an Australian volunteer said that he grew to hate fascism from newspaper accounts.[68] A Dutch volunteer said nearly the same thing.[69] Some might also have said the same thing about apartheid in South Africa, but none volunteered for the African National Congress. A character in William Herrick's autobiographical novel makes the same point, that anger at dislocations at home, intellectual hatred of fascism, and the military revolt against the Popular Front government somehow fused.[70] In one pamphlet, an American volunteer despairs of the hardship and hunger in the

American Appalachian Mountains and then pledges himself for Spain saying, "this" is worth dying for.[71] What "this" is remains obscure, but somehow hardships in the Appalachian Mountains and Spain are connected.

Of course, the Great Depression was not limited to the United States. In Canada only single men could qualify for public assistance. Families disintegrated to meet this criterion, with women and children returning to the maternal home. Men gained such assistance as provided in Unemployment Relief Camps at a few locations across the continent. In the nearly four years between October 1932 and June 1936 an estimated 170,000 single, unemployed men spent some time in one or another of these camps,[72] which were disbanded because they became hotbeds of agitation and recruitment for radical causes. For men who weathered this experience, the transference of their diffuse anger to Spain may have made sense, though the burden of George Orwell's study of coal miners argues against this facile conclusion. Orwell found miners interested in their own lives, and not in the big issues during the Great Depression.[73]

A fragment of more systematic evidence confirms Orwell's conclusion. One American survey in February 1938 found no simple relationship between unemployment and support for the Spanish Republic. Among those who expressed an opinion, the business community and professionals were more likely to favor the Republic than workers or the unemployed. Specifically, the levels of sympathy were: the business community, 31 percent; professionals, 41 percent; skilled workers, 27 percent; unskilled workers, 30 percent; and the unemployed, 25 percent.[74] Perhaps middle-class individuals in this early instance of public opinion polling, moved by the Republic's democratic character, did not appreciate how much Spanish democracy differed from American democracy.

Displacement has secondary effects on persons not directly touched by it. Political failures demonstrated in the Great War, as it was still called then, were made all the more painful by the 1920s and 1930s publication of accounts by foot soldiers, like Eric Remarque's sobering *All Quiet on the Western Front.* These combined with economic failures of the seven years of the Great Depression to rob the nation-state of much legitimacy in the eyes of many intellectuals and others. Anti-fascism and democracy would have broadly appealed to them in connection with the Spanish Republic. Free-floating, intellectual cosmopolitans, inconvenienced by the Depression, did not cause their anger so much as the corrupt system to which they attributed the Depression. Worldly wise and jaded beyond their years, they were enveloped in a feigned air of *ennui.*[75] Once they were aroused, Spain would be a natural place to go, if going was to be done, Iberia being so much nearer and more familiar than China or Abyssinia (alternative places where demon fascism could have been joined). As English volunteer Esmond Romilly, said: "However strongly I sympathized with the cause of the Spanish people, no doubt if my circumstances in London had been completely satisfactory, I should have gone no further than sympathy."[76] Romilly confessed that political convictions were not the only reason he joined the International Brigades,[77] a sentiment echoed nearly 40 years later by South African volunteer Jason Gurney.[78] The cosmopolitans are difficult to categorize because the sincerity of their disenchantment brings them close to the displaced, but they differ in not suffering personally and in not being angry. On the other hand, their ennui makes them more like adventurers. They were probably something of both, and they are no less difficult to number. Recalling how few members of the bourgeoisie were in the ranks, there must have been even fewer cosmopolitans.

Jews, a more distinct and numerous group similar to the displaced, were among German, Italian, and other exiles.[79] Their motivation rings clear enough as exiles, albeit of a special kind. Some Jews were not exiles, as their enemies were quick to note, for instance Ben Leider, mentioned above.[80] One historian estimates that 30 percent of the Lincolns were Jews.[81] Peter Wyden, a volunteer, said the same.[82] On the other hand, *Life* magazine estimated that only 10 percent were, calling the statement "I know what Hitler is doing to my people" a normal explanation for volunteering.[83] Even with no discussion of specifics, the reaction seems provoked more by Hitler's race rhetoric than by any facts known at the time. Although not factually grounded, the reaction was more foresighted than most people's; the connection between Hitler and Spain was assumed in silence. The number of Jews will be further discussed under the identity of members of the International Brigaders.

6. The Anticipators

If the exiles continued yesterday's fight and if the displaced struck an angry blow, then others anticipated tomorrow's war. Amateur strategists and politically conscious men attracted to the International Brigades saw that a Fascist Spain would encircle France and threaten English access to sea lanes.[84] The official Comintern slogan declared, "Madrid is the universal frontier that separates liberty and slavery."[85] Years later, Steve Nelson, the dedicated American Communist, described a perfect domino theory from Madrid to Paris

. . . to Pearl Harbor.[86] A domino theory may also be found in the words of Welsh volunteers.[87] However, the domino theory is not repeated in Steve Nelson's 1982 autobiography after a similar domino theory was used to justify the policy of Communist containment during the Cold War.[88]

On the face of it, anticipation of another great war must have been most widespread and disturbing for central European countries like Czechoslovakia and Western Europeans like France. If another German war came, these countries would be the battlefields.[89] The Spanish Civil War offered to some a preventive war where fascism could be defeated and an all-out war including invasion of their own countries could be avoided, much in the way that Winston Churchill would have preferred to fight the Germans in Norway than in England. Such a widespread sentiment in France together with sheer proximity, would account for the preponderance of French volunteers in the International Brigades. Historian Delperrie de Bayac concludes that the threat of fascism mobilized the International Brigades.[90]

7. Adventurers

The idealist wants all his army to be as pure as he is, wrote volunteer John Sommerfield, who quickly acknowledged the impossibility.[91] Only Gabriel has ever had an army of angels. That old soldier, Socrates, to be sure, would have gently reproved the idea that any person is pure. The International Brigades comprised an army of strangers among whom was more than one fallen angel. Mercenaries, defined as those motivated by pay, were mainly if not exclusively in the air corps of the Spanish army.[92] Infantry war offered a less enticing prospect to those with pecuniary interests: little pay, long hours, flesh-tearing risks, bone-breaking labor, and death. If no mercenaries enlisted in the International Brigades, there definitely were adventurers, men who came to Spain to fight, caring not a bit for the cause. The adventurers have their own ennui. A confessed adventurer, Belgian volunteer Nick Gillain said

> Si l'on me demandait pourquoi je suis parti pour l'Espagne, je répondrais que c'est par ésprit d'aventure, et par lassitude, en cet automne pluvieux de 1936, de voir la mer grise et le ciel chargé de nuages.[93]
>
> (If I was asked why I went to Spain, I would have said that it was a spirit of adventure and of lassitude, in that rainy fall of 1936, seeing the grey sea and the cloudy sky.)

War in sunny Spain seemed preferable to autumn rains and another winter of snow in Belgium.

Others have hotly denied the presence of either adventurers or idealists in the International Brigades, probably because such sorts belittle the importance of the struggle.[94]

8. Conclusion

Each person went to Spain for a reason, but knowing this does not complete the discussion of motivation. At the same time men also had reasons for not going, as was the case of the vast majority of their peers, who stayed home. Those who went had a reason because they wanted one; they searched for a cause. As one participant noted in his diary, "Undoubtedly the great majority are here for the sake of an ideal, no matter what motive prompted them to seek one."[95] Alvah Bessie, the American volunteer, said, "Men went to Spain for various reasons, but behind almost every man I met there was a common restlessness, a loneliness."[96] In a time of causes, a time of movements, a time of social mobilization, and a time of loneliness, many people were available for recruitment or recruited by all kinds of organizations and causes that explained the present strife and offered quick, if painful, solutions. In the first instance, the choice of volunteers differed in degree, not in kind. Once in Spain, volunteering took on new dimensions. Protesting in Ottawa or Washington, moving a step ahead of the secret police, battling rightists in the streets, suffering insomnia because of stress, all of these made Spain a not-so-outlandish place to go.

No logical reason dictated that a loyal Communist, committed idealist, or desperate unemployed man go, and most did not. Consider that if every one of the 3,000 American Internationals had been a member of the Communist party, unlikely as that is, they would have represented only a tiny fraction of the party. Its membership has been estimated at 350,000 at the time.[97] The American Internationals were less than one percent of the Communist party's members. Those who did must have been like so many others caught up in the plethora of social movements of the time. Being marginal men—objectively, or subjectively, or both—the exiles and the displaced had a place in a society but had been dispossessed. For the exiles, fascism was the culprit responsible for their plight and Spain became the place to continue the fight. The displaced required a more tenuous series of abstractions to connect their plight with fascism, but once done, the sign Fascist was easily hung on the Spanish Nationalists with the help of the press, a process eased by the volunteers' ignorance of both fascism and Spain.[98] Cosmopolitans and Jews were marginal as well: the cosmopolitans by choice, Jews by chance and perhaps after that by choice. Fascism would represent the worst things to both. The adventurer, a little like the cosmopolitan, chose a personal withdrawal from his society. In different ways and to different degrees, they were all available, and for them all fascism presented a target of choice, and of opportunity for the adventurer.

The anticipators, who are the hardest to pin down, were available to embrace fascism as the enemy. The proof is that they went. In this way, they differed from those who stayed, but the nature and origin of that difference is not plain. Everything that they said and saw in their Cassandra moods was said and seen by many others who chose to cling to normal life, like a possum turning its back on the enemy and wishing it away, as a volunteer might have said. Perhaps this clinging to normality needs explanation more than does going. A more fine-grained conclusion would require even more knowledge of the anticipators' social identities. They might have been found chiefly among the French for whom Hitler's aggression meant only one thing.

Acknowledging the limitation posed by the anticipators may leave things more than a little vague. The Great Depression created an enormous amount of latent social and political frustration which, together with the aftermath of the Great War, must have made striking a blow highly desirable.[99] If, as Edwin Rolfe said, "There is a no-man's land between conviction and action into which the great majority of mankind never venture," then the Spanish Civil War occurred at a time that might have been calculated to arrest world attention, invoke powerful symbols, and galvanize a partly mobilized audience.[100] The Spanish Civil War was something that people cared about; people who cared nothing about Spain cared about the Spanish Civil War and still do. As with opposition to the Vietnam War, support for the Spanish Republic seemed the one pure cause of a generation. In the words of observer Murray Kempton, "It was the passion of that small segment of my generation which felt a personal commitment to the revolution."[101] The less one knew about Spain, the more pure the cause and the occasion to concentrate anger and relieve frustrations. Listen to the words of volunteer Jason Gurney:

> The Spanish Civil War seemed to provide the chance for a single individual to take a positive and effective stand on an issue which appeared to be absolutely clear. Either you were opposed to the growth of Fascism and went out to fight against it, or you acquiesced in its crime and were guilty of permitting its growth.[102]

This voice perceives the world to be morally incoherent and sees the need to act. Armageddon was at hand. Who but a knave or a fool would hold back at the last trumpet call? Gurney honestly admits in the next breath that ultimately going, while politically right, was motivated by personal reasons. Not to have gone would have made him feel a knave or a fool, and he was free to go, unrooted in work or family.

Another equally honest volunteer, Walter Gregory, disarmingly confessed in retrospect that he had no ready answer to the question why he went to Spain.[103]

Other volunteers have said that they went ". . . so as not to be left out . . .," to seize the opportunity to "participate" in history, to fulfill a "general feeling of commitment" for a "better society," and to follow what "was romantic," to remain loyal to friends.[104]

This is the human comedy. If their actions proved that the International Brigaders were not knaves, to some extent the advent of anti-Fascist World War II proved that they were not fools in their distorted judgment, something that cannot be said of all politicians of the era. Of course, J. Edgar Hoover was right to say that Americans were fools for not knowing a thing about the Spanish conflict, but he was wrong to suppose that they needed or wanted to know anything to convince them to go. They wanted to go somewhere and do something. The propaganda did not create this impulse but the brilliant propaganda conveyed on a new scale by radio, newsreel, and still photographs lighted the way to Spain. If the propaganda fooled some about the conduct of the war, it did not create the desire to go from nothing, any more than did the propaganda that recruited the armies of the Great War.[105] Spain became an opportunity for moral and political therapy for the exiles, the displaced, the anticipators, the cosmopolitans, the Jews, and the adventurers alike.

Had there been a civil war in France or Italy in the 1930s, the same types of men would have gone for the same reasons. The same men would have gone under the banner of anti-fascism, however appropriate or inappropriate that label might have been. It was Europe's civil war, not Spain's, involving men from the New World and beyond, and it became the world's civil war as all great wars are. At Guadalajara, Italians stood against Italians, as Germans often stood against Germans elsewhere in what was Italy's civil war, Germany's, Poland's, and so on.[106] The volunteers who knew and cared nothing of Spain, shared this common characteristic.

Nothing in the publicity or in volunteers' reports shows an initial knowledge of or affection for Spain. It was simply the forum for conflict. Once there, some International Brigaders toyed with living in Spain after the war, but they were reacting to the euphoria of arrival.[107] A few tried to learn Spanish in those first days.[108] In the end, little if any interaction bonded Spaniards and International Brigade volunteers, although the International Brigades always had a large number of Spaniards, 60 percent at the end.[109] Moreover, the first spontaneous volunteers enlisted in the Spanish army and militia.

By the same token, precious little sign of interaction exists among the Internationals themselves. After the glow of the unity between the proletarians and progressives faded in the maelstrom of battle, slogans remained only on posters, not on lips. For most of the men the multiple language barrier made impossible the exchange of more than the clenched first salute of the Popular Front: it truly was an army of strangers.

More important, volunteers did not come to Spain to know Spain, to know each other, or to fight together. Each nationality, if not each individual, came to fight a private war. Once in the fray, each soldier battled the eternal war every soldier has always fought, the war to survive without shame. A Republic triumphant would have changed nothing for these men. They could not have stopped with Spain; the war they yearned to win was both at home and ultimately within themselves.

The analogy must be a crusade, one that volunteers have repeatedly chosen for themselves.[110] Promoters of the First Crusade to the Holy Land hoped for an army of knights and got an army of peasants.[111] The promoters of the International Brigades hoped for an army of experienced soldiers and got an army of neophytes. The promoters of the Crusades, who were doubtful of more than a handful of respondents to the appeal, were overwhelmed by the spontaneous response of dispossessed peasants in search of heavenly and earthly salvation.[112] Tom Wintringham, who first conceived the idea of recruiting volunteers to join the spontaneous volunteers already in Spain, doubted that 50 Englishmen could be raised; yet within months 50 Englishmen would die in a single hot afternoon at the Jarama River.[113] The International Brigaders must have seen themselves like the "mythological hero" who "is the champion not of things become but of things becoming, the dragon to be slain by him . . . precisely."[114] When any new order is in the making, to be chosen, one must choose, as the volunteers did. Whether that makes them heroes remains to be seen.

ENDNOTES

1. J. Edgar Hoover, *The Masters of Deceit* (New York: Pocket Books, 1959), 71. For the record, International Brigaders reportedly received the conscript's pay of ten pesetas a day when they were paid. This was equivalent to four shillings, according to Geoffrey Cox, *The Defense of Madrid* (London: Gollancz, 1937), 172, or perhaps $ 0.60 at the time, according to Marion Merriman and Warren Lerude, *American Commander in Spain: Robert Hale Merriman and the Abraham Lincoln Brigade* (Reno: University of Nevada Press, 1986), 189. By the way, many Nationalist volunteers in Falange units received even less, three pesetas a day, according to Stanley G. Payne, *The Franco Regime, 1936–1939* (Madison: University of Wisconsin Press, 1987), 165.
2. Impressions of other observers about the percentage of the Americans who were Communists raises the question, if it need be raised, of Hoover's accuracy. The political affiliations of the International Brigaders will be treated in Chapter 6.
3. See U.S. Congress, 83rd Congress, 1st Session, 1953, Senate, Committee on the Judiciary, Sub-Committee to Investigate the Administration of the Internal Security Act, *Hearings on Interlocking Subversion in Government Departments,* 765–772.
4. Hoover, 72.
5. Variations on this slogan advertised the Republic throughout the world, thanks to the Comintern.
6. Joseph North, *Men in the Ranks* (New York: Friends of the Abraham Lincoln Brigade, 1939), 5.
7. Jason Gurney, *Crusade in Spain* (London: Faber and Faber, 1974), 36.
8. On the political dimensions of the International Brigades, see Hugh Thomas, *The Spanish Civil War* (3rd ed.) (Harmondsworth: Penguin, 1977), 152–151.
9. When demobilization parades were held later Negrín was present for photographs, which were was useful publicity, as was La Pasionaria's incomparable oratory.
10. League of Nations, *Official Journal, Special Supplement, Number 183,* Records of the Assembly, 19th Session, 21 September 1938, p. 90.
11. Ibid.
12. The screenplay improved upon the novel, Dorothy B. Hughes, *The Fallen Sparrow* (New York: Carroll & Graf, 1988 [1942]). On Garfield's political sympathies and their affect on his career, see Larry Ceplair and Steven England, *The Inquisition in Hollywood* (Garden City: Anchor, 1980), 144 ff.
13. See *L'Humanité,* 18 October 1937, p. 3.
14. Herbert Matthews, *Two Wars and More To Come* (New York: Carrick and Evans, 1938), 207. See also his *The Yoke and the Arrow* (New York: Braziller, 1957), 33 and 35.
15. Judy Keene, *The Last Mile to Huesca: An Australian Nurse in the Spanish Civil War* (Sydney: University of New South Wales Press, 1988).
16. See, for example, Andreu Castells, *Las Brigadas Internacionales de la Guerra de España* (Barcelona: Editorial Ariel, 1974), 21-23.
17. Tom Wintringham, *English Captain* (London: Faber and Faber, 1939), 26–28.
18. "Fascists Massed 60 miles North of Madrid," *New York Times,* 26 July 1936, p. 24.
19. Randolfo Pacciardi, *Il Battaglione Garibaldi* (Lugano: Nuove Edizioni di Capolago, 1938), 7.
20. Robert Rosenstone, *Crusade of the Left* (New York: Pegasus, 1969), 96.
21. J. Schleimann, "The Life and Work of Willi Münzenberg," *Survey* 55 (April 1965): 78–79.
22. R. Dan Richardson, *Comintern Army: the International Brigades and the Spanish Civil War* (Lexington: University Press of Kentucky, 1982), 32.
23. Ibid., 35.
24. Hywel Francis uses "catalyst" in "Welsh Miners and the Spanish Civil War," *Journal of Contemporary History* 5 (1970) 3, pp. 179 and 181.

25. Gurney, 66.
26. Victor Hoar, *The MacKenzie-Papineau Battalion* (Toronto: Copp Clark, 1969), 20–21.
27. William Rust, *Britons in Spain* (New York: International, 1939), 18.
28. Virginia Cowles, *Looking for Trouble* (London: Hamilton, 1941), 46.
29. See Antonio Candela, *Adventures of an Innocent in the Spanish Civil War* (Cornwall: United Writers, 1989), 64.
30. So say the victors in *Las Brigadas Internacionales* (Madrid: Officina Informativa Española, 1949), 19, and the vanquished in Rust, 4.
31. Massimo Mangilli-Climpson, *Men of Heart of Red, White and Green* (New York: Vantage, 1985), 22.
32. *New York Times*, 26 July 1936, p. 24.
33. Ibid., 13 August 1936, p. 11.
34. "Last Hours of Madrid," *Times*, 9 November 1936, p. 12.
35. Douglas W. Foard, "A Chronology of the Spanish Civil War: 1930–1939," *Historical Dictionary of the Spanish Civil War*, p. 504.
36. *New York Times*, 21 November 1936, p. 7.
37. Wayfarer, *The International Brigade* (Sussex: Ditching Press, n.d.), 7.
38. See "Foreign Colonies in Barcelona," *Times* (London), 24 July 1936, 14.
39. "Italians" Ordeal in Barcelona," ibid., 28 July 1936, p. 13.
40. Paolo Spriano, *Storia del Partito Communiste Italiano* (Turin: G. Einaudi, 1970), 3: p. 90.
41. Pacciardi, 2.
42. Gustav Regler, *The Great Crusade*, trans. W. Chambers and B. Mussey (New York: Longmans, 1940), 140.
43. Carlo Rosselli, *Oggi in Spagna, Domani in Italia* (Turin: Einaudi, 1967 [1938]), 70.
44. Regler (1940), 374.
45. *Interbrigadisten: Der Kampf deutscher Kommunisten und anderer Antifaschisten in national-revolutionären Krieg des spanischen Volkes 1936 bis 1939* (Dresden: Deutscher Militarverlad, 1966), 13.
46. Ibid., 147.
47. "Fascists" Rising Feared," *Times*, 17 July 1936, p. 1.
48. *New York Times*, 26 July 1936, p. 24.
49. Ibid., 2 December 1936, p. 26.
50. George Orwell, *The Road to Wigan Pier* (Harmondsworth: Penguin, 1982 [1937]), 150.
51. André Malraux speaks of the German and Italian exiles in *L'Espoir* (Paris: Gallimard, 1937), 410; cf. Cox, 83–85.
52. Sources are cited in the bibliography.
53. *New York Times*, 10 November 1936, p. 20.
54. Wintringham, 36.
55. See the letter attributed to Joe Monks in Marcel Acier, ed., *From Spanish Trenches* (New York: Modern Age Books, 1937), 123.
56. See Patricia Fagen, *Exiles and Citizen* (Austin: University of Texas Press, 1973).
57. One propaganda piece boasted 12 languages alone in the Dimitrov Battalion, enough to limit any researcher. See *The Book of the XV Brigade* (Madrid: Commissariat of War, 1938), 25.
58. Rosenstone, 368–369.
59. The effort to make the volunteers seem ordinary was unsparing if ineffective, for example, in "Americans have died fighting for Democracy in Spain," *Life* 4 (1937), 14–28.
60. Hywel Francis nominates 18 percent in "Welsh Miners and the Spanish Civil War," 182, and 20 percent in *Miners Against Fascism: Wales and the Spanish Civil War* (London: Lawrence and Wishart, 1984), 213.
61. Joseph Staróbin, *The Life and Death of an American Hero: The Story of Dave Doran*

(New York: New Age, 1938). For a different view of hero Doran see Sandor Voros, *American Commissar* (Philadelphia: Chilton and Co., 1961), 340.

62. *Ben Leider American Hero* (New York: Ben Leider Memorial Fund, n.d.), 4 and 5. Cf. Acier, 151, where the same is written of Leider.
63. North, 30, and Acier, 157.
64. Rosenstone, 136.
65. Tisa, 14.
66. Louis Fischer, *Men and Politics* (New York: Duell, Sloan, and Pearce, 1941), 394.
67. Rosenstone, 73.
68. Nettie Palmer, et al., *Australians in Spain*, rev. ed. (Sydney: Current Books, 1948), 15.
69. Jef Last, *The Spanish Tragedy*, trans. D. Hallett (London: Routledge, 1939 [1938]), 200.
70. William Herrick, *Hermanos!* (London: Weidenfeld and Nicolson, 1969), 66.
71. *Ben Leider*, 11.
72. Hoar, 27–29.
73. Orwell, *The Road to Wigan Pier*, 80.
74 Allen Guttmann, *The Wound in the Heart* (Glencoe: Free Press, 1962), 65. Guttmann cites as the source of this information Hugh Jones Parry, "The Spanish Civil War: A Study in American Public Opinion, Propaganda, and Pressure Groups" (Unpublished thesis, University of Southern California, 1949), 367–370. Where we find that not only were those with no opinion excluded from the analysis, but also those who did not take sides. Those with no opinion comprised 24 percent of the sample. Of the remaining 76 percent, more than half (54 percent) declared for neutrality, the official American policy at the time. That means that only about 35 percent of the original sample was analyzed by occupation. Other public opinion polling information from the time is found in the American Institute of Public Opinion, "Surveys 1938–1939," *Public Opinion Quarterly*, 3 (1939) 4, p. 600. Asked which side of the Spanish Civil War they favored, those that took sides favored the Republic; specifically, in February 1937, 65 percent; February 1938, 75 percent; and December 1938, 76 percent. These published figures were misleading because they excluded those who offered no opinion. The full distribution is reported in Parry's dissertation:

	Loyalist	Franco	Neutral
February 1937	30%	16%	54%
February 1937	50%	17%	33%
December 1938	46%	14%	40%

These results show a preference for the Republic, but it is not as overwhelming as to be inferred from the figures published at the time.

75. Cowles, 51.
76. Esmond Romilly, *Boadilla* (London: Hamish Hamilton, 1937), 26.
77. Ibid., 27.
78. Gurney, 36.
79. Malraux, 410.
80. Wayfarer, p. 31, and Adolfo Lizón Gadea, *Brigadas Internacionales en España* (Madrid: Editora Nacional, 1940), 65.
81. Rosenstone, 110.
82. Wyden, 5.
83. "Americans have died fighting for Democracy in Spain," *Life* 4, 14–28 March 1937, pp. 56–57.
84. For example, Henry Blythe, *Spain over Briton* (London: Routledge, 1937); Phillippe Lamour and André Cayette, *Sauvons la France en Espagne* (Paris: Baudiniere, 1937), 16-17; Acier, 171; and Hywel Francis, *Miners Against Fascism*, 213.

85. So said Fernando Valera, a Republican deputy, on Madrid Radio on 8 November 1936, see Thomas, 481.
86. Steve Nelson, *The Volunteers* (New York: Masses and Mainstream, 1953), 181. (At the publication of this book, Nelson was imprisoned under the Smith Act; see Joseph North's introduction, 9.) Cf. Last, 53 and 116.
87. Hywel Francis, "Welsh Miners and the Spanish Civil War," 188.
88. Steve Nelson, J. R. Barrett, and R. Ruck, *Steve Nelson: American Radical* (Pittsburgh: University of Pittsburgh Press, 1982), 183–249.
89. Edwin Rolfe, *The Lincoln Battalion* (New York: Random House, 1939), 23.
90. Delperre de Bayac, 366.
91. John Sommerfield, *Volunteer in Spain* (New York: Knopf, 1937), 29.
92. See, for example, Oloff de Wet, *The Patrol is Ended* (New York: Doubleday, 1938), 13.
93. Nick Gillain, *Le Mercenaire* (Paris: Libraire Arthéme Fayard, 1938), 7; cf. Sommerfield, 57.
94. Hywel Francis, "Welsh Miners and the Spanish Civil War," *Journal of Contemporary History*, 5 (1970) 3, p. 182.
95. The diary of Miles Tomalin, quoted by Thomas, 455.
96. Alvah Bessie, *Men in Battle* (New York: Scribner's, 1939), 181.
97. Harvey Klehr estimates 350,000 in *Communist Cadre* (Stanford: Hoover Institute Press, 1978), 83. Vivan Gornick suggests that there were more than a million members at the time in *The Romance of American Communism* (New York: Basic, 1977), 23. If so, then those who volunteered were a tiny fraction of the whole.
98. It continues in, for example, "Arthur Koestler . . .," *The Australian*, 5 March 1983, p. 10.
99. Hoar, p. 17.
100. Rolfe, p. 15.
101. Murray Kempton, *Part of Our Time* (New York: Dell, 1955), 317.
102. Gurney, 36. Similar sentiments may be found in many other memoirs, e.g., Milt Felsen, *The Anti-Warrior: A Memoir* (Iowa City: University of Iowa Press, 1989), 100 and Laurie Lee, *A Moment of War* (London: Viking, 1991), 46.
103. Walter Gregory, *The Shallow Grave* (London: Gollancz, 1986), 157.
104. Gerassi, 43, 44, 75, and 49 and Louis Fischer, "Worshippers from Afar," *The God That Failed*, ed. R. H. Crossman (New York: Harper & Row, 1949), 187.
105. Voros, 270.
106. See John F. Cloverdale, *Italian Intervention in the Spanish Civil War* (Princeton: Princeton University Press, 1975), 205–263.
107. For example, the letter signed Hank, dated 2 April 1937 in Acier, 160.
108. Bessie, 33.
109. In the months at the Jarama River, the Lincoln Battalion had a Spanish Battalion on its left flank, but there is no sign of any interaction, see Gurney, 142. Volunteers' accounts neglect the 60 percent of the men in the International Brigades who were Spanish.
110. Note how often "crusade" appears in books by International Brigaders and in books about them, e.g., Gurney and Regler for the former and Rosenstone for the latter.
111. See Steven Runciman, *A History of the Crusades* (Cambridge: Cambridge University Press, 1957), 1: 108.
112. Ibid., 108–110.
113. Wintringham, 29.
114. Joseph Campbell, *The Hero with a Thousand Faces* (London: Abacus, 1948), 284. This description would fit neither Hector nor Achilles, nor for that matter most of Shakespeare's heroes.

CHAPTER 5

How Many Went?

1. The Spear Carriers

The story of the International Brigades in the Spanish Civil War has often been told by veterans and admirers, and such books continue to appear.[1] These works brightly illuminate every aspect of the creation and activities of the International Brigades, and yet in the center of the stage the men in the ranks of the International Brigades remain shadowed. Organization tables and orders of battle give only unit names and designations that comprised the five International Brigades, also providing the names of commanding officers. To fathom the motivations of the men in the ranks, the spear carriers, requires reliance on testimony and impression. Moreover, points of brute fact must also be decided from the same kind of evidence. Few if any records seem to have been kept; none are cited even by the veterans such as Louis Fischer, who was briefly an International Brigade quartermaster.[2] Records that once existed may not have survived the defeat of the Republican government. Not keeping records was a deliberate policy to frustrate enemy agents (from the other Spain, Germany, and Italy) bent on disrupting recruitment and organization of the International Brigades.[3] The secrecy surrounding the entire enterprise served many purposes: to avoid provoking neutral countries where recruiting occurred; to mask the sponsorship of the local Communist parties, the Comintern, and the Soviet

Union; and to protect many of the volunteers, like the exiles, who had long since adopted aliases to suit the occasion. The enterprise was possible only as long as few if any questions were asked. The host government refrained from questioning the local fund raising activities of Spanish Republican supporters to see if more than funds were being raised. Volunteers refrained from questioning who was recruiting them and paying their fares to Spain. The recruiter refrained from questioning the birth certificate, identity card, or passport the recruit presented.

The difficulty of characterizing the identities of the men in the International Brigades begins with the brute question: how many were there? Their nationalities, ages, classes, and politics are all equally obscure. Only that small number of Internationals whose biographies were produced for propaganda purposes during the war, or who were described by writers in Spain, or who have since written books, have identities. These individuals are unlikely to be representative or to be taken at face value. In spite of their suffering and the mythology that has surrounded them for so long, most of the remainder have nearly disappeared. Because identifying the men of the International Brigades is so difficult, most observers forego the attempt; instead, writers in the primary and secondary literature alike settle on estimates of number and composition, often without a word on their basis.[4] At best, those who discuss wider aspects of the Spanish Civil War include a guarded paragraph or footnote on problems of number, and these estimates differ enormously, with little or no effort made to reconcile or prove them.[5] To illustrate; Robert Whealey in James Cortada's *Historical Dictionary of the Spanish Civil War* has estimated 59,000 as the size of the International Brigades, while less than 50 pages later Robert Rosenstone has suggested 35,000. Nowhere is the discrepancy between these figures noted and resolved.[6] Franco's physique receives more space than the number of men in the International Brigades, despite the many entries devoted to them. When there is insufficient light, one proceeds carefully by touch, one step at a time.

2. The Number

Though world-wide recruitment for the International Brigades was disorganized and hampered by secrecy, it was effective. Between December 1936 and June 1938, the Comintern program directed many thousands of men to Spain. In the early days of the conflict, when the idea of the International Brigades had just been formed, an anti-Semitic, anti-Republican pamphlet published in England asserted that 100,000 villains had already flocked to the cause.[7] In early 1937, the Paris newspaper *Le Figaro* reported an estimated 70,000 to 75,000 International Brigaders.[8] Well after the war, a publication from the Spanish Information Office surpassed this prediction by declaring no fewer than 125,000 red hooligans made up the International Brigades.[9] This figure appeared in other Nationalist sources in the war's aftermath.[10] About a decade ago, one writer blithely numbered 100,000.[11] Many years later, a Nationalist historian, Ricardo de la Cierva y de Hoces, arrived at 80,000 in a general history of the war.[12] However in another of his works devoted to the International Brigades he settled on 90,000.[13] Another Spanish historian published a comprehensive study of the Republican army repeating that 70,000 foreigners were with the Republic.[14] Shortly thereafter, Luis Aguilera Duran opted for 63,000, consciously drawing back from the Spanish Information Office's 1948 claim of 125,000.[15] Andreu Castells, whose book was published in Franco's Spain a year later in 1974, estimated 59,380 with a great show of precision based on testimony and impressions but not on documentation.[16] This estimate was accepted and was repeated by one of the most impassioned keepers of the International Brigades faith, volunteer Paul Preston.[17] Many have regarded Castells's book as authoritative.[18]

On the other hand, some estimates set the number far lower. La Pasionaria, Spanish Communist leader during the civil war, and her collaborators in exile after the war suggest between 30,000 and 35,000.[19] The figure 35,000 has also been stated by American and English volunteers,[20] a figure accepted by two sympathetic historians,[21] and by French veterans.[22] One book categorically noted 37,351 in May of 1938, claiming that this number represents nearly 25 percent of the Spanish Republican army.[23] Some indication of the confusion surrounding the question is shown by another source whose best estimate was 35,000; six pages later this author produced a table that totals to 37,000 or 38,000.[24] References to Soviet army archives showed the number to be exactly 31,237.[25] This lower range of estimates around 35,000 comes mainly from the Republican perspective. Ludwig Renn, a German Communist with the International Brigades, confidently declared that there were 32,000 International Brigaders.[26] There is no simple concurrence within the Republican camp just as there is not in the Nationalist one. One American volunteer, John Gates, numbered 25,000 in the International Brigades,[27] while another, Sandor Voros, claimed 50,000.[28] Both were commissars and might have been in positions to know. This figure also appears in a book by British volunteer Peter Wyden.[29] A figure of 46,000 exists,[30] as does 45,000.[31] David Mitchell in his widely screened television documentary said that 35,000 men in the International Brigades were commanded by a cadre of 5,000, making 40,000 in all.[32] More interesting still, Michael Alpert's comprehensive study of the Republican army omits foreigners altogether.[33]

How many foreign volunteers in total were in the International Brigades? Answering this fundamental but all too often neglected question requires examining a range of sources as set out in Table (3).

The partisan interests of the persons involved explain a good portion of the difference between low and high estimates. Table (3) above illustrates that all higher estimates, except Bauman, Prittie and *Le Figaro*, come from Franco's Spain. Presumably, Prittie simply repeated one of these sources in his biography of Willy Brandt, the post-

Table 3
The Range of Estimates

32 sources

The number	The sources and years
140,000	*Spain* (1938)
125,000	Lizón Gadea (1940) and the Spanish Information Office (1948)
100,000	Prittie (1974), Wayfarer (nd)
90,000	de la Cierva y de Hoces (1973) and Salas Larrazabal (1973)
80,000	de la Cierva y de Hoces (1970)
75,000	*Le Figaro* (1937)
63,000	Aguilera Duran (1974)
60,000	Bauman (1979)
59,380	Castells (1974), Whealey (1981), Viñas (1985), Preston (1986)
50,000	Voros (1961) and Wyden (1983)
46,000	*Adelante!* (1976)
45,000	Alba (1948), Geiser (1988), and Fernandez (1975)
40,000	Stewart (1972), Mitchell (1982), Mangill-Climpson (1985)
37,000	*Vrijwilligers* (1978)
37,351	Bolin (1967)
35,000	Wintringham (1939), Rolfe (1939), Delperrie de Bayac (1968), Thomas (1977), and Diamant (1979)
31,237	García (1956), Maidanik (1960), and Payne (1967)
30,000	La Pasionaria (Ibarruri) (1967).
25,000	Gates (1958)

Sources: The full citation of each source is to be found in the bibliography.

war German political leader, who visited Spain as a young exile during the Spanish Civil War. *Le Figaro's* estimate might be attributed to the heat of the moment. Bauman claims to follow Castells but rounds Castells's figure up to 60,000. On the other hand, the lower estimates come from International Brigaders like Voros, Geiser, Wintringham, Rolfe, and Gates, or Republicans like La Pasionaria and Garcia.

If the sources are divided into Republican and Nationalist, within both camps the range is 100 percent or more, from 59,380 to 140,000 for the high estimates of the Nationalists and from 25,000 to 50,000 for the low of the Republicans; such data make further statistical analysis unreliable. Thomas, Delperrie de Bayac, Stewart, and Whealey are historians and their estimates range from 35,000 to 59,380. That Luis Bolín, a Nationalist diplomat, offers a middling estimate seems surprising. Preston still follows Castells who wrote in Franco's Spain, as does Vixas writing in Spain after Franco's death. For reasons of their own, Nationalists have generally stressed the magnitude of the foreign intrusion on behalf of the Republic, an exaggeration made all the easier by pro-Republican hyperbole of early war days. Bolín is an exception to this rule of thumb. At times, Republicans wanted to maximize the size of foreign involvement to portray the struggle as global, and at other times they wanted to minimize it to portray the struggle as Spanish on their side. As Pierre Broué and Emile Témine have written, the number of foreign volunteers is very difficult to determine with precision. Those survivors in positions of authority disagree about such basic questions, and documentation, such as it was, did not survive. Add the tendency to exaggerate, and the picture clouds even further, a tendency not limited to the Nationalists alone, contrary to the claim of Broué and Témine.[34]

More than a little guess-work figures in these estimates because evidence is scarce. Take, for example, the International Brigade identity card for Georges Enrique Halley, reproduced by Delperrie de Bayac (and nowhere else in the vast oeuvre on the International Brigades) who makes little of it.[35] A casual reader might overlook it as a curious relic, but the Frenchman Georges Enrique Halley has not been left to rest in peace. The Nationalist historian de la Cierva y de Hoces cited this card in Delperrie de Bayac's reproduction as evidence—the only evidence—for his claim of 90,000 men in the International Brigades.[36] Georges Enrique Halley's military card, as reproduced by Delperrie de Bayac, carries the number 91,468. De la Cierva inferred that this number represents foreigners in the International Brigades, but nothing suggests that the card number played this role. De la Cierva's inference has also been made by

Stewart Cameron using the number 44,986 on American volunteer Sandor Voros's card.[37]

To use the number in this way assumes that the foreigners in the International Brigades were assigned numbers in a uniform series, regardless of their individual date of entry, point of registration, language group, or method of recruitment. Voros was a cadre, but it is assumed that his number is part of the same sequence as that of Halley. It assumes that when the International Brigades were formed after many foreign volunteers had already formed military units in Spain, there was a retrospective enrollment. It assumes that anti-Communist Italian Socialists allowed themselves to be registered on a master list along with the German Stalinists and others. These assumptions stretch the imagination too far. One of the things we know about the International Brigades is that they were disorganized. To take a mundane example, the number on my driver's licence is 8,351, but this does not mean that 8,350 other expatriate Americans are licensed to drive in New South Wales, Australia. Delperrie de Bayac did not cite this reproduction as proof of 90,000 International Brigaders.[38] Though Bauman reproduces an identity card numbered 72,086 in his book, that of José Naga-Venero, a native of Peru and a Chicago resident, this card has not yet been used to prove the existence of 72,085 other International Brigaders.[39] One day it will.

The problem becomes even more difficult without good will. Who, after all, counts as an international? Many foreigners arrived in Republican Spain throughout the civil war. Like the writers and journalists, some visited, but some bore arms. Individuals, like George Orwell, were scattered throughout Republican Spanish military units.[40] These men were not members of the International Brigades, but they were foreign volunteers. Since they were not organized as foreigners, there is no way to enumerate them, though Hugh Thomas's educated guess is 5,000.[41] In addition, men were recruited for the Republican air corps, some were volunteers, like André Malraux,[42] but others were mercenaries.[43] Some flyers were organized as an International Air Service for a time, but not all foreign flyers were placed in that unit. Moreover, the International Air Service had no connection with the International Brigades on the ground. This International Air Service did not work exclusively or mainly with the International Brigades and there is little sign of personal contact between the Internationals of air and earth, as is typical in any army. Malraux's artistic curiosity made him exceptional in seeking contact with other foreigners in Spain, including those in the International Brigades. There were also non-combatant volunteers, mainly women and men working in ambulance and medical services;

Thomas suggests as many as 10,000 of these, an estimate exceedingly difficult to substantiate.[44] No one seems to have kept track of noncombatant volunteers. In addition, another 500 to 1,000 International Brigade recruits reportedly perished before reaching Spain, many of them when the Republican ship, *Ciudad Barcelona*, was sunk in May 1937.[45] No doubt others, too, perished along the way, some of them frightened and alone.

Conversely, certain members of the International Brigades were foreigners but not volunteers, and these formed the cadre. Officers and commissars, the cadre, were all steadfast Communists nearly to a man, except the Italians who were dominated by anti-Communist Socialists.[46] Though none was Russian, many had taken up residence in the Soviet Union, and they were sent to Spain. During the purges, many of them were later called back to Moscow from the firing line in Spain to the firing squad of Stalin's justice. These men were extremely important to the International Brigades and to the men in the ranks, but they in no way represent the International Brigaders in identity or motivation, nor would all of them number more than a few thousand. Mitchell suggests 5,000 compared with 35,000 for the ranks, making every eighth man a cadre.[47] If cadres were all officers that may be too many; however the International Brigades did feature a double command structure with a political commissar next to every military officer. Accordingly, a cadre of one-eighth might be closer to the truth than first appears. Some of those who became commissars probably were among the exiles living in Russia who had pestered Stalin to fight Hitler. The idea of an international brigade, reminiscent of the international column that fought with the Bolsheviks in the Russian Civil War, allowed Stalin to send these pests off to fight Hitler.[48] Those earlier internationals allied to the Bolsheviks were also the subject of a bitter and enduring propaganda battle.[49]

Soviet citizens were not permitted to volunteer for service. In 1943 in "Looking Back on the Spanish Civil War," George Orwell predicted that if Franco remained in office one of the chief lies infecting history would be a "Russian army that never existed will become historical fact."[50] The French ambassador to Spain in 1936 put the number of Russian infantry at 21,000.[51] More than a generation later, Nationalist historian Salas Larrazabal echoed this figure, citing 20,000. In 1937, *Le Figaro* published 75,000.[52] Thirty years later Luis Bolín, a Nationalist diplomat, reported the existence of 9,000 Russian infantry.[53] In 1979, Geraldo Gino F. Bauman writing in Lima, Peru, asserted there were 8,000 Russians.[54] Later in 1982, Anthony Beevor named a modest figure of 4,000, attributing it to recent but unnamed

Figure 2. War as glamor, a single handsome and youthful individual strikes an idealized pose. The man is Juan Modesto (a Republican military leader of early note). This picture was widely published in Spain and abroad. Its image of the dramatic individual would have been known to many in the International Brigades, and so perhaps set a standard for them. It is reproduced in Hugh Tomes, *The Spanish Civil War* (Rev ed) (New York: Harper, 1977), p. 464.

Figure 3. This is perhaps the most famous picture from a war that generated many famous pictures. It has a title, 'Muerte en accieón' (Death in Action). We can be confident it was staged. It is by Robert Capa. The man does not look like an International Brigader from his uniform, but his image was well known to many of them. It appeared in *Life*.

Figure 4. A man carries a wounded comrade up a mountain road. Another Robert Capa picture from *Life* and it, too, looks staged. I reproduced it from Tomas Salvador, *La Guerra de España en sus Fotografias* (Barcelona: Ediciones Madrid, 1966), p. 222.

Figure 5. Defeat and retreat in the snow after the brutal battle at Teruel in the bitter cold of February 1938. These are Republicans climbing out of the valley, an escape only possible because the bad weather limited the Nationalist air force. It is reproduced from Vincente Rójo, *España Heroica* (3d ed) (Barcelona: Ariel, 1975 [1942]), p. 96.

Figure 6. A group of severely wounded Internationals awaiting repatriation. The one-armed man is placed carefully in the center to show his loss. It is reproduced in *The Spanish Civil War: A History in Pictures* (New York: Norton, 1986) on page 90, 173.

Figure 7. Marching through the streets of Madrid. These men are not armed or uniformed. The small number of spectators show no enthusiasm (at upper left or across the street on the right). This must have been a memorable occasion for the marchers, giving what was probably a full-throated rendition of the 'Internationale.' It is reproduced from Hugh Tomes *et al.*, *La Guerra Civil Española* (Madrid: Ediciones Urbion, 1980), Volume II, p. 365.

Figure 8. This is an action photograph that looks less staged than most. The closer man has an arm patch which looks like the Saint George Cross (which would make him English). It is clearer in the photograph than the photocopy. The other man has on a helmet that looks French from this angle. Reproduced from Ricardo de la Cierva, *Historia ilustrada de la guerra civil España* (Madrid: Danae, 1970), p. 27.

research.[55] The irony here is that while Beevor admired Orwell, he did exactly what Orwell feared; he created a Russian army, albeit a small one, out of hardened air. Such a claim has been made repeatedly since the war and for some the claim proves the existence of such a Soviet force.

Parades of incoming volunteers may have looked like Russians, especially since many Republicans desperately wanted Russian intervention.[56] However, many sources in a position to know say unequivocally that there were no Russian infantry.[57] Instead, Soviet soldiers acted as advisers to the Spanish Army, some technicians in signals, instructors to teach pilots, and some pilots and tank crews who did enter battle. Thomas cautiously suggests 2,000, though their number would be guess work.[58] Since they never seem to have known contact with the men of the International Brigades, who would have been delighted to meet a Soviet comrade in arms, they may have numbered as few as that. Nor were captured Russians a feature of Nationalist propaganda, which they would have been had any been taken. Presumably, Russians in Spain would have been under strict discipline to keep to themselves and to avoid publicity. The story goes that Stalin personally ordered the Soviets he sent to Spain to stay well clear of cannon fire, a concern not for their safety, but for fear of bad publicity. Since the International Brigades received constant publicity, especially when going into battle as shock troops as they invariably did, the few Russians in Spain would have steered well clear of them. In the political calculus of the time, a presence in Spain would have undermined the moral superiority of the Soviet position in criticizing Italy and Germany for direct intervention.

Some discrepancies in estimates of the number of men in the International Brigades arose because not all men in them were foreigners. One reason for forming the International Brigades was to create a model army raised from veterans of the Great War. A neutral in that earlier war, Spain had no body of trained veterans. While the Spanish Republican conscript army was being trained and equipped, this model army would provide an example of efficiency and discipline to inspire the Spanish to the *levée en masse*.[59] That they might benefit from the object lesson of this model army, Spaniards themselves were included in the formations of the International Brigades from the start. Hence, a military commission from the League of Nations, which supervised the evacuation of the foreign combatants from Republican Spain in 1938 and 1939, found that 60 percent of men in the five International Brigades were Spanish.[60] Perhaps 80,000 or 100,000 or 120,000 men served in the five

International Brigades, but only about 32,000 of them were foreign volunteers with another 3,000 to 4,000 officers and commissars.

A further margin of error occurs because some foreigners adopted Spanish citizenship, particularly the stateless persons who had their national passports revoked. The number was not great, and the League of Nations commission included these people to the extent possible. Finally, a certain number of Spanish-speaking foreigners were in the International Brigades or in Spain. If they had wanted to pass themselves off as Spanish, few other foreigners would have been the wiser, including the League's commission. However, there were no great numbers of these Spanish-speakers or of those who had any great desire to be taken for Spaniards, especially at the end.

In short, estimating the size of the International Brigades is complicated because not all foreigners were in the International Brigades and not all members of the Brigades were foreigners. Moreover, some members who were foreigners were not volunteers, namely the bulk of the political and military officers. In addition, enumerating the foreigners on the Republican side is confused by the presence of Russians.

If 32,000 foreign volunteers served in the ranks of the five International Brigades from November 1936 to September 1938, they were not all under arms simultaneously. Perhaps judging from the accounts of battles, Thomas opines that no more than 18,000 foreigners were members of the International Brigades at any one time.[61] A figure of 18,000, filed by the American consul general in Barcelona, Mahlon Perkins, on 2 December 1936 seems excessive for that early date in the life of the International Brigades.[62] Raymond Carr estimates 14,000 in August of 1937, a smaller number which sounds better. We should note that Carr's figure includes more than 7,000 Spaniards.[63] There was simple algebra to the size of the International Brigades. On one side of the equation were the recruiters and volunteers, minus some attrition along the way, and on the other side were the casualties and desertions. The casualty rate ran high, due to the lack of training, the foolishness of many orders, and the absence of medical care.[64] Desertion, a taboo subject in the propaganda of the time and in most of the remembrances, was not uncommon.[65]

At the end on 21 September 1938, the Spanish Republican Government supplied the military commission of the League of Nations with a figure of 12,208 foreigners serving in the army.[66] Of this total, 7,102 belonged to the International Brigades and 1,946 enlisted elsewhere in the Spanish army, with more than 3,160 in hospitals. The commission noted that the Spanish-speaking foreigners were mainly integrated into the army.[67] Whether or not this ratio was maintained throughout the existence of the International Brigades, excluding those in hospitals, it shows that at conclusion 78.5 percent of the foreigners were in the International Brigades and 21.5 percent were not, whereas Thomas suggests that only 5,000 of 40,000 foreigners were not in the International Brigades, meaning that 87.5 percent were in and 12.5 percent were not. Whether this League list consists only of foreign volunteers or includes the International Brigades officer corps is unknown, but it is unlikely, and it certainly did not include any of the Russian technicians, as they were called. Also listed were another 3,160 men undergoing hospital treatment, men who were not categorized by the Spanish government in either the International Brigades or the Spanish Republican army.[68] On 12 January 1939, the commission itself counted and listed 12,673 foreigners by using the pay records of the Spanish Republican army, but these records were destroyed in 1940 after the fall of France, when League officials feared that Germany would next invade Switzerland.[69] More than once in these pages, the claims of eyewitnesses have not been taken as authoritative, because they cannot always be believed. Few of them would have been in a position to know whereof they have sometimes spoken. For instance, Commissar Sandor Voros, an American in the International Brigades, confidently declared there were 8,000 men in the brigades at the end when the League of Nations supervised repatriation. This figure is incorrect.[70]

3. Conclusion

In summary, about 36,000 foreigners belonged to the International Brigades. Temporarily excluding the Communist party cadres of about 4,000 who were ordered to Spain, approximately 32,000 men made a personal decision that took them from their homes to Spain. The cadre of 4,000 was the Comintern army. A generous margin for error must be allowed in these estimates.

The remaining 32,000 were as numerous as residents of a small city, a city of men alone, but unlike the residents of a city, they did not and could not know each other. This city of men, like Xenophon's marching polis of the *Anabasis*, was an army of strangers who had traveled many long and separate ways to make war, and as it happened, to make war together. None was conscripted; few were subjected to social pressures to enlist; some gave up a secure life; all risked much, even if they themselves did not fully appreciate that at the time. As many as 18,000 were in service at one time in Spain, with a little more than 12,000 of the total of 32,000 who continued in service and survived to repatriation in 1938. Survival, as will be seen, became no small achievement in the International Brigades.

ENDNOTES

1. See, for example, Verle Johnston, *The International Brigades in the Spanish Civil War* (Stanford: Hoover Institution Library, 1952) and Vincent Brome, *The International Brigades* (New York: Morrow, 1966). An abridged version of Johnston's book appeared later under the title *The Legion of Babel* (Philadelphia: University of Pennsylvania Press, 1967).
2. Louis Fischer, *Men and Politics* (New York: Duell, Sloan, and Pearce, 1941).
3. *New York Times*, 22 September 1937, p. 13.
4. Richardson, the most recent example, offers a general estimate of the number of men in the International Brigades with no word on the scarcity of evidence or variety of claims and ignores other dimensions of identity. See Richardson, 191.
5. For example, Stanley G. Payne, *The Franco Regime, 1936–1975* (Madison: University of Wisconsin Press, 1987), 157 n. 103.
6. James W. Cortada, ed., *A City at War* (Wilmington: Scholarly Resources, 1985), 222 and 266. Whealey has adopted a different strategy in a later publication where he continues to cite Castells and puts "a liberal's figure" of 35,000 in parentheses. The liberal referred to is Hugh Thomas. See Robert Whealey, *Hitler and Spain: The Nazi Role in the Spanish Civil War, 1936–1939* (Lexington: University Press of Kentucky, 1989), 24.
7. Wayfarer, *The International Brigade* (Sussex: Ditching Press, n.d.), 7.
8. David W. Pike, *Les Français et La Guerre d'Espagne* (Paris: Presses Universitaires de France, 1975), 160.
9. *Las Brigadas Internacionales* (Madrid: Oficina Informativa Española, 1948), 156.
10. See Adolfo Lizón Gadia, *Brigadas Internacionales en España* (Madrid: Editoria Nacional, 1940), 11 and José Manuel Martinez Bande, *Communist Intervention in the Spanish Civil War* (Madrid: Spanish Information Service, 1966), 142.
11. Terrance Prittie, *Willy Brandt* (London: Weidenfeld and Nicolson, 1974), 31.
12. Ricardo de la Cierva y de Hoces, *Historia Ilustrada de la Guerra Civil Española* (Barcelona: Ediciones Danue, 1970), 1: 404.
13. Ibid., 33.
14. Ramón Salas Larrazabel, *Historia del Ejército Popular de la República* (Madrid: Editora Nacional, 1973), 2: 2141 and 2153.
15. Luís Aguilera Duran, *Orígenes de las Brigadas Internacionales* (Madrid: Editora Nacional, 1974), 127 and 126.
16. Andreu Castells, *Las Brigadas Internacionales de la Guerra de España* (Barcelona: Editorial Ariel, 1974), 383.
17. Paul Preston, *The Spanish Civil War, 1936–1939* (London: Weidenfeld and Nicolson, 1986), 160.
18. Geraldo Gino Bauman, *Extranjeroes en la Guerra Civil Española* (Lima: no publisher given, 1979), 138; Alister Hennessy, "Cuba," *The Spanish Civil War, 1936–1939: American Hemispheric Perspectives*, ed. Mark Falcoff and Frederick Pike ed. (Lincoln: University of Nebraska Press, 1982), 132; Mark Falcoff, "Argentina," ibid., 318; and Manuel Tunon de Lara et al., *La Guerra Civil Española* (Barcelona: Editorial Labor, 1985), 153.
19. *Guerra y Revolucion en España 1936–1939* (Moscow: Editions Progreso, 1966), 2: 234.
20. Tom Wintringham, *English Captain* (London: Faber and Faber, 1939), 37. Also Edwin Rolfe, *The Lincoln Battalion* (New York: Random House, 1939), 8.
21. Hugh Thomas, *The Spanish Civil War* (Harmondsworth: Penguin, 1977), p. 982

and Jacques Delperrie de Bayac, *Les Brigades Internationales* (Paris: Fayard, 1968), 386.

22. David Diamant, *Combattants Juifs dans L'Armée Republicaine Espagnole, 1936–1939* (Paris: Editions Renouveau, 1979), 127.
23. Luis Bolín, Spain: *The Vital Years* (London: Cassell, 1967), 213.
24. *Vrijwilligers voor de Vriheid* (Amersfoort: Kritak, 1978), 21 and 27. The table on page 21 cites a range for one nationality and so totals either 37,000 or 38,000.
25. K. L. Maidanik, *Ispanskii Proletariart v Natsionalno-Revoliusioni Voine* (Moscow: Academy of Sciences of the U.S.S.R., 1960), 206, which featured a reference to Juan García's article in Russian "The International Brigades in Spain, 1937–1938," *Voprosy Istorii* 7 (1956): 33–48. García cites a file number in the Soviet Central Archives, but the response was "not owned" when I requested this file. Maidanik gives an incorrect reference. This table is reprinted in Stanley G. Payne, *The Spanish Revolution* (London: Weidenfeld, 1970), 328.
26. Ludwig Renn, *Der Spanische Krieg* (Berlin: Aufbau-Verlag, 1956), 359.
27. John Gates, *The Story of an American Commissar* (New York: Nelson, 1958), 66.
28. Sandor Voros, *American Commissar* (Philadelphia: Chilton Co., 1961), 271.
29. Peter Wyden, *The Passionate War* (New York: Simon & Schuster, 1983), 19.
30. *Adelante! Pasaremos!* (Cologne: Verlag Internationale Solidarität, 1976), 29.
31. In both Victor Alba, *Histoire des Républiques Espagnoles* (Vincennes: Nord-Sud, 1948), 334, and Carl Geiser, *Prisoners of the Good Fight: The Spanish Civil War 1936–1939* (Westport: Lawrence Hill, 1988), 5. Alba was a journalist who sympathized with POUM, the anarchist force with which Orwell served, and Geiser was an American volunteer in the 15th International Brigade.
32. David Mitchell, *The Spanish Civil War* (London: Granada, 1982), 63.
33. Michael Alpert, *El Ejército Repúblicano en la Guerra Civil* (Barcelona: Ruédo Iberico, 1977).
34. Pierre Broué and Emile Témine, *La Révolution et la Guerre d'Espagne* (Paris: Les Editions du Minuit, 1961), 351.
35. Jacques Delperrie de Bayac, *Les Brigades Internationales,* (Paris: Fayard, 1968), 49.
36. Ricardo de la Cierva y de Hoces, *Leyenda y Tragedia de las Brigadas Internacionales* (Madrid: Editorial Prensa Española, 1973), 176.
37. Cameron Stewart, "Summoned to the Eternal Field," (unpublished PhD dissertation, Claremont Graduate School, 1972), 99 n. 53. Voros cited a figure of 50,000 and reproduced his card as the frontispiece of his book, *American Commissar* (Philadelphia: Clifton & Co., 1961).
38. Aguilera Duran, 126.
39. Geraldo Gino F. Bauman, *Extranjeros en la Guerra Civil Española* (Lima: no publisher given, 1979). The photographs in this book are not on numbered pages.
40. See George Orwell, *Homage to Catalonia* (London: Secker and Warburg, 1959).
41. Thomas, 982.
42. See André Malraux, *L'Espoir* (Paris: Gallimard, 1937).
43. For example, Oloff de Wet, *The Patrol is Ended* (New York: Doubleday, 1938), 12–13.
44. Thomas, 983.
45. Artur London, *Espagne* (Paris: Réunis, 1955), 173. Cf. James W. Cortada, ed., *A City at War* (Wilmington: Scholarly Resources, 1985), 134.
46. Randolfo Pacciardi, *Il Battaglione Garibaldi* (Lugano: Nuove Edizioni di Capolago, 1938).
47. Mitchell, 63.
48. W. G. Krivitsky, *I Was Stalin's Agent* (London: Hamilton, 1939), 112.
49. Marc Janson, "International Class Solidarity or Foreign Intervention? Internationalists and Latvian Rifles in the Russian Revolution and the Civil War," *International Review of Social History,* 31 (1986) 1, pp. 68–79.
50. Orwell, *Homage to Catalonia,* 235.
51. Pike, *Les Français et La Guerre d'Espagne,* 160.

52. David Pike, *Conjecture, Propaganda, and Deceit and the Spanish Civil War* (No city is given: California Institute of International Studies, 1968), 74.
53. The number 9,000 is given in Bolín, 213. Bolín was involved in the Nationalist deceptions about the bombing of Guernica; see Herbert Southworth's seminal study, *Guernica! Guernica!: A Study of Journalism, Diplomacy, Propaganda, and History* (Berkeley: University of California Press, 1977).
54. Bauman, 139.
55. Anthony Beevor, *The Spanish Civil War* (London: Orbis, 1982), 123.
56. Fischer, *Men and Politics*, 393.
57. See Claude Bowers, *My Mission to Spain* (London: Gollancz, 1954), 316 and Herbert L. Matthews, *Two Wars and More to Come* (New York: Carrick and Sons, 1938), 208.
58. Thomas, 984.
59. Wintringham, 139.
60. See "Withdrawal of Non-Spanish Combatants from Spain," *Official Journal of the League of Nations*, 104th Session of the Council, January 1939, p. 132.
61. Thomas, 984.
62. Cortada, *A City in War*, 72.
63. E. H. Carr, *The Comintern and the Spanish Civil War* (London: Macmillan, 1984), 58. The breakdown by nationality that Carr provides at this point does not total 16,000 but more like 15,308.
64. Wintringham, 324.
65. Carl Geiser, *Prisoners of the Good Fight: The Spanish Civil War 1936–1939* (Westport: Lawrence Hill, 1988), 82; cf. Cecil Eby, *Between the Bullet and the Lie* (New York: Holt-Rinehart, and Winston, 1969), 55.
66. "Withdrawal," 127.
67. Ibid.
68. Ibid.
69. Ibid., 129.
70. Voros, 438.

CHAPTER 6

Who Were They?

Having now some idea of what motivated the International Brigaders and how many there were, the next question is who they were. What was their social identity? Quite clearly, the limited available information makes nothing definite, but some points warrant close consideration. Four characteristics will be examined: nationality, age, class, and politics (that is, Communist party membership).

1. Nationality

Investigation into the national composition of the International Brigades leads to two impressive reconstructions in the secondary literature, one in French and the other in Spanish. Each was assembled from first-hand accounts of participants and journalists and from other secondary sources to which this study also refers. Whatever the difficulties of that method and the deficiencies in each execution, the two efforts are each comprehensive and independent of the other, conducted by experts on the International Brigades. These estimates are as authoritative as any to be found. Two other sources also apply to nationality, one comprehensive and the other detailed. The comprehensive source is drawn from the Soviet army archives and the detailed one from the League of Nations military commission. The phrase 'army archives' may suggest authoritative material, but no such assumption should be made because so few

Soviet records are known to have been kept. One possible source of national identification would be passports. A great effort was made at Albacete, the International Brigades base camp, to collect the passports of all foreign volunteers in the International Brigades. Whatever the reason given to the men, these passports were turned over to the NKVD, the Soviet state security service of the day.[1] Was the information from the passports available to clerks of the Soviet army archives? Was there a historian at the archives who anticipated the need to record the characteristics of the foreign volunteers? Many of the volunteers, however, the French for example, probably did not carry passports. Because none of these passports were returned to the demobilized men when they were repatriated, the League's commission had to establish their nationalities by interviewing them individually.[2] These data are detailed but limited to the men interviewed by the military commission.

Comparisons among these four sources become all the more cumbersome because they do not use the same national categories. Castells uses the largest number of nationalities, 70 in all, and Delperrie de Bayac uses the smallest, 10. The League used 13 and the Soviets 17. With no means to disaggregate any of the totals these sources use, the data of the others will be aggregated into Delperrie de Bayac's categories as the lowest common denominator to gain a comparison across the board. Inevitably other problems occurred, including the misperception of nationalities like the Spanish-speakers, especially when they were integrated into the Spanish Army or when Canadians were taken as Americans or English. In addition, some stateless persons did not claim nationality or lied about their nationality to avoid drawing unwanted attention to themselves. German and Italian volunteers, worried that evacuation might take them back to Germany and Italy, respectively, may have had reason to lie to the military commission of the League and even to hide from it. Finally, Castells, Delperrie de Bayac, and the Soviet Army archives all refer to the Spanish Army as the League does, as distinct from the International Brigades.

In Table (4) below, the category "Other" includes in Castells's figures some 2,148 Hungarians (3.5 percent of his total); 1,057 Dutch (1.8 percent); 673 Swiss (1.1 percent); and 615 Romanians (1.0 percent). In the Soviet Army archives, this designation includes 862 Balts (1.8 percent of that total); 586 Dutch (1.9 percent); 510 Hungarians (1.6 percent); and 406 Swiss (1.3 percent). The League of Nations lists 143 Dutch (2.2 percent) and 80 Swiss (1.2 percent).

All sources presented in Table (3) agree on one thing, that the French formed the largest national group in the International

Brigades, ranging from 25 to 33 percent in each of the four samples. This result, which is confirmed by the impressions of many witnesses and participants, coincides with the central role of the French Communist party in the organizing of the International Brigades. Two of the five International Brigades spoke French. Castells, who cites a figure far larger than the other two comprehensive sources, acknowledges in a footnote that a figure of 8,500 Frenchmen was given by a French source at the time of the war, but he suggests no reason for rejecting that figure, which would be very similar to the other two, or for citing the figure 15,400.[3] An even larger number of Frenchmen, 25,000, was cited by *Le Figaro* on 17 February 1937.[4]

Though their number and the percentage of the whole that they constitute varies, Germans[5] and Austrians (who are combined by Delperrie de Bayac),[6] Poles[7], and Italians rank next in significance both absolutely and relatively in that order in each source apart from the League. Germans and Austrians, Poles, and Italians are under-represented in the League's findings, and other groups are over-

Table 4
Nationalities of the Foreign Volunteers

Nationality	Delperrie de Bayac Number	%	Castells Number	%	Soviet Army Number	%	League of Nations+ Number	%
French	9,000	25.4	15,400	25.9	8,778	28.1	3,278	22.0
German[6]	5,000	14.1	5,831	9.8	3,026	9.7	1,744	11.7
Polish	4,000	11.3	5,411	9.1	3,034	9.7	1,560	10.4
Balkan	4,000[5]	11.3	2,614[1]	4.4	2,056[1]	6.6	667	4.5
Italian	3,100	8.7	5,108	8.6	2,908	9.3	1,553	10.4
Canadian	—	—	847	1.4	510	1.6	377	2.5
British	2,000	5.6	3,504	5.9	1,806	5.8	469	3.1
Belgian	2,000	5.6	3,072	5.2	1,701	5.4	432	2.9
U.S.A.	2,000	5.6	3,890[3]	6.6	2,274	7.3	839	5.6
Scandinavian	2,500[5]	7.0	1,177[2]	2.0	6,62[2]	2.1	434[2]	2.9
Other	2,000	5.6	12,526	21.0	4,482	14.0	3,583[4]	24.0
Total	35,600	100.2*	59,380	99.9*	31,237	100.0	14,936	100.0

*Rounding error.
+Based on League of Nations archives which are more complete than published information.
[1]Includes Albanians, Bulgarians, Greeks, and Yugoslavs.
[2]Includes Danes, Norwegians, and Swedes.
[3]Excludes Jews whom Castells lists separately. Puerto Ricans are included in this figure.
[4]Includes some 1,500 men designated as stateless.
[5]Not stated which nations are included.
[6]German includes Austrains.

represented compared to other sources. Those overrepresented include Americans, Balkans, and Scandinavians. That the League's data depart from others on this point is easy to understand. When the volunteers were evacuated, the Nationalists had divided Republican Spain into two zones, as Sherman's march to the sea had divided the Confederacy in the American Civil War. Supervised evacuations occurred only in the Barcelona zone and comprised 66 percent of the 9,843 foreign volunteers there. Another 2,830 men were stationed in the Valencia zone. Because men in the International Brigades were organized into common language groups wherever possible, perhaps the German, Polish, and Italian formations were in the Valencia zone though the International Brigades were withdrawn during the battle at the Ebro when they were all in the firing line. If the Germans and Austrians, Poles, and Italians are not visible in the report of the military commission of the League of Nations, they might have avoided evacuation since they had no place to go, or were counting themselves as stateless persons, or were stationed in Valencia. These best guesses about who the avowed stateless persons were still do not answer the question why *all* Italians, Germans, and Poles did not declare themselves stateless. Of course, being stateless does not affect nationality since the two are conceptually distinct; however, in the matter at hand the concepts seem confused.

According to the order of battle at the Ebro River from 19 August to 23 September, all five of the International Brigades became involved.[8] When the 129th Brigade, composed partly of central Europeans in the Valencia zone, was withdrawn from the line for evacuation, each of the five International Brigades was demobilized between 25 September and 5 October 1938.[9] Apparently, no one from the 129th was evacuated while the commission was in Spain, since it did not visit the Valencia zone. This is an inference. Castells notes that elements of the 11th International Brigade, mainly German; the 12th International Brigade, mainly French; and the 129th International Brigade, mainly central European, fought out the war in the final defense of Catalonia on 9 February 1939 when these men crossed the French border.[10] One eyewitness to a contingent of international volunteers marching across the border at Le Perthus counted 750 of them, the national composition of which he estimated at 170 North Americans, or 22.7 percent; 300 Italians, or 40.0 percent; and 250 Czechs and Hungarians, or 33.3 percent.[11] It is surprising that any Americans missed repatriation but evidently some did. If they did, it is quite possible those with reason to fear repatriation might have escaped it, too.

On the other hand, the proportion of the International Brigades constituted by some nationalities is very consistent. Consider the Belgians and British in all four sources in Table (3).

In the case of the Canadians, one writer claims that as many as 1,200 Canadians went to Spain.[12] Yet the largest number cited by sources is 847 in Castells, who mentions but rejects for reasons not given another writer's reference to 1,300 Canadians.[13] Delperrie de Bayac omits Canadians completely. That Canadians do not show up in these four sources as significantly as 1,200 would dictate does not impeach the sources. The first writer who mentions 1,200 emphasizes the significance of this number against the Canadian populace of 12 million at the time, compared to 3,000 Americans from a population of 140 million.[14] He goes on to undermine this point by allowing that many of these 1,200 Canadians may have been recent immigrants from Europe, judging by the names and birthplaces on an incomplete card file used to recruit for the Canadian MacKenzie-Papineau Battalion when Canadians were separated from Americans of the Lincoln Battalion. Such new Canadians may not have even had a Canadian passport, or if they did, it may have been the only thing Canadian about them. Upon examining 600 names in that card file, Victor Hoar concluded that 262 of them gave homelands suggesting that they were new Canadians.[15] These men would not strike many observers as Canadians. Nor would they identify with other Canadians. Moreover, such individuals may have been counted twice, once as Canadian and once as Finnish or Yugoslavian. In addition, an English-speaking Canadian would often be mistaken for or conveniently counted with the Americans' especially when Canadians first served with the Americans.

On the point of languages, an earlier reference was made to Spanish-speaking foreign volunteers who were integrated into the Spanish army rather than assigned to the International Brigades. Only eight Latin Americans were repatriated under the League of Nations' aegis. Castells includes entries for every Latin American nationality, totaling 1,081, to which might be added the 16 Puerto Ricans, 16 Filipinos, and 133 Portuguese that he also lists for a grand total of 1,246, or 2.1 percent of his total.

To take the Mexicans as an example, Castells's total is 781 for the International Brigades. Two others agree with Castells that Mexican volunteers were concentrated in the International Brigades, but both cite far smaller numbers. In 1955, Lois Smith estimated 150 Mexicans,[16] while in 1973 Juan-Simeon Vidarte said 300.[17] Odder still, Hugh Thomas says 90 Mexicans probably fought in Spain and cites Lois Smith for this figure.[18] However, other no-less-well-placed writers have estimated the total at 330, of whom some few were in the International Brigades but most were scattered throughout the Republican army.[19] Castells appends a footnote to his figure referring the reader to Garcia's article in a Soviet history journal, but he neither agrees with it nor criticizes it.

The Soviet army archives cite 2,274 Americans and 2,908 Italians, although any number of participants and observers in a position to know number 3,000 to 3,200 Americans.[20] As for Italians, Palmiro Togliatti notes 3,354 in Spain, 3,108 of whom were combatants.[21] Togliatti, a highly placed Communist and later the leader of the party, stayed in Spain after the International Brigades were withdrawn. He surely was in a position to know. Other sources suggest that there may have been another 750 Italian volunteers in Republican Spain serving in a variety of other capacities.[22] If the Italian number were used as a bench-mark, then Delperrie de Bayac fares best; but he is as wrong as the Soviets about the number of Americans.

A pattern is elusive in these sources. Castells works with a larger total number than the other three comprehensive accounts, a total of 167.3 percent that of Delperrie de Bayac and 190.0 percent that of the Soviet Army archives. Yet Castells's total for each nationality is not always greater than that of the other two and where greater, it is not always greater by the same degree as his total. His estimates for the two composite groupings, Balkan and Scandinavian, run lower than Delperrie de Bayac.

Comparing Delperrie de Bayac's total to the Soviet Army archives yields 113.6 percent that of the Soviets. Yet his national totals do not always exceed those of the Soviets at all or to the degree of his total. Delperrie de Bayac estimates fewer Americans than the Soviets do and places fewer in the "Other" category.

On the whole, Castells's totals seem most doubtful. His totals depart greatly from both Delperrie de Bayac and the Soviet army archives and a host of impressions by participants and observers. Moreover, the documentation he claims for each nationality is often a general figure, sometimes at odds with his own data cited from other secondary sources. For example, Garcia is quoted as saying that there were 500 Latin Americans, the only authority produced by Castells who lists 94 Argentines, 14 Bolivians, 41 Brazilians, 136 Cubans, 24 Ecuadoreans, 25 Guatemalans, 15 Haitians, 14 Hondurans, 464 Mexicans, 12 Nicaraguans, 22 Paraguayans, 22 Uruguayans, and 149 Venezuelans, totaling 1032! Castells, a widely and frequently cited authority, is too exact to be credible. He is not alone in such unconvincing precision: Unencumbered by documentation of any kind, scholar Neal Wood has asserted 2,762 British volunteers, neither more nor less.[23] Castells's may compromise his value because he tried to be precise and honest about documentation, whereas Delperrie de Bayac gives no references for his admitted estimates of each nationality and he offers global figures. Nor do we know on what the Soviet account is based. Totals for both Delperrie de Bayac and the Soviet army archives are similar and approximate the estimates of other observers.

Which observers to believe is by no means easy to decide. David Cattell, in a brief reference to the International Brigades, accepts the word of Tom Wintringham on the size of the International Brigades, though he makes no effort to show that Wintringham could estimate the size or to show evidence of Wintringham's sound and honest judgment.[24] Instead Cattell vindicates Wintringham by saying that he was not a Communist.[25] Since he was not a Communist, it is implied that he is to be believed, a poor way in general to evaluate sources and false in this case. Wintringham was a Communist, a fact he omitted from the book Cattell cites. When Wintringham was arrested in 1925 he admitted his party membership.[26] Wintringham, one-time editor of *The Left Review* and military writer for the *Daily Worker* in London, was assigned to visit Spain early in the war and was often named one of the architects of the International Brigades.[27] He helped sell the idea of the International Brigades to Maurice Thorez, leader of the French Communist party, and through him to the Comintern and Stalin.[28] Wintringham was definitely a Communist, well placed, of good judgment, honest, and a Communist all the same.[29] His estimates may have done duty for propaganda purposes but they are worth close consideration.

In sum, the French dominated nationality, constituting 25 percent and more with the next largest group exiles from Germany and Italy and also Poland and the Balkans, from 33 percent to 40 percent of the total. The remainder comprised smaller groups of around 5 percent each for Americans, Belgians, British, and Scandinavians.

2. Class

The class background of the foreign volunteers in the International Brigades is as hard to ascertain as nationality, because so little evidence exists. Considering the paucity of evidence, all fine points of class that so delight theorists must be discarded, leaving only the perceived background of a few individuals and some general impressions about the national groups within the International Brigades. One veteran, Jason Gurney, remarked many years later that one benefit he expected in going to Spain would be an escape from his own (middle) class identity; Spaniards would not be able to distinguish between middle-class and working-class Englishmen, and, of course, Comintern propaganda emphasized the proletarian nature of the conflict without neglecting the contributions of right-thinking members of the middle-class.[30] From our remove we can neither respect Gurney's wish nor believe the propaganda.

Some middle-class intellectuals throughout the International Brigades have largely preserved the story of the brigades in their writings; however, only a few of the total number of brigaders ever wrote. Gurney, a South African by birth, estimates that among the British with whom he served, about 30 out of 600 or 5 percent, were middle-class intellectuals, the rest workers.[31] Another British volunteer writing at the time noted that the British were mostly workers with some middle class intellectuals.[32] Examples of middle class intellectuals among the British would include Giles Romilly who was, according to Gurney, the informal leader of about a dozen homosexuals.[33] Giles's cousin, Esmond Romilly, remarked at the time that most of the Germans were working-class.[34] Early British volunteers like Esmond Romilly served with the Germans until there were enough men to form a British unit, although Esmond's proficiency in German is not stated. One writer, Dutchman Jef Last, was not a middle-class intellectual but a miner and sailor.[35]

Working with a card file of 1,804 names for American volunteers, Robert Rosenstone concludes that nearly all these men—who represent more than half the Americans—were from working class homes,[36] but then so are many intellectuals, whether middle-class or not. Occupations were listed on only slightly more than half the cards (53.8 percent), the most common being dock worker, seaman,[37] and student.[38] Of approximately 970 names with an occupation, 38.2 percent were seamen, 33.3 percent students, 10.6 percent teachers, 6.37 percent miners, 5.8 percent longshoremen, and 5.8 percent steel workers.[39] Students and teachers, who comprised 43.9 percent, are hardly working class, whatever their sympathies.

One other treatment of class composition of the International Brigades comes from the Italians. In his history of the Italian Communist party, Palmiro Togliatti provided an account of the social origins of 1,794 Italians, more than half, including 1,471 industrial workers at 81.9 percent; 254 peasants at 14.2 percent; and 69 professionals (including 19 lawyers) at 3.8 percent.[40]

Two other nationalities, Bulgarians and Welsh, have been examined for their class. Luis Aguilera Duran pieced together the activities of 334 of the 460 Bulgarians he thinks joined the International

Brigades, about 65 percent of whom were classed as laborers and artisans, with six peasants. Another 26 percent were styled intellectuals who were either students or possibly middle-class, the remaining 9 percent unknown.[41] Clearly a sizable majority of Bulgarians were workers, all the more so if unknowns are deleted from calculations, making workers 72 percent of the total. For the 170 Welsh identified by Hywel Francis, the working class origin is even more pronounced at 95 percent. Francis's study of Welsh miners means that nearly all his subjects were working class, yet according to Francis only 65 percent of the total were miners.[42] Perhaps this figure represents the employed miners.

The importance of this small amount of evidence on class origins should not be overlooked. Because a few veterans of the International Brigades have written so much, the impression may be that they were a middle class group of intellectuals, an impression that thrives because the heroes of Hemingway and Malraux novels are intellectuals. The fictional contrast would be Herrick's and Sinclair's blue-collar, low-brow heroes. *Hermanos!* by William Herrick, a memorable account of the experience of foreign volunteers, lacks the literary merits of Malraux's *L'Espoir* and Hemingway's *For Whom the Bell Tolls,* but more than compensates for any deficiency of style with the intensity of emotions. Evidence for Americans and Italians suggests that most volunteers were proletarian.

The greater mystery revolves around the relationship between middle-class intellectuals in the International Brigades and members of the working class, a subject neglected in most personal accounts. To imagine any of the spear carriers from the working class in conversation with today's self-appointed, middle-class leaders of the political left—Militant Tendency in Great Britain, the Western Maoists of the 1960s, technocratic socialists in Germany, or the De-Constructors of bourgeois liberty in France—is difficult. Why? First, the International Brigaders wanted an improvement in the material conditions of life for workers, and much of that has been achieved. But subsequent leaders of the left consider this is a special, new form of repression. Second, many International Brigaders were patriots at heart, proud of their identity as American, French, English, Dutch, Italian, German, and so on, they affected none of the national self-loathing that is a hallmark of the learned left today.

3. Age

Although age may not be as important a factor as nationality or class, still knowing the recruits' ages would provide the basis for estimating how many had military training and service in World War I. Recall that one point made in promoting the International Brigades was that the men would have had experience in the Great War. A Nationalist writer flatly stated later that the men of the International Brigades were veterans of the Great War.[43] German, Italian, and French volunteers would be likely examples of this experience. One of Malraux's characters in *L'Espoir* notes that 60 percent of Italians in the Garibaldi battalion in the first winter of the war were over age 45.[44] Francis has hazarded the guess that the average age of the Welsh volunteers was more than 30.[45] Any men over 35 might well have had training and experience in the Great War.

Sufficient data exist only to describe the ages of the Americans and Canadians; in each case, a record shows the recruitment age of a small number of men as set out in Table (5).

Even this fragmentary evidence on age indicates the possibility that the national groups may be very different. Whereas information about class composition all told very much the same story, for age it does not. Volunteering for Spain was the preserve of youth in the United States where 70 percent of this sample of American International Brigaders was under age 30. Cameron Stewart's study of American records for the International Brigades found 60 percent of those for whom an age was recorded were 29 or under, while nearly 80 percent were 34 or under. With the birth dates for 1,758 American volunteers he calculated the mean age of his sample as 29 with a median of 28.[46] The relatively young Americans, many of whom were later denied service in World War II because their loyalty was questioned, have often lived long enough to write and to be interviewed. Also notable is that ages given for letter-writing Americans in one

Table 5
Ages of Some American and Canadian Volunteers

	American		Canadian	
		Cumulative		Cumulative
Age	%	%	%	%
Under 20	2.4	2.4	2.0	2.0
20–29	67.8	70.2	35.7	37.7
30–39	21.2	91.4	52.7	90.4
40 or more	7.9	99.3	9.0	99.4
Total	99.3*	99.3*	99.4*	99.4*
	N = 291		N = 366	

Source: For the Americans, Rosenstone, 368–369, and for the Canadians, Hoar, 31–32.
* Does not total 100.0 percent due to rounding error.

source are 22, 36, and 39.[47] Some photographs from the time, like that of John Gates acting as American commissar, look as if they should be published in high school or college yearbooks.[48] By contrast, more than 60 percent of the Canadians at age 30 were older, more mature men when they made their separate decisions to go to war. These additional years could well mean that Canadians were or had been married and had more confidence and independence. One American commissar claimed that Canadians were more durable than Americans, but this may have been only flattery to be filed under diplomacy and forgotten.[49] Mature men would have been both more cautious and more self-reliant than romantic youth from the United States, inspired by Robert Capa's Spanish photographs in *Life*, viewing Spain in the deceiving light that lies on the world when one is young and innocent, and unconscious of being either.

4. Race

The International Brigade literature devotes small space to determining how many volunteers were Jewish. Earlier discussions of motivations of the volunteers noted Jews who said they went to Spain because of the identification of Fascism with anti-Semitism. Nationalist propaganda quickly decried the Jewish influence.[50] Advocates of the Republic were no less eager to enlist Jews in the propaganda war.[51] One highly placed German volunteer noted many Jews in the International Brigades.[52] Certainly many observers note that a third of the American volunteers were Jewish.[53]

Castells specifies 366 Jews from nine nations, but he notes the difficulty in establishing the number of Jews, citing another source that suggests between 2,000 and 3,000.[54] A year later, an article published in Franco's Spain detailed more than 7,000 Jews among the volunteers.[55] See Table (6).

These figures reportedly emerged from an interview with an

Table 6
Jewish Volunteers

From Poland	2,250
From the U.S.A.	1,236
From France	1,043
From the U.K.	214
From Palestine	267
From elsewhere	2,695
Total	7,705

Source: Fernandez (1975).

International Brigade veteran now living in Israel, though no documentation is cited. The range in estimates of Jews is canvassed by Albert Prago, himself an International Brigade veteran, who drew no conclusion in this, one of very few, investigations into the role of Jews.[56] In his 1979 *Combattants Juifs dans l'Armée Républicane Espagnole* David Diamant estimates 6,000 to 7,500 Jews in the International Brigades, out of a total of 35,000 foreign volunteers.[57]

Blacks are also identified among the Americans and much emphasized in the propaganda with their numbers estimated at 60 to 80 by Arthur Landis,[58] and at 100 by Robert Rosenstone.[59] Black American volunteer James Yates listed 83 black Americans in his book.[60] It is true that propaganda emphasized Blacks, but unlikely that the higher figure of 250 mentioned by historian Cameron Stewart obtained.[61] Their motivation is routinely described as a variation on the one-fight thesis discussed below. Blacks are mentioned to show the universality of the anti-Fascist appeal and nothing more. The propaganda emphasis is another example of the Comintern seizing opportunities. It tells little about the minds of individuals in which the real decisions were made.

5. Politics

The political character of most armies can be located in a sense of patriotism; however, this address would be inappropriate for the multi-national International Brigades. Under law none of their nations was at war in Spain, and many governments discouraged their own citizens from joining the International Brigades. These included Belgium, Canada, and Switzerland.[62] Recruiting offices were raided.[63] Service in a foreign army was often said to jeopardize citizenship, a comment that was not made when Americans like William Faulkner joined the Canadian armed service to participate in the Great War as others did later to contribute to World War II. Other nations, like France, tolerated the recruitment of the International Brigades but after a time only most reluctantly. The Soviet Union publicly supported the idea of the International Brigades yet refused to allow its own citizens to volunteer, with the consequent irony that the 50 nationalities in the International Brigades did not include the Soviet Union. The International Brigades were recruited around the world, but not in Moscow.[64] Only Mexican volunteers were given moral support by their government which, along with the Soviet Union, was the only positive ally of the Republic. This lack of public support might not have bothered the men once they met their comrades in Spain, but it must have been harder for those whom they left behind without the normal moral support of other families in the same situation, especially widows. The men themselves would have noticed it most when they returned. For the foreign volunteers in Spain, there was no moral support, except from the Communist party. Worse off were the German and Italian volunteers, most of whom had already been exiled from their homelands and had been portrayed as traitors, once for leaving their countries and now a second time for fighting in Spain.

In most wars, the conscript has a political identity, like it or not, in fulfilling a duty to the nation. That sense of duty, with patriotism, characterizes the politics of most armies. Not so for the International Brigades.

In the absence of patriotism, two themes dominate: anti-fascism and the Communist party. Anti-fascism applies more to the recruits from the New World and England, while the role of communism runs deeper among the Europeans, especially the exiled Germans. Anti-fascism was the umbrella term for all those champions of embattled democracy and opponents of rising tyranny in those times, or so at least they said of and to themselves. Even in 1937, the need to resist fascism was deeply felt by some people apart from Communists. A super-imposed vision, like a Braque painting, overlaid the distantly perceived fascism of Germany and Italy on indigenous movements like Oswald Mosley's in Britain or demagogues of the left and right in the United States.[65] A revulsion against fascism, without seeming knowledge of it, is ritually repeated in the propaganda for the International Brigades.[66] The matter is not without complications, for even a sensible man moved by anti-fascism, like Jason Gurney, also admitted that ultimately his decision to go was not political but a personal test of himself.[67] The personal and the political are not mutually exclusive nor jointly exhaustive, nor is the personal the political. For others, anti-fascism became a handy slogan, used as a prophylactic against serious justification by one International Brigade volunteer to fend off awkward questions from a girlfriend.[68] Anti-fascism was the side of the angels. Even so, many reports claim that the men in the ranks were apolitical![69]

As noted above, some American volunteers were working-class men, as far as can be judged. A great many of these workers had been militant union activists.[70] Though published propaganda of the time is the main source on the attitudes of these militant unionists, like compilations of letters, memorials to the fallen, and leaflets, there is the ring of truth to it. Sometimes the attitudes are so simple as to be naive, say in the faith expressed in the union movement, but these views are resonant with attitudes expressed at the time by an intellectual, Upton Sinclair, and with attitudes reported later by a critic and veteran of the International Brigades, William Herrick. Sentiments that seem naive to an observer at this remove did exist, and, moreover, exerted a force that is now difficult to judge because we do not feel it. Remember, too, that the 1930s were very troubled times, times when democracy had many enemies even in the heart of democratic institutions.[71]

In the propaganda for the Americans, the oft-repeated central point was that there is One Fight. A part of this struggle went on at the picket line in Pittsburgh and another part in the trench warfare in Spain.[72] According to the One-Fight thesis, the oppressor in Spain is related materially and morally to the oppressor in the United States.[73] A volunteer allegedly carried his union card into battle just as he would into a picket line.[74] Steve Nelson's book opens with an account of strike activity in the United States and then goes on to Spain as if it were another front in the same campaign.[75] Volunteer John Tisa does the same.[76] So did a Mexican volunteer.[77] Perceived oppressors in the United States were called Fascists.[78] Sometimes the threat is not indigenous fascism but imported European fascism.[79] These experienced unionists among the Americans were seasoned radicals.[80] The One-Fight thesis was also expressed by Mexican volunteers.[81] A Welsh labor leader, Anthony Harner, said shortly before the Spanish Civil War:

> The fight against fascism is the fight for trade unionism . . . [and] is the most important safeguard against fascism .... Scale Unionism is fascism in embryo.[82]

The Spanish conflict was readily assimilated to this *Weltanschauung*. Many comparable men among the British[83] and the Dutch[84] felt themselves prepared, trained, and qualified for war thanks to their experiences in strikes and riots.[85] As a study of their training and casualties will show, this was a grievously mistaken assumption. Robert Rosenstone guesses that perhaps a third of the 3,000 Americans had seen industrial violence.[86] For others, like the pseudonymous Comintern agent Jan Valtin in a German prison, the Spanish Civil War became the fight to free himself.[87]

With all the radicalism of so many volunteers, they remained their countries' sons at heart. The letters of one Australian volunteer, Lloyd Edmonds, dwell on the coming of the Spanish Civil War no more than on the dalliance of the king of England with Mrs. Simpson.[88] Even for committed Americans, nationalism was the complement of radicalism, not the antithesis. One recurrent minor point, both in the propaganda of the time and in later accounts by veterans, is a faith, not just in democracy in the abstract, but in American democracy. The proof of American democracy was the election of President Franklin D. Roosevelt.[89] Here is a clear example of what Eric Homberger has called American Exceptionalism.[90] First the woes of oppression in the United States will be detailed, and then the New Deal and FDR will be mentioned, as if to say that the battle is won in the United States, the savior has come. Social change will be produced by the heroic president, but only in America! On to Spain! The clearest expression of this attitude is in Upton Sinclair's *roman-à-clef, No Pasarán,* where he suggests that the Spanish Republican government was modeled on the New Deal administration.[91] A young John F. Kennedy expressed a similar view at the time.[92] If that is the clearest expression, the most moving account concerns a group of cold, hungry, frightened Americans under bombardment singing the "Star-Spangled Banner" to keep up their spirits.[93] No doubt at moments of truth the Italians and Germans sang their own songs and not just the "Internationale."

In this time of the Popular Front, anti-fascism was promoted by the Comintern and national Communist parties, but these promotional efforts did not so much create the attitudes suggested above as give them a vent.[94] Even if much has to be disallowed as propaganda, the basic dislike of abstract fascism and the fundamental nationalism remain. No doubt, one political bond among the International Brigaders was this vague but genuine anti-fascism.

The other common bond was communism. For the German and Italian refugees, their Communist parties formed the opposition in exile, voicing nationalism and communism simultaneously.[95] Momentarily by-passing such a delicate, difficult, and deep issue as the relationship between nationalism and communism in these times we concentrate on a simple, concrete question: how many of the men in the International Brigades were members of a Communist party? This, too, becomes a mystery worthy of Sherlock Holmes. Testimony shows that party members were enjoined to keep secret their membership once in Spain, the better to catch Trotskyists.[96] In the absence of any facts, impressions are varied. As noted earlier, J. Edgar Hoover, for example, claimed that the volunteers of the International Brigades were duped, tricked by the lure of gain into service by the devious Reds.[97] From a similar political perspective, a publicist for the victorious Nationalists in 1940 declared that 90 percent of the Internationals had been party members.[98] More recently, de la Cierva y de Hoces has written that 65 percent of the foreigners were Communist before they arrived in Spain and another 15 percent joined while in Spain, 80 percent in all.[99] For him they were Moscow

Zombies. Angel Viñas estimated 85 percent, in one of the few books published in Spain for the 50th anniversary of the war.[100]

Both the proportion of volunteers who were party members and the propensity of party members to volunteer must have varied from one nationality to the next. In the 1930s, only Communists seemed able and willing to fight fascism. Throughout Europe, liberals were perceived to be reluctantly accommodating fascism while conservatives were eagerly abetting it. Since the Communist party was strong in European countries, having become the moral opposition to fascism throughout the continent, German, Italian, French, and Polish volunteers probably included many Communists. Hans Beimler is reported to have claimed that 80 percent of the Germans were Communist.[101] Togliatti claims that 56 percent of the Italians were Communists.[102] In the German case, the exiled party's central committee met in Paris to pass a resolution calling for members to volunteer for Spain,[103] as did the Italian Communist party.[104] In the American case, party members and cadres were at first not allowed to volunteer because they were too rare.[105] When the American contingent in Spain later manifested indiscipline while serving under European officers, American cadres who had earlier volunteered were ordered to go to Spain to provide some national leadership.[106] Communism paid homage to nationalism in this small way. To be explicit; untrained Americans were sent to the slaughter in their first battle by European Comintern officers who treated them as cannon fodder. The Americans had no stomach for more battle. A decision was made on high to recruit American cadres to serve as officers in the hope of creating harmony among the ranks. In the pages of *Volunteer for Liberty* these same European Comintern officers routinely praised the prowess of American volunteers who in fact broke in battle and mutinied. These same officers are now sometimes cited with affection by American volunteers; memory has faded. A similar inner-party conscription occurred in Wales, too.[107] One of the American cadres, John Gates, said that 25 percent of the Americans were party men,[108] while the American party leader Earl Browder said 60 percent.[109] In 1986, John Gerassi concurred with Browder,[110]and also claimed another 24 percent were fellow travelers. All these men would have been in a position to know. But the cloth may have been cut to suit each occasion. This same figure of 60 percent is also cited for the Canadians.[111] Francis suggests 72 percent of the Welsh were Communists while Gregory says 50 percent of the English were.[112] One of the English had been convicted as a Soviet spy, and another was subsequently convicted.[113] If it were true for them and for the Americans, more of them would have been Communist than the

Italians. If that were so it would not necessarily impeach the thesis implied above about anti-fascism in the New World and England and communism in Europe, but it would require that it be revised. For Communist parties did not all occupy the same social and political space in each country at the time. In the 1930s in the U.S.A. the Communist party had the ground of anti-fascism almost to itself, and that brought it many recruits, sympathizers and friends, some of whom were probably among those who went to Spain.

The Popular Front goal of a broad coalition against fascism is compromised if 60 percent of the American volunteers were communist party members—or is it? Anti-fascism was a Communist front to organize opposition to fascism outside the Soviet Union, that much is sure. Hence a man proclaiming anti-fascism might simply be mouthing the party line. On the other hand, might it not also be the case during the middle 1930s that Communism was an umbrella that sheltered all manner of disaffected individuals, including those who opposed fascism? As anti-fascism was a convenient fiction for Communists, communism might have been a fiction for anti-fascists in those days before much was known about Stalin's Soviet Union, apart from its high-profile opposition to fascism until the Nazi-Soviet pact, which came well after the end of the Spanish Civil War. No less an authority than J. Edgar Hoover has acknowledged that a concerned idealist might have joined the Communist party and volunteered for Spain.[114] The Communists were doubtless anti-Fascists, and some were anti-Fascist before (in time if not in importance) they were Communist, but not all anti-fascists were Communists.

In sum, available evidence shows half or more of the International Brigades to have been party men from nations as different as Italy, Bulgaria, Wales, the United States, and Canada. Moreover, even more men seemed to have been party members among the Germans. Jason Gurney, who served with both the British and American battalions, believed that the International Brigades' Communists—and he estimated only 20 percent—were "from the lowest echelon of the Party structure."[115] To his knowledge, "nobody was invited to join the Communist Party while in Spain,"[116] though Hugh Thomas, among others, speaks of 60 percent of the International Brigades being members at recruitment and another 20 percent joining in Spain.[117] Did an International Brigader join the Spanish Communist party, his national party's Spanish branch, or some international section of the party? In one case, a volunteer joined the Communist party of Spain, which would have been normal procedure all other things being equal.[118] The *Volunteer for Liberty*, the International Brigades' newspaper and propaganda sheet, gave no evidence of recruiting for the party; its main preoccupation was the demon Trotsky. Jacques Delperrie de Bayac estimates that "60 à 80 des Allemands, des Italiens, des Polonais et des Balkaniques sont communistes quand ils arrivent en Espagne" (60 to 80 percent of the Germans, of the Italians, of the Poles, and of the Balkans were Communists when they arrived in Spain) and that once there, more of them joined. For the Scandinavians, Belgians, and British, the percentage is lower, and "chez les Français elle est de l'ordre de 40 à 50%" (among the French it [party membership] was of the order of 40 to 50 percent).[119] The French were the largest nationality and the closest nation.

At times Communist propaganda sought to diminish the role of Communists in Spain to promote an all-party coalition against fascism and at other times the aim was to emphasize the Communist contribution. Against such a shifting background, focus bends like a stick in water.

6. Conclusion

The when and the how of the International Brigades have been as well documented as possible in the historical accounts of the Spanish Civil War. The purpose here has been to ascertain something of who they were from available evidence, first considering their numbers, a challenging undertaking in itself with no authoritative sources. Going beyond number to nationality, age, and politics of the volunteers quickly reveals the inadequacy of erstwhile sources and the absence of other information.

Some sources affect an air of precision on nationality; however, close inspection reveals that one of these sources, Castells, is poorly substantiated and compromised overestimating the size of the International Brigades. Another source, which has no documentation appended to it, provides nationality figures at odds with credible estimates for Italians and Americans. The most reliable but limited information available on both number and nationality comes from the League of Nations' military commission, once certain qualifications are realized.

Relying on the observations of participants and others regarding class provides evidence; though no precision is possible, all writers agree that the vast majority of International Brigaders were proletarians. Many were experienced in politics, such as Italian or German refugees from fascism and militant unionists from the United States.

Another widespread argument—that a majority of most nationalities were members of their countries' Communist parties—particularly specifies Italians, Americans, Germans, and Canadians, but these estimates do not pass unchallenged. Some participants suggest a much lower figure in one nationality or another, like the French. A man's speech will tell an observer something of his nationality and even class background, but there is no similar sign of party membership. If Communist party members were urged to secrecy, then there is room for error. In the circumstances some would claim membership but not have it, while others would not claim it but have it. Different estimates are to be expected. Higher party officials would be likely to be more accurate in that they knew who was a member when recruited, but sometimes the party wanted to reduce, and at other times to enlarge, the perception of its role in Spain. Never was it committed to the unvarnished truth for the historical record.

Information on age for two nationalities shows differences; the American volunteers were much younger than the Canadians. Americans also seem to have been junior to Bulgarian, Italian, and Welsh volunteers. As a whole, however, 60 percent of both Americans and Canadians were party members. American party members may have been younger than their Canadian colleagues, though that conclusion may press limited information too far. Perhaps many students who came from working-class homes were not themselves workers.

Whatever suffering men of the International Brigades endured and whatever they accomplished, they massed as an army of strangers. Strangers to Spain they came, and so they remained, strangers to each other in their different linguistic nationalities at the start and at the end. Hardly a single case in the mountain of literature produced by the bourgeois intellectuals in the International Brigades identifies any but the most superficial interaction between the International Brigaders and Spanish people or between men of different nationalities within the International Brigades. With the language barriers, how could it have been otherwise? Worse still, these men have become strangers to history without any documentation and so they largely remain.

However incomplete the puzzle, certain pieces can be used. Why did they go to Spain? What did they do and become in service there? Examination of their own answers to that question will tell something about the minds of the volunteers. And we can also ask what they did and what happened to them to see what they became in Spain.

ENDNOTES

1. W. G. Krivitsky, *I Was Stalin's Agent* (London: Hamish Hamilton, 1939), 113.
2. The League's military commission conducted 254 investigations and built a card index with a double entry for each of the 12,000 men. See "Withdrawal of Non-Spanish Combatants from Spain," *Official Journal of the League of Nations*, 104th Session of the Council, January 1939, pp. 131–132.

3. Andreu Castells, *Las Brigadas Internacionales de la Guerra de España* (Barcelona: Editorial Ariel, 1974), 381 n. 40.
4. *Le Figaro,* 17 February 1937.
5. Arnold Krammer, "Germans Against Hitler," *Journal of Contemporary History*, 4 (1969) 2, p. 65.
6. Castells lists 1,507 Austrians, 2.5 percent and 4,324 Germans, 7.3 percent, while the Soviet archives list 846 Austrians, 2.7 percent and 2,180 Germans, 7.0 percent, and the League's reported 1 Austrian and 46 Germans evacuated, 0.7 percent.
7. Recently, one author has claimed 30,000 Slavs (including Poles) in the International Brigades; see the reference and discussion in Hugh Thomas, *La Guerra Civil Española, 1936–1939* (Barcelona: Ediciones Exito, 1978), 3: 1051 n. 42.
8. Castells, 331–370, and cf. Vincente Rójo, *España Heroica* (Barcelona: Editorial Ariel, 1975 [1942]), 147–159.
9. "Withdrawal," 140.
10. Castells, 501, 506, and 525, respectively.
11. Matthews, *Education of a Correspondent* (New York: Harcourt, 1946), 158.
12. Hoar, 109.
13. Castells, 381 n. 33.
14. Hoar, 109.
15. Ibid., 32. Identifying Canadians was complicated at the end because the Canadian government refused to incur the expense of repatriating its own citizens, leaving that job to others; see Matthews (1946), 141.
16. Lois Smith, *Mexico and the Spanish Republicans* (Berkeley: University of California Press, 1955), 106.
17. Juan-Simeon Vidarte, *Todos fuimos Culpables: Testimonio de un Socialista Español* (Barcelona: Ediciones Grijalbo, 1978), 546.
18. Hugh Thomas, *The Spanish Civil War,* 3rd ed. (Harmondsworth: Penguin, 1977), 984.
19. David Alfaro Siqueiros, *Me Llamaban el Coronelazo* (Mexico: Biografias Gandes, 1977), 348, and Roberto Vega Gonzalez, *Cadetes Mexicanos en la Guerra de España* (Mexico: Compania General de Ediciones, 1954), 201–217. Cf. T. G. Powell, "Mexico," *The Spanish Civil War, 1936–1939: American Hemispheric Perspectives,* ed. Mark Falcoff and Frederick Pike (Lincoln: University of Nebraska Press, 1982), 71.
20. Matthews (1946), 141. Observers often give different figures at different times, further confusing the issue. Alvah Bessie, for example, says there were 3,800 Americans in his book *Men in Battle* (New York: Scribners, 1939), p. v, but many years later the number 3,200 is given in his *Songs of the Spanish Civil War* (New York: Folkways, 1961), 2. The publicist Joseph North varies his estimates from 3,800 in his "The Lincoln Battalion in Pictures," *New Masses* 30 (14 February 1939), 4 but in the same year he cites 3,200 in his book *Men in the Ranks* (New York: Friends of the Abraham Lincoln Brigade, 1939), 5, which dropped to 3,000 in his "No Pásaran: 1940," *New Masses,* 34 (9 January 1940), 9.
21. Palmiro Togliatti, *Le Parti Communiste Italien,* R. Paris, trans. (Paris: Maspero, 1961), 102.
22. In 1966 the Fratellanza ex-Garibalidini di Spagna put the total number at 4,110. See Massimo Mangilli-Climpson, *Men of Heart of Red, White and Green* (New York: Vantage, 1985), Appendix 2, p. 136.
23. Neal Wood, *Communism and British Intellectuals* (London: Gollancz, 1959), 56. Columnist Dick Beddoes confidently says there were 1,239 Canadians in "Remembering the Mac-Paps," *Toronto Globe and Mail,* 10 January 1980, p. 8.
24. David Cattell, *Communism and the Spanish Civil War* (New York: Russell and Russell, 1955), 83 and 230, n. 54 and n. 55.
25. One of the most common methods in documentation of the Spanish Civil War

is the argument from the authority of the enemy. To a Nationalist historian, Wintringham would be an authority if, perhaps only if, he had been a Communist. Martinez Bande, *Communist Intervention in the Spanish Civil War* (Madrid: Spanish Information Service, 1966), 33, declares argument from the authority of the enemy to be a policy in writing the official history of the war. To prove the International Brigades saved Madrid and prolonged the war in the winter of 1936, he quotes three unfriendly sources. For their part, such sources prove the same point by quoting other Nationalist historians; cf. Robert G. Colodny, *The Struggle for Madrid* (New York: Paine-Whitman, 1958), 186–187. In neither case is an effort made to evaluate sources and claims. Myths become reality by their repetition. Early in the war, a Republican tract claimed 20,000 Portuguese with the Nationalists; see Hispanicus, *Foreign Intervention in Spain* (London: United Editorial, n.d.), 341. This figure is reproduced in the first two editions of Thomas and also appears in Jacques Delperrie de Bayac, *Les Brigades Internationales* (Paris: Fayard, 1968), 35; Richard Kisch, *They Shall Not Pass* (London: Wayland, 1974) 124; Irving Weinstein, *The Cruel Years* (London: Bailey Bros., 1974), 177; David Mitchell, *The Spanish Civil War* (London: Granada, 1982), 67; and Marjorie A. Valleau, *The Spanish Civil War in American and European Films* (Ann Arbor: University Microfilm Research Press, 1982), 1. In 1986 this phantom army was boosted threefold to 60,000 in John Gerassi, *The Premature Antifascists* (New York: Praeger, 1986), 15. What is the proof? Hispanicus cited a selection of journalistic hyperbole from a Portuguese newspaper. Full stop. To put this figure of 20,000 in perspective, the *Statesman's Yearbook* for 1936 put the total of the Portuguese army in Portugal at 27,000. Not everything read in newspapers at the time was true. Rumors were endless in number and amazing in variety, for example, "3,000 Japanese Reported En Route to Join Franco," *New York Times*, 11 January 1937, p. 2, while an article in England spoke of Amazon battalions of Popular Militia in the Republican army ("The Recapture of Albacete," *Times*, 27 July 1936, p. 12). Many Portuguese served in the war, including some with the Republicans but not 20,000, let alone 60,000; Ricardo de la Cierva y de Hoces, *Leyendu y Tragedia de las Brigadas Internacionales* (Madrid: Editorial Prensa Española, 1973), 100–101. But like the Soviet infantry with the Republic, this Portuguese legion has been created from the imagination.

26. Great Britain, Home Office, *Communist Papers*, Command 2682 (London: His Majesty's Stationary Office, 1926), 1, and *Times*, 16 October 1925, p. 11.
27. Fred Copeman, *Reason and Revolt* (London: Blandford Press, n.d. [1948?]), 79.
28. Hugh Thomas, *The Spanish Civil War* (Harmondsworth: Penguin, 1977), 452. There is no mention of his role in Maurice Thorez, *Fils du Peuple* (Paris: Editions sociales, 1960), 155, where the International Brigades are mentioned. At the time, the party's interest in the International Brigades was not always advertised, for example, "La bataille pour Madrid," *L'Humanité*, 11 November 1936, p. 3.
29. Thomas, 590. Cf. Peter Stansky and William Abrahams, *Journey to the Frontier* (London: Constable, 1966), 317.
30. Jason Gurney, *Crusade in Spain* (London: Faber and Faber, 1974), 46.
31. Ibid., 69.
32. Rust, 6.
33. Gurney, 66–67.
34. Esmond Romilly, *Boadilla* (London: Hamilton, 1937), 26.
35. Jef Last, *The Spanish Tragedy*, trans. D. Hallet (London: Routledge, 1939), 136.
36. Rosenstone, 98.
37. For example, Joseph Starobin, *The Life and Death of an American Hero* (New York: New Age Publishers, 1938), 10 and 12.
38. Rosenstone, 98.
39. Ibid., 368–369. Rosenstone lists percentages based on the 1,804 names where 46.2 percent have no occupations. The percentages in the text have been re-

calculated against the baseline of the 970 with occupations or 53.8 percent of the total.

40. Togliatti, 102.
41. Aguilera Duran, 130.
42. Hywel Francis, "Welsh Miners and the Spanish Civil War," 179–181.
43. Lizón Gadia, 10.
44. André Malraux, *L'Espoir* (Paris: Gallimard, 1937), 521.
45. Francis, "Welsh Miners and the Spanish Civil War," 185.
46. Cameron Stewart, "Summoned to the Eternal Field" (Unpublished PhD dissertation, Claremont Graduate School, 1972), 322.
47. Marcel Acier, ed., *From Spanish Trenches* (New York: Modern Age Books, 1937), 144 and 148.
48. Tom Wintringham, *English Captain* (London: Faber and Faber, 1939), 257. Cf. Edwin Rolfe, *The Lincoln Battalion* (New York: Random House, 1939), 14.
49. Hoar, 99.
50. See Adolfo Lizón Gadea, *Brigadas Internacionales en España* (Madrid: Editoria Nacional, 1940), 65, and Wayfarer, *The International Brigade* (Sussex: Ditching, n.d.), 31.
51. See Upton Sinclair, *No Pasarán* (London: Werner Lawrie, 1937), 233.
52. See Gustav Regler, *The Owl of Minerva,* trans. N. Denny, (New York: Farrar and Strauss, 1959), 284.
53. See Robert Rosenstone, *Crusade of the Left* (New York: Pegasus, 1969), 110 and Cameron Stewart, "Summoned to the Eternal Field," 333. Cf. Victor Hoar, *The MacKenzie-Papineau Battalion* (Toronto: Copp Clark, 1969), 22.
54. Castells, 382 n. 48.
55. Alberto Fernandez, "Judios en la Guerra de España," *Tiempo de Historia,* September 1975, p. 8.
56. Albert Prago, "Jews in the International Brigades," *Jewish Currents,* February 1979, pp. 16–17.
57. Diamant, 128 and 127.
58. Arthur Landis, *The Abraham Lincoln Brigade* (New York: The Citadel Press, 1967), 73.
59. Robert Rosenstone, 100.
60. James Yates, *Mississippi to Madrid: Memoirs of a Black American in the Abraham Lincoln Brigade* (Seattle: Open Hand, 1989), 176–177.
61. Cameron Stewart, "Summoned to the Eternal Field," 277.
62. See Colodny, 63, regarding Belgium and Switzerland and Hoar, 14, regarding Canada.
63. *New York Times,* 22 September 1937, p. 13.
64. See Adam Ulam, *Expansion and Coexistence,* 2nd ed. (New York: Praeger, 1975), 244.
65. Gurney, 27, and also cf. Rosenstone, 73.
66. See the remarks attributed to Bill Young in Nettie Palmer et al., *Australians in Spain,* rev. ed. (Sydney: Current Books, 1948), 15, or the echo many years later in Sam Aarons, "Reminiscences of the Spanish Civil War," *Australian Left Review* 39 (March 1973): 24–29.
67. Gurney, 27, and also Rosenstone, 73.
68. Peter Elstob, *The Spanish Prisoner* (London: Macmillan, 1939), 23.
69. John Sommerfield, 166. Cf. Vincent Brome, *The International Brigades* (New York: Morrow, 1966), 17.
70. Staróbin, 10–12, and cf. Rosenstone, 98.
71. Jane Morgan, *Conflict and Order: The Police and Labour Disputes in England and Wales, 1900–1930* (Oxford: Oxford University Press, 1988).
72. *Ben Leider: American Hero* (New York: Ben Leider Memorial Fund, n.d.), 8.
73. Joseph North, *Men in the Ranks* (New York: Friends of the Abraham Lincoln Brigade, 1939), 24–25.

74. Ibid. This thesis is still asserted; see William L. Katz and Marc Crawford, *The Lincoln Brigade: A Picture History* (New York: Atheneum, 1989), 7-11.
75. Steve Nelson, *The Volunteers* (New York: Masses and Mainstream, 1952), 15–19.
76. John Tisa, *Recalling the Good Fight*, 5.
77. Pablo de la Torriente-Brau, *En España, Peleando con los Milicianos* (Mexico: Editorial Grijalbo, 1972), 52.
78. Ibid., 151.
79. Sinclair, 151 and passim. Robert Jordan says that many do not know that they are Fascists but will find out when the time comes, Ernest Hemingway, *For Whom The Bell Tolls* (New York: Scribner's, 1940), 208.
80. Rosenstone, 112.
81. Torriente-Brau, "Mexico," *Hemispheric Perspectives*, ed. Falcoff, 131.
82. Francis, "Welsh Miners and the Spanish Civil War," 177.
83. William Rust, *Britons in Spain* (New York: International, 1939), 6.
84. Last, 69.
85. North, 15, and also Cook, 3 and 40.
86. Rosenstone, 100.
87. Jan Valtin, *Out of the Night* (London: Heinemann, 1941), 572–573.
88. Lloyd Edmonds, *Letters from Spain* (Sydney: Allen & Unwin, 1985), 46 and 69.
89. Ibid., 71, and Eby, 10.
90. Eric Homberger, *American Writers and Radical Politics* (London: Macmillan, 1987).
91. Sinclair, 51, 123, and 129.
92. James M. Burns, *John Kennedy* (New York: Harcourt, 1960), 32.
93. Landis, 557.
94. For the opposite conclusion, see Richardson, 32–44 and passim.
95. Gabriel Almond, *The Appeals of Communism* (Princeton: Princeton University Press, 1954), 241.
96. Gurney, 72.
97. J. Edgar Hoover, *The Masters of Deceit* (New York: Pocket Books, 1959), 65–66. Steve Nelson was jailed later under the Smith Act.
98. Lizón Gadia, 13.
99. How de la Cierva y de Hoces could possibly know this remains veiled.
100. Angel Viñas, "Los Condicionantes Internacionales," *La Guerra Civil Española*, Manuel Tunon de Lara, 153.
101. So says Rosenstone, 112.
102. Togliatti, 102.
103. Krammer, 66.
104. Paolo Spriano, *Storia Del Partito Communista Italiano* (Turin: G. Einaudi, 1970), 3: 94.
105. So say Staróbin, 23, and Voros, 271.
106. An example is Steve Nelson; see Rosenstone, 115.
107. Hywel Francis, "Welsh Miners and the Spanish Civil War," 182.
108. According to Rosenstone, 112.
109. Rosenstone, 112.
110. Gerassi, 11.
111. Hoar, 36.
112. Francis, "Welsh Miners and the Spanish Civil War," 182, and Walter Gregory, *The Shallow Grave* (London: Gollancz, 1986), 35.
113. Phillip Knightly, *The Second Oldest Profession* (London: Pan, 1986), 81 and 202.
114. Hoover, 109.
115. Gurney, 72.
116. Ibid.
117. Thomas, 455.
118. Lardner, 275.
119. Delperrie de Bayac, 85.

CHAPTER 7

What Purpose Was Served?

1. Introduction

The stated justification for the creation of the International Brigades was not to provide an outlet for the politically, socially, economically, and morally frustrated men who eventually joined. In the heat of July and August of 1936 when spontaneous volunteers of one kind and another were coming to the Republican cause, several individuals made suggestions to members of the Spanish government about the organization of an international column.[1] These suggestions were rebuffed on the grounds that the government needed material; men it had aplenty.[2] When the idea of an international column aroused the interest of Stalin for reasons of his own, the Spanish government was persuaded to accept volunteers,[3] with the justification that foreign volunteers would be a model army.[4] A model of military efficiency was needed, it was said, to aid the development of the popular militia then being integrated with that part of the Spanish army loyal to the government and the conscripts being raised to fill out the ranks.[5]

In the word of Tom Wintringham, speaking as an International Brigader,

> The important thing, over all, is not our success ... but our example. People learn from example more quickly than from lectures or other

forms of talk. We have to show the Spanish militia what a real army looks like, how it marches, how it defends, and how it attacks.[6]

Here was the first justification for the International Brigades: to set an example of military skill and commitment, an intention the volunteers were aware of even if they did not often mention it.[7] The lessons of example would be brought home to the Iberian levies by integrating their units into the International Brigades. The brigades were thus mixed from the start, though a British veteran has seen fit to deny it.[8] It was not training that would make the International Brigades into a model army. That took time, for both Spaniards and foreigners, far too much time. Rather the International Brigades were to be recruited from men who already had military training and who perhaps had served in the Great War. Spain, neutral in the Great War, had no experience of conscription and so no mass training of men between ages 20 and 30 during the 1914–1918 period. Consequently, no cohort of 40-year-olds with such military experience was available, as in England, France, Germany, and Italy.

Already trained, foreign volunteers could fight while the new Spanish army trained, a second and related justification for the International Brigades. Not only were they to provide a military object lesson, but they were also to fight until the new army could take over. In particular, this fighting meant the defense of endangered Madrid when the International Brigades were organized.[9]

Last and significantly, the International Brigaders offered another kind of model, a third justification that will be treated in the next chapter. Volunteers would, as one of them said later, offer a model of moral commitment to the cause that would inspire both the Spanish and the world.[10] The more disparate the class and origins of the men and the more plainly they were volunteers, the better this third purpose would be served. The more determined and tenacious the men proved themselves to be in battle and the more willingly they obeyed the high command, the more they would show the Spanish what had to be done. The watching world would learn the lesson that fascism had to be and could be fought. However, the more varied and independent the volunteers, the less likely they could quickly be formed into effective fighting units. Moreover, men most likely to follow all orders blindly would not be those with military training and experience. Veterans regard orders with a healthy skepticism, especially veterans of the Great War, once described as the war of officers against men. A tension existed from the start in the justifications of the International Brigades, even (mistakenly) assuming the mutual good will of those involved.

The moral commitment that the International Brigaders manifested had its due effect. Those who observed them were struck by the uniqueness of the event. The safe, sane, sensible, sober *New York Times* war correspondent, Herbert Matthews, exhibited unaccustomed eloquence when he wrote:

> There had been nothing like the International Column in modern history. I suppose that one would have to go back to the Crusades to find a group of men, from all over the known world, fighting purely and simply for an ideal. Many men have given their lives and many more will do so before the conflict ends . . . not for home or country or money or because they were drafted and ordered to go, but because of the deep conviction that this world will not be worth living in if Fascism triumphs.[11]

In the words of another observer, a publicist, "most of" the volunteers "were poor men who ... went partly for adventure, but chiefly for an idea . . .," knowing "that if they were killed they would die unremembered."[12] Despite the library of books about the International Brigaders, most of them are unremembered. That they were poor and that they were animated by fundamental ideas are judgments corroborated in the study of their social identities and motivations. When it was all over, one veteran reportedly said that "something which could never happen again in the history of the world had come to an end."[13] A contemporary historian of the International Brigades responds to this sentiment—that the International Brigades were unique—by noting that no comparable upsurge occurred to aid solitary England after the fall of France to fascism in 1940.[14] Another historian has gone as far as to say, in passing, that the "ultimate result" of the Spanish Republic was the International Brigades.[15] Of course, many individuals did go to England to fight, among them more exiles from Poland, the Netherlands, and France, along with those who anticipated a wider war from the United States, and the nations of the Commonwealth, while the Swiss and Swedes mobilized. For the occupied countries like Denmark, the war seemed to be over. In short, the analogy is limited.

The International Brigaders were not the only volunteers of the epoch. Thousands of Swedes and some other foreigners joined the Finns in the Winter War with the Soviet Union, about 12,000 in all.[16] Later, thousands of Spanish soldiers, veterans of their civil war, went to fight in Russia as volunteers in World War II, some 40,000 in all.[17] Other examples could be named, including the Irish and Portuguese who took the part of the rebel Spanish nationalists during the civil war. This unique feeling is, as will be shown, an outgrowth of that third purpose, exemplary moral commitment.

Events must be taken in context. For example, many Dutchmen volunteered for the Waffen S.S. during the German occupation of the Netherlands in World War II.[18] From this small country of the Netherlands, which historically has always looked west to France and England, 40,000 volunteers came, more than all the foreigners in the International Brigades, from 50 countries. Leo Palacio has argued there can be no similarity between those who volunteered for the International Brigades and those in occupied Europe who volunteered for the Waffen S.S, but he acknowledges that some who served in the International Brigades also later served in the Waffen S.S.[19] The difference Palacio cites is that the S.S. volunteers were well paid.

In sum, the International Brigades as organizations had three justifications:

(1) to provide a model of military efficiency,
(2) to defend Madrid, and
(3) to be a moral example of the cause of anti-fascism.

In addition to the motivations of the exiles, the displaced, and the others and whatever personal atonement by expiation particular individuals sought, these three were the purposes of the men as a whole, as an institution. How well the International Brigades achieved these purposes requires analysis of what the volunteers did and what was done to them. The military history of the campaigns in which the International Brigades were involved can be found in many sources. Such a history is not the purpose here. The aim is rather to summarize, explain, and reflect on the experiences of the foreign volunteers through impressions and other data.

2. Military Model

Starting with the first justification of the International Brigades, that of providing a military model of excellence, many of the earliest spontaneous volunteers were experienced soldiers who understood and accepted martial discipline, like the Germans and Italians. At the squad level of a dozen men or a *centura* of 100, there was no denying that effective fighting units existed within the International Brigades. Here, Spanish conscripts and militia could learn through example.[20] However, battalion and brigade levels of the International Brigaders were doomed to failure by their very nature, as was the hero of Greek tragedy. The very characteristics that made the International Brigades unique also made it impossible to function efficiently. Diversity of national languages, emphasis on volition, political differences, ignorance of Spain, all of these things and more made operations nearly impossible under conditions of campaign and battle. Nor were the International Brigades' relations with the Spanish government and army particularly cordial. In the excitement of being mistaken for Russian troops and cheered, the volunteers failed to notice, judging from their accounts, that the Republican government did not warmly welcome them. The official welcome was invariably at the remote, autonomous base camp of the International Brigades at Albacete where the speaker was André Marty, a nominee from the French Communist party. Richardson has written that the Comintern wished to isolate the International Brigades for its own purposes, which suited the uninterested Republican government.[21] First-hand accounts of volunteers show no sign that they found their greeting a disappointment; nor were Spanish conscripts in the International Brigades noticeably eager to learn from their mentors.[22]

If the first German volunteers were veterans of the Great War, as were many Italians, well and good, because no signs are evident that anyone ever received any training once posted to Albacete. Instead, they were subjected to speeches on the class struggle and repeatedly told of the need for military training that was promised but not provided.[23] All this talk about training has convinced some writers, including International Brigade veterans, that the International Brigades were a well-trained and equipped force.[24] Though some participants attest that volunteers for the International Brigades were rejected, none were rejected for not already having had real military training. I say "real" military training because occasionally the claim is that some volunteers were rejected because "they were too old or because they lacked military experience," as Hywel Francis has said of the Welsh.[25] This assertion is best digested slowly.

As shown earlier, many men motivated by the Spanish Civil War, including the Welsh in Francis's study, subscribed to the one-fight doctrine, one implication of which was that soldiering was no different from picketing or protesting. The plausibility of the doctrine rests on the violent nature of these activities in the 1930s and, more importantly, on ignorance of war. Knowledge of war today, thanks to the electronic media, and of violent strikes, apart from those in South Africa, proves otherwise. Any Welsh rejects would have been those without such union experience that was readily and falsely equated to military experience in the enthusiasm of the moment. If so, the point remains: men with no military experience were accepted. Francis himself in a later work quotes, without registering a demur, a Welsh volunteer who said, "If I can shoot rabbits, I can shoot fascists."[26] Paul Preston, like Francis, disinclined to be critical of the

International Brigades, admits that "most of them [the volunteers] had no experience of warfare" when they arrived in Spain.[27]

At Albacete they mainly waited. So removed were they from the reality of war that a group of Poles allegedly agreed that a "man isn't supposed to worry about his own skin in a war."[28] Since few Americans served in the Great War, they as much as any other nationality would have needed training, but veterans make it clear that they received none in Spain.[29] Volunteers John Tisa and Lloyd Edmonds refer to some lectures on matters military, not to training.[30] But as Wintringham had said from the outset, lectures were useless. In the terror of battle, no man saves himself or anyone else by remembering something from a chalk talk. In the confusion of combat, no officer sees the light thanks to lecture notes. Not only was training generally not provided, but it would have been unwelcome to some. An English sailor balked at the prospect of training, having come to kill Fascists, he said, not to be made into a soldier.[31] A man rebellious enough to volunteer for Spain was not likely to be a man to accept meekly martial discipline. A fortunate batch of volunteers did receive some instruction on one occasion, limited to advancing over open country. Missing was any practice with the use of cover, the formation of defensive position, or retreat.[32] Of using and reading tracer rounds, they knew nothing. The deadly secrets of cross fire, enfilading fire, and traversing fire remained mysteries to the untrained volunteers.[33] As if it were a sport, one subsequent book speaks of the International Brigaders being trained on the battlefield.[34] No amount of experience with ruthless, strike-breaking police could have prepared a volunteer for what he found on the battlefield, and it is pointless to speak of it as battlefield training.

After a time at Albacete, sometimes weeks, men were taken in trucks to battlefields where they would hold a rifle for the first time in their lives, or so said Polish, Hungarian, and American International Brigaders.[35] On at least one occasion, these completely inexperienced men had one practice shot on the road to a battlefield, the sum total of military training and experience of these ostensibly model soldiers.[36] Lack of training and comic opera disorganization of the International Brigades, together with the spontaneous volunteers, permitted the rapid deployment of the International Brigades, not any advance preparation, contrary to one propaganda claim made at the time.[37] Later still, half the International Brigaders at the Ebro River went into that offensive battle unarmed as well as untrained.[38] Once in battle, the international volunteers found that the Fascists whom they had come to kill fought back.[39]

The reaction of the International Brigades was surprise and anger as they were injured and killed. The Englishman Tom Wintringham, who had done so much to promote the idea of the International Brigades, declared his surprise that so many of the volunteers were men who had never handled a gun before.[40] Yet within the space of 23 pages, he goes on to boast of the International Brigades as a martial model for the Spanish militia.[41] Men who had handled a gun and knew its powers might well have been the ones least likely to volunteer, a thought never admitted by the architects and publicists of the International Brigades. Another publicist says first that the International Brigades were an amateur army and then two pages later that the International Brigades taught the Spanish militia to fight.[42]

Mostly, the publicity material produced for and about the International Brigades falls silent on training. The *Volunteer for Liberty* omitted the subject in favor of devoting space to the several threats posed by the devil, Trotsky. A pamphlet produced in Canada boasts of the ill-training of the volunteers.[43] Writers implicitly praise the willingness to do battle so unprepared as a measure of faith in the cause and as a kind of indirect proof of the justice of the cause. On the battlefields there was different counting and the feeling waned that "war is fun," as one volunteer had said in the early days of his service.[44]

In general, the men of the International Brigades knew as little about making war as they did about conjugating Spanish verbs. Ignorance made them as incandescent and extraordinary as a shooting star, possessed of neither origin nor destination. They were men literally prepared to stand up to machine gun fire, once. Said an English volunteer, "knowing nothing of war, nothing surprised me in the way it was fought."[45] The International Brigaders did things no trained soldiers would have done, as Wintringham wrote:

> The Americans obeyed orders. They attacked at "all costs." There are not many units, in regular armies, that will renew an attack without support or stiffening of any sort, when casualties have risen to more than 50 per cent of those engaged. The Lincoln battalion did so.[46]

(Nationalist historian Ricardo de la Cierva y de Hoces sees in this combat Spanish revenge for 1898.)[47] Enduring 50 percent casualties, being given orders like "at all costs," attacking without support; properly trained soldiers know these measures to be the terrible failures they were. Not so the International Brigaders. Once in pitched battle, these inexperienced men found the Fascists damnably difficult to kill. Esmond Romilly said of his first day against fire, "I never took aim. I never looked up to see what I was firing at. I never heard the order to open fire. I never saw the enemy."[48] Dying, on the other hand, was easy.

That day for which Wintringham praised Americans for their obedience, 298 out of 400 fell, a good deal more than 50 percent. In the assault upon Pingarron Hill alone on that day, 127 men died, men who did not know how to recognize enemy fire, who did not know how to use weapons still coated in packing grease.[49] These men were ordered to attack by their commander, American Robert Merriman, who was the focus of propaganda because he was tall and good looking, not because he was a capable officer.[50] In 1983, volunteer Peter Wyden made him sound like a Hollywood hero,[51] while in 1985, volunteer John Tisa attributed to Merriman virtues of leadership. These testimonials are belied by the casualties suffered by those inexperienced men unfortunate enough to be under Merriman's command. So impenetrable is myth that volunteer Tisa went on to assert that Merriman's previous experience as a teaching assistant in economics at the University of California prepared him to deal scrupulously with a multitude of details and military problems that forever challenge a battlefield commander—from tutorial room to trench in one mortal lesson.[52] Merriman, said to be a model for Hemingway's Robert Jordan in *For Whom the Bell Tolls*, questioned his orders but ultimately he dared not refuse them.[53] Those who glamorize him fail to associate the debacle at Jarama with his culpability.[54] More generally, one searches in vain for instances of line officers in the International Brigades who protected their men by resisting foolish orders often designed for propaganda effect rather than military advantage. Only with the Italians is there evidence that line officers tried to resist the stupidity of staff officers.[55] Though at times the Italian brigade probably had a majority of Communists, its command was in the hands of virulently anti-Communist Socialists who made up their own minds. The truculence of Italian Socialists led to an unremitting effort to oust them. Compliance was hardly surprising since political loyalty or propaganda value were the criteria for selection and promotion of most officers.[56]

In another famous case, propaganda value led to the promotion of a black American to command white Americans in military service for the first time.[57] Enlightened though that may have seemed, it could not compensate for his incompetence, which proved fatal for the men in his command.[58] When veteran William Herrick criticized this officer's competence in an interview in 1986, he was vilified by defenders of the faith.[59] Furthermore, volunteer veteran Gerassi in 1986 bestowed a place in the pantheon of heroes to this black man.[60]

Contrary to cinema stereotypes, questioning superior orders is not at all uncommon in campaign and battle. Line officers at brigade and battalion level do not always submissively concur with the schemes concocted by staff officers, nor do all officers in combat accept without question the orders of a direct superior. Part of officer training in any army is obedience, but another part is to voice one's own estimate of the situation for the information of superiors and to protect one's men. World War II, so often linked to the Spanish Civil War, is replete with examples of officers of all ranks who questioned, resisted, and refused superior orders in the interest of protecting their men from what these officers perceived to be useless sacrifice. These examples, which can be drawn from the German and Soviet armies as readily as from the American, British, French, Canadian, and other armies, do not appear in the record of the International Brigades.

With this compliance and incompetence, only three months in battle saw 400 of the first 600 Englishmen dead.[61] New, untrained men pressed into the ranks blundered into their deaths before their names were known to others in their units.[62] At Jarama, a veteran said later (without identifying his sources) that the International Brigades suffered casualties of 63.8 percent.[63] Three weeks at Jarama took 750 of 1,000 Germans to a better world.[64] Wintringham estimated that the International Brigades were suffering a loss of 15 percent a month in dead, missing, and wounded unable to return to the line.[65] There were also plenty of desertions.[66] Over a year, this rate of loss would come to 180 percent, reduced for any time that International Brigades were out of the line on leave or in transit. This means that in 12 months, all the men in the International Brigades in January would be lost by the end of July and by December eight out of ten of the mid-year replacements would have suffered the same fate as well. One writer, who acknowledged the high casualty rate at the time, disingenuously attributed it to the German and Italian weapons possessed by the rebels, not to the misconception, inexperience, or malfeasance of the International Brigades.[67]

Compare this rate of loss with that suffered by Allied countries in World War II. As a percentage of troops who served overseas, the Australian dead, wounded, and captured was 15.86 percent; the American was 18.90 percent; the Canadian 20.42 percent; the British 21.57 percent; and the New Zealanders 30.83 percent.[68] Of course, each of these figures derives from a baseline that includes troops who never saw combat, whereas the International Brigaders saw little else. Even allowing this difference and multiplying the Allied figures by two, three, or four, the result still falls below the rate Wintringham mentions. Or to take an example from the Great War, consider the

French debacle at the third battle of Champagne in April 1917. About 1.2 million French troops took part in the assault, and 120,000 of them were casualties, a rate of 10 percent, again below Wintringham's figure.[69]

Still more apt comparisons would be with those who fought against the International Brigades. One estimate for the Italian expeditionary corps in the Spanish Civil War is 4.5 to 6 percent killed and 20 to 25 percent wounded.[70] Some of these troops were nearly as poorly led, trained, and equipped as the International Brigades. Another writer estimates that the Falangist and Carlist militia on the Nationalist side suffered 6 percent killed and 31 percent wounded. These troops were amateur zealots.[71] Again, these rates in both cases are below those cited by Wintringham.

This happens when untrained men play soldier, especially when they are used as shock troops, the first into attacks and the last out in retreat. While in existence the International Brigades were the shock troops in every offensive save one, though they never accounted for more than about 3 percent of the Spanish army.[72] In the propaganda of the time and to some historians, this use proves that the International Brigades were recognized as the best troops in the Republican army.[73] A cynic might think that the Spanish generals and politicians preferred to use foreigners as cannon fodder wherever possible, another taboo subject in the hagiography of the International Brigades, though Mahlon Perkins, an American diplomat in Barcelona, reported in 1937 hearing the foreigners "referred to as 'carne de canon' (cannon meat)."[74] Comintern and Soviet generals and politicians found dead heroes a treasure beyond price in the propaganda war. Live heroes could be an embarrassment, but dead ones could not. The International Brigaders had no one to defend them from the greatest threat to soldiers' lives, their own leaders. In this respect, the Spanish Civil War continued the Great War, the war between the men and the officers, rather than anticipating World War II, the war between men and machines. If the number of men who served in the International Brigades cannot be established, saying how many of them of them died may also be impossible; however, many sources offer estimates that must suffice to set some limit to the casualties (see Table 7). None of these estimates is unimpeachable and different estimates can be found for each case.[75]

Table (8) shows that Castells provides figures for each of these nationalities, different from the estimates of Table (6).[76]

Castells distinguishes between seriously wounded soldiers and those who were not. That only seriously wounded have been included in Table (8) may account for some of the differences. If all wounds

Table 7
Estimates of Casualties by Selected Nationalities

Nationality	% Killed	% Wounded	Total Served	Killed
Germanic[1]	40.0%		5,000	2,000
Italians[2]	20.0%	67.6%	3,108	662
French[3]	11.8%		8,500	1,003
British[4]	19.7%	63.8%	2,762	544
Yugoslav[5]	"about half"	20.0%	1,500	750
American[6]	32.1%		2,800	898
Composite	24.7%		23,670	5,857

[1]Includes Austrians; Alfred Kantorowicz, *Spanische Tagebuch* (Berlin: Aufbau-Verlag, 1948), 15.

[2]Palmiro Togliatti, *Le Parti Communiste Italien*, trans. R. Paris (Paris: Maspero, 1961), 102.

[3]*L'epopée de L'espagne* (Paris: Amicale des anciens volontaires français en Espagne républicaine, 1957), 80.

[4]Neal Wood, *Communism and British Intellectuals* (London: Gollancz, 1959), 56.

[5]Tito with V. Dedijer, "Tito Speaks, II," *Life*, 12 (28 April 1952), 67.

[6]Edwin Rolfe, *The Lincoln Battalion* (New York: Random House, 1939), 7.

are counted, the British rate is 57.3 percent; the Italian 82.8 percent, and the Yugoslav 49.5 percent, results more in line with Table (7).

Overall, Castells asserts that 9,934 out of 59,380 died in Spain, or 16.7 percent.[77] He also asserts that only 3 percent of the international volunteers escaped injury completely.[78] For his part, Delperrie de Bayac estimates that 10,000 out of 35,000 died, a total of 29.2 percent.[79] Note a convergence in the number of the dead in these two sources. No one, not even Castells, can guess how many volunteers died of their wounds later, outside Spain where none had pensions or veterans' hospitals and many had only French internment camps or worse when the Germans occupied France. In these circum-

Table 8
Castells's Estimates of Casualties by Selected Nationalities

Nationality	% Killed	% Wounded	Total Killed
Germanic	22.0%	26.4%	5,831
Italian	18.0%	30.0%	5,108
French	17.3%	30.6%	5,400
British	16.2%	28.3%	3,504
Yugoslav	34.7%	26.3%	1,512
American	13.4%	26.8%	3,874
Total			25,229

stances, those who lived through their baptism of fire quickly settled on survival as their only goal.[80]

Like the universal soldier, the International Brigaders suffered from every other aspect of war in addition to the dying and the maiming of battle—hunger, stench, lice, filth, disease, fatigue, and so on. Though most of the untrained men did not expect this, Jason Gurney admits he was foretold, but the privilege of joining the just cause outweighed these burdens, or so he thought when he was recruited.[81] Like the universal soldier, they suffered from the confusion and incompetence of command.[82] Communication through the languages of the International Brigades was very difficult.[83] In staff meetings, chains of amateur translators conveyed the babel of life and death information. Imagine the difficulties for these amateurs with technical terms from the lexicons of topography and military science. The European Community deals with only nine official languages but nearly one in five employees is a translator in the Brussels establishment of just under 20,000. Political pressures presumably guarantee that a high standard is set for each language. By contrast, no specific allowance was made for translation in the International Brigades. Those most proficient in languages deemed important wound up writing propaganda like *Volunteer for Liberty*. Others with rudimentary knowledge of languages served as translators.

Nor was deceit completely absent. International units were ordered to undertake suicide attacks, spurred on by the claim that other units on their flanks had already gone over the top, and would be exposed to slaughter if the International Brigaders failed to support them. At times, the call's receiver could see that flanking units had not moved and were making no preparation to move. Standard operating procedure may have been to compel obedience to incredible orders through moral blackmail.[84] When the offensive is due and the promised aerial, artillery, and ground support does not come, what does come is a call on the field telephone that is nothing but a lie. Even the most naive learn something from this.

Moreover, the NKVD tirelessly searched for Trotsky's followers in the International Brigades, dutifully fabricating villains to appease Stalin's paranoia. Men who had survived combat did not always survive purges in the trenches.[85] Most accounts are silent on the NKVD, though some attribute these murders to the undoubted lunacy of André Marty.[86] However, Ludwig Renn, a German political commissar, and Carlo Penchienati, commander of the Garibaldi Brigade, have acknowledged the NKVD murders.[87] Marty reportedly admitted—even boasted of—500 executions.[88] According to some calculations, 500 deaths would equal 10 percent of all the International

Brigades' deaths in Spain.[89] Other veterans excuse these executions by claiming that the International Brigades attracted many spies and saboteurs.

The claim that the International Brigades were replete with spies was curiously vindicated in a book ascribed to one Henri Dupré, entitled *La Légion Tricolore*, which appeared in German-occupied Paris in late 1942.[90] The thesis emerges from this garbled book that a certain number of Frenchmen secretly formed "La Légion Tricolore" to infiltrate and sabotage the International Brigades. Dupré has written that "mon plan était placer aux postes importants les moins qualifiés et les incapables" (My plan was to place in important posts those least qualified and incapable).[91] Dupré could do this because he was an authority in the French brigade for a time. Whatever Dupré did, as distinct from what this book claims he did, the norm in the International Brigade favored incompetence. Nevertheless, more than 40 years later, Leo Palacio, a French journalist who observed the International Brigades first hand, treated Dupré's claim seriously.[92] A wit might say that service in the International Brigades was the punishment hardest to bear for any spy.

More than one foreign volunteer saw Trotsky's hand in the revolt of the anarchists in Barcelona against the Republican government in May 1937. In 1989 an American volunteer reasoned that the anarchist uprising was suspect because they had held back their revolt against the monarchy all those years.[93] It is an argument unencumbered with any knowledge of Spanish history, which was at the time full of examples of anarchist revolts against central authority.[94]

In any event, Trotsky excited the purges, not enemy spies.[95] After deaths in battle during the day, there would be executions in the night. The commanders of the International Brigades did not suffer from the constraints of imposing discipline on a volunteer force dedicated to liberty such as served under General George Washington, after whom one American formation was named.

The fighting of the International Brigades was as harrowing as trench warfare in the Great War or the jungle warfare in World War II. First and always, the men were confronted by the man-killing enemy, then the deadly blunders of one's own shot and shell falling on friend not foe, then the rigors of nature—snow, cold, mud, sun, heat, flies, hard earth, dust, and so on. Add to that each man's own private fear, blisters, ulcers, infections, decay, and exhaustion. Little food or water and no medicine were available. Next comes the incompetence of command, poorly informed, indecisive, divided, and the like. This much would be true of any army. Now add the multiple language barrier in staff and line command to compound incompetence with misunderstanding. Add deep political differences within and between the Spanish and the foreigners. These differences introduce malfeasance to the picture. Add the machinations of the NKVD. In these difficulties, the International Brigaders were unlike other soldiers in what they endured. In addition, they did not enjoy the moral support of their compatriots at home. German and Italian International Brigaders were renegades to the good citizens of Germany and Italy in 1937. If the American volunteers received good press occasionally that was all they received from the public at large. Yet they went on.

The International Brigaders did not comprise a model of military organization unless this means an illustration of every conceivable mistake. Training was a subject of indifference with unscreened and untrained recruits. Command was divided by language, and politics took precedence over military matters in operations and in promotions.

3. Defenders of Madrid

Model army or not, no one can gainsay the contribution of the International Brigades to the cause of the Republic. One purpose of the International Brigades was to hold the line of defense until the new Spanish Republican army could be created; this they did and more. Undoubtedly, the entry of the German International Brigaders into the battle at the University City in Madrid lifted Republican morale. The Republic no longer perceived itself as alone against the might of fascism. Until this entry in November 1936 the war had been a Spanish war for all that mattered. Spontaneous volunteers were too few to hold attention and, more importantly, too scattered to seem an important factor in themselves. The rebels had accepted only limited assistance from Nazi Germany and Fascist Italy. Everyone expected a fast finish to the war, as everyone contemplating a war always does. Many observers of both Republican and Nationalist sympathies have since concluded that the war would have ended before the dawn of 1937 had it remained Spanish.[96] According to these writers, the successful defense of Madrid prolonged the war, and that defense was successful because of the German International Brigaders.[97] The Nationalist strategy was to force the Republican government to capitulate by a quick occupation of Madrid without having to fight for it or to destroy it. Franco concentrated his attack on Madrid on the *Casa del Campo* to avoid damaging the city of Madrid in a street fight. With that strategy thwarted, a war of attrition followed since neither side possessed the strength for a knock-out blow.[98]

When those German exiles invested a building on the then incomplete university campus, some took shelter behind stacks of thick books of metaphysics, according to one survivor.[99] Perhaps a tome by Kant or Hegel stopped a dum-dum bullet otherwise bound for some ardent Marxist's breast.

The defense of Madrid by the International Brigades has contributed to one of the most persistent and pernicious myths of all, namely that outsiders did most of the fighting on each side.[100] First the Republic was saved from certain death at Madrid by the International Brigades, and then Franco turned to the Germans and Italians for assistance. Volunteer Arthur Landis 50 years later emphasized the great role played by the American volunteers.[101] Historian Richardson invariably attributes the Republic's military successes—and survival was a success in the circumstances—to the staff work and line command provided by Soviet and Comintern officers, together with Soviet air and tank units and the International Brigades.[102] Venerated historian E. H. Carr implicitly lays greatest stress on Soviet tanks and planes.[103] George Orwell wrote that "the outcome of the Spanish War was settled in London, Paris, Berlin—at any rate not in Spain."[104] A skeptic might say that the intrusion of these officers and the independence of the air, tanks, and international units made for confusion and disorganization. The patient survived despite the medicine not because of it. Only occasionally does a Nationalist source complain of over-emphasis on the role of foreigners.[105] Usually it is just ignored.[106] One Republican writer has complained that "the International Brigades figured in the press dispatches as though they were the sole saviours of Madrid."[107] The Spanish were largely ignored.

Franco's rebel army, suffering no less from its own confusion and disorganization, had been exhausted and over-extended by November 1936 in an audacious bid to take Madrid as much by bluff as by storm. The resistance of the popular militia was fanatical if inept.[108] One of the few commentators to credit the Spanish with the defense of Madrid is David Mitchell.[109] The arrival of 2,000 or so International Brigaders lifted Republican morale greatly but did not decide the day, contrary to Richardson.[110] The grim logic of war reigned. If there were heroes among the defenders of Madrid, there were also heroes among the attackers of attacked Madrid.[111] Unprepared to assault Madrid, Franco gathered his strength and tried to manoeuvre to the Jarama River in February 1937, a campaign that looms large in the mythology of the International Brigades. Here again Madrid was saved, and here once again the International Brigades were the saviors. Richardson concurs, yet as his own subsequent references show, at the Jarama River five of the nine Republican brigades called international were wholly Spanish in composition.[112] Moreover, another five Republican brigades of Spanish troops were present.[113] In sum, the battle was carried by ten Spanish and four International Brigades on the Republican side.

4. Conclusion

Whether or not the conventional estimate of the importance of the International Brigades is regarded skeptically, they did their share of fighting and dying. Not being misled by the supposed glories of the International Brigades should force attention on what is really extraordinary about them: the fact that these men chose to go to Spain and to fight as well as they did once there, rather than the military prowess Richardson and others attribute to them. This fact will not be made to seem more important by alleging that they saved Madrid or anything else. Accounts of orders of battle throughout the war show that the International Brigades were always to the fore, and their casualties show that they suffered commensurately. More impressive, considering their diversity, lack of training, poor leadership, and suffering, is the moral fact that the International Brigades remained intact, some until February 1939. Desertion, though a problem, was not wholesale; neither was mutiny nor the slow disintegration that usually occurs in military units beaten white upon the anvil. While the men of the International Brigades were certainly not model soldiers, they fought. In fighting, they contributed greatly to the defense of Madrid in 1936 and more at other times and places. The significance of that contribution, compared to that of other units of the Spanish army, remains a matter best left to military historians. If their defense of Madrid prolonged the war, then it made possible more deaths of International Brigaders and Spaniards alike. In conclusion, the International Brigades were to defend the Republic while a new army formed, and they did throughout their existence, even after the withdrawal.

Herbert Matthews, describing the last parade of the International Brigades in Barcelona on 28 October 1938, said of the thin, drawn, shabby, diseased men:

> Those men had learned to fight before they had learned to parade. They were not clad in spic-and-span uniforms; their garb was nondescript; they had no arms, and they could not seem to keep in step or in line. But every one who saw them—and above all those who fought with them—knew that these were true soldiers.[114]

This description may recall for American readers the lean and haggard men in butternut rags at Appomattox court house in early April of 1865. In Spain there was no magnanimous victor.

The sight of such men, reduced by enduring so much out of choice, must have been a profound moment. Whatever may be thought of the cause and the result, the nobility of their endurance, like King Lear's, claims admiration as a tragedy for the inevitable outcome because of the composition of the International Brigades, and as bathos because so much of the dying could have been prevented by basic training. Wintringham states that these true soldiers proved that "raw and inexperienced lads from Milwaukee could be very dangerous in war"—very dangerous to themselves.[115] If the survivors, tempered in trial by fire with mortal on-the-job training were true soldiers, what of those who died needless deaths and those who were mutilated, all out of ignorance? For the fallen and for those who bear its marks, war never ends. Perhaps Matthews would agree that these men—the dead and the wounded—are true soldiers.

A dictum in charity work is that those with the least give the most; a person who has little is more likely to be generous than one who has more. It has to do with social and psychological distance. The analogy to the ordinary men who went to Spain seems clear: With nothing to give, they gave themselves. In this they unconsciously heeded the injunction of First Corinthians, Chapter 13, which says that virtue does not lie in doing the good deed without hope of recompense but in doing the good and willing the good, as the International Brigaders did. Either doing or willing without the other is of no value. If these volunteers meet this double requirement, are they the heroes Dr. Negrín declared them to be? This question will bring us in the next chapter to consideration of the third purpose of the International Brigades, that of serving as a model of moral commitment to the cause.

ENDNOTES

1. Hugh Thomas, *The Spanish Civil War*, 3rd ed. (Harmondsworth: Penguin, 1977), 452–454.
2. Consider the omission of any reference to the International Brigades in the book of the Republican Commissar General, J. Alvarez del Vayo, *Freedom's Battle* (London: Heinemann, 1940).
3. R. Dan Richardson, *The Comintern Army* (Lexington: University Press of Kentucky, 1982), 30 ff.
4. Carl Geiser, *Prisoners of the Good Fight: The Spanish Civil War 1936–1939* (Westport: Lawrence Hill, 1988), 3.
5. On the state of the army when the rebellion occurred, see Michael Alpert, *El Ejército Repúblicano en la Guerra Civil* (Barcelona: Ruédo Iberico, 1977).
6. Wintringham, 6.

7. Alvah Bessie, *Men in Battle* (New York: Scribner's, 1939), 152. See also Sulpice Dewez, *Gloire aux volontaires internationaux* (Madrid: Dianh, 1937), 20.
8. Bill Alexander, *British Volunteers for Liberty* (London: Lawrence and Wishart, 1982), 144.
9. Wintringham, 138.
10. Robert Colodny, *El Asedio de Madrid*, trans. J. Tomas de Salas (Paris: Ruédo Iberico, 1970), 64.
11. Herbert Matthews, *Two Wars and More to Come* (New York: Carrick and Evans, 1938), 207. This is the same Matthews who was thought unsympathetic by some International Brigaders (see Rolfe, 69), and who was later clubbed by a French soldier at Le Perthus for protesting the treatment International Brigaders crossing into France were receiving. Matthews modestly does not mention this incident himself, but see Louis Stern, *Beyond Death and Exile* (Cambridge: Harvard University Press, 1979), 34.
12. G. T. Garratt, *Mussolini's Roman Empire* (Harmondsworth: Penguin, 1938), 182.
13. Vincent Brome, *The International Brigades* (New York: Morrow, 1966), 266.
14. Ibid., 300.
15. Robert Colodny, "Preface," Carl Geiser, *Prisoners of the Good Fight: The Spanish Civil War 1936–1939* (Westport: Lawrence Hill, 1988), p. viii. Colodny quotes his own earlier *The Struggle for Madrid* (1958).
16. Max Jakobson, *The Diplomacy of the Winter War* (Cambridge: Harvard University Press, 1961), 273 n. 32.
17. Gerald Klenfield and Lewis Tambs, *Hitler's Spanish Legion* (Carbondale: Southern Illinois University Press, 1974), 1.
18. Robert Lewis Koehl. T*he Black Corps: The Structure and Power Struggles of the Nazi SS* (Madison: University of Wisconsin Press, 1983), 216. See also Rupert Butler, *The Black Angels: A History of the Waffen SS* (New York: St. Martins, 1979).
19. Leo Palacio, *1936: Le Maldonne d'Espange* (Paris: Privat, 1986), 58.
20. Ronald Fraser, *The Blood of Spain* (New York: Pantheon, 1979), 263. Burnett Bolloten concedes more in *The Spanish Civil War: Revolution and Counterrevolution* (Chapel Hill: University of North Carolina Press, 1991), 316.
21. Richardson, 50.
22. Bessie, 44.
23. See, for example, copies of the *Volunteer for Liberty* (The Organ of the International Brigades), 1 (6 September 1937) 13 and succeeding numbers. Cf. volunteer Keith S. Watson, *Single to Spain* (New York: Dutton, 1937), 51.
24. See, among others, volunteers Robert Goldston, *The Civil War in Spain* (London: Phoenix, 1966), 74, and Richard Kisch, *They Shall Not Pass* (London: Wayland, 1974), 127 (which the author contradicts on p. 131, quoting Gustav Regler as saying, "we were all amateurs").
25. Hywel Francis, "Welsh Miners and the Spanish Civil War," 181.
26. Francis, *Miners Against Fascism*, 215.
27. Paul Preston, *The Spanish Civil War*, 94, and also David Corkill and S. Rawnsley, *The Road to Spain*, xviii.
28. Gustav Regler, *The Great Crusade*, trans. W. Chambers and B. Mussey (New York: Longman's, 1940), 129–130.
29. Milt Felsen, *Anti-Warrior: A Memoir* (Iowa City: University of Iowa Press, 1989), 53, 57, and 60 and James Yates, *Mississippi to Madrid: Memoir of a Black American in the Abraham Lincoln Brigade* (Seattle: Open Hand, 1989), 114.
30. John Tisa, *Recalling the Good Fight*, 29, and Edmonds, *Letters from Spain*, 102.
31. Esmond Romilly, *Boadilla* (London: Hamish Hamilton, 1937), 238.
32. Wintringham, 11, 116, and 139.
33. Ibid., 278.
34. William Katz and Marc Crawford, *The Lincoln Brigade: A Picture History* (New York: Athenaeum, 1989), 19.

35. Romilly, 100; Tisa, 47; and Gerassi, 88.
36. Eby, *Between the Bullet and the Lie*, 2.
37. Wayfarer, *The International Brigades* (Sussex: Ditching Press, n.d.), 7.
38. Verle Johnston, *The International Brigades in the Spanish Civil War 1936–1939*, rev. ed. (Stanford: Hoover Institute Library, 1958 [1952]), 75. An abridged version of this work was published under the title *The Legion of Babel* (Philadelphia: University of Pennsylvania Press, 1967). At the Ebro, as elsewhere, the International Brigades found themselves facing another international brigade, namely the Spanish Foreign Legion; see J. H. Galey, "Bridegrooms of Death," *Journal of Contemporary History*, 4 (1969) 2, pp. 47–69.
39. Harold Smith, "Action at Brunete," *The Heart of Spain*, Alvah Bessie, ed. (New York: Veterans of the Abraham Lincoln Brigade, 1952), 181 and 183.
40. Wintringham, 116. Cf. William Rust, who said the majority of the International Brigaders had training, *Britons in Spain* (New York: International, 1939), 6. Even if true it would have been no help. Untrained soldiers in adjacent units can be just as dangerous to trained soldiers as to themselves.
41. Wintringham, 139.
42. Garratt, 181 and 183.
43. *Hello Canada* (Toronto: Friends of the MacKenzie-Papineau Battalion, n.d.), 7.
44. See *Letters from Spain* (New York: Friends of the Abraham Lincoln Brigades, 1937), 8.
45. Romilly, 100.
46. Wintringham, 258.
47. De la Cierva, 82.
48. Romilly, 166.
49. Matthews ([illegible]), 220–221.
50. There is a touching memento of Merriman by his widow, for he, like so many whom he commanded, did not survive Spain; see Marion Merriman and Warren Lerude, *American Commander in Spain: Robert Hale Merriman and the Abraham Lincoln Brigade* (Reno: University of Nevada Press, 1986).
51. Wyden, 237.
52. Tisa, 77.
53. Cecil Eby, "The Real Robert Jordan," *American Literature*, 38 (1966) 3, pp. 380–386.
54. Wyden, 294.
55. Richardson, 65.
56. Victor Hoar, *The MacKenzie-Papineau Battalion* (Toronto: Copp Clark, 1969), 122.
57. Considering the publicity generated, it is disingenuous of veteran Milt Felsen to say that the men hardly noticed that their officer was black; Felsen, *The Anti-Warrior: A Memoir* (Iowa City: University of Iowa Press, 1989), 58.
58. See the account in William Herrick, *Hermanos*! (London: Weidenfeld and Nicolson, 1969), 267 ff.
59. The Herrick interview appears in Paul Berman, "Spanish Betrayals: A Lincon Vet Remembers," *Village Voice*, 14 July 1986. The immediate response was Marc Crawford, "Vets Defend Black Commander Killed in Spanish Civil War," *Daily Challenger*, 30 July 1986, 9-11. Crawford followed up this hagiography in William L. Katz and Marc Crawford, *The Lincoln Brigade: A Picture History* (New York: Athenaeum, 1989), 14, 32-33.
60. Gerrasi, 5.
61. Wintringham, 324.
62. Hoar, 157.
63. Robert Colodny, *The Struggle for Madrid* (New York: Paine-Whitman, 1958), 229 n. 3. The same figures are confirmed in José Luís Alcofar Nassaes, *Spansky: Los Extranjeros Que Lucharon en la Guerra Civil Española* (Barcelona: Dopesa, 1973), 1: 383.
64. A. Krammer, "Germans Against Hitler," *Journal of Contemporary History*, 4 (1969)

2, p. 69 n. 16 where Colodny (1958), 318 is quoted, and who in turn gives no source.

65. Wintringham, 324.
66. Cecil Eby, *Between the Bullet and the Lie* (New York: Holt, Rinehart, and Winston, 1969), 55.
67. Corkill, p. x.
68. John Ellis, *The Sharp End of War* (London: David and Charles, 1980), 377.
69. R. E. and T. N. Dupuy, *The Encyclopedia of Military History*, rev. ed. (New York: Harper and Row, 1970), 969.
70. John F. Cloverdale, *Italian Intervention in the Spanish Civil War* (Princeton: Princeton University Press, 1975), 418.
71. Stanley G. Payne, *Politics and Military in Modern Spain* (Stanford: Stanford University Press, 1967), 461.
72. Johnston, 75.
73. Sulpice Dewez, *Gloire aux volontaires internationaux* (Madrid: Dianh, 1937), 24 and R. Dan Richardson, *Comintern Army* (Lexington: University Press of Kentucky, 1982), 82 and 2.
74. Cortada, *A City at War*, 72.
75. For example, see Eby, 302 for the Americans, and Arthur Landis, *The Abraham Lincoln Brigade* (New York: The Citadel Press, 1967), 326.
76. Andreu Castells, *Les Brigades Internacionales de la Guerra España* (Barcelona: Editorial Ariel, 1974), 381–383.
77. Ibid., 383.
78. Ibid.
79. Jacques Delperrie de Bayac, *Les Brigades Internationales* (Paris: Fayard, 1968), 386.
80. Romilly, 270 and Bessie, 187.
81. Jason Gurney, *Crusade in Spain* (London: Faber and Faber, 1974), 38.
82. See, for example, the description of André Malraux, *L'Espoir* (Paris: Gallimard, 1973), 387–395.
83. Sandor Voros, *American Commissar* (Philadelphia: Chilton Co., 1961), 356. Cf. Robert Rosenstone, The Crusade of the Left (New York: Pegasus, 1969), 356.
84. See the letter of Alfred Kantorowicz in Marcel Acier, ed., *From Spanish Trenches* (New York: Modern Age Books, 1937), 75.
85. Herrick, 257 and passim.
86. Gurney, 144. Cf. Illya Ehrenberg, *Eve of War* (London: Macmillan, 1963), 167; Gustav Regler, *Owl*, 277–279; or Louis Fischer, *Men and Politics*, 387–388.
87. Ludwig Renn, *Der Spanische Krieg* (Berlin: Aufbau-Verlag, 1955), 187 and Carlo Penchienati, *Brigate Internazionali in Spagne: Delitti della "Cheka" Communista* (Milan: Echi del Secolo, 1950), 125. Commissar Gustav Regler is silent in his two books on the Spanish Civil War on this subject; cf. Jef Last, *The Spanish Tragedy*, D. Hallet, trans. (London: Routledge, 1939 [1938]), 276. The NKVD was no secret to the men; see Herrick, 263.
88. Stanley Weintraub, *The Last Great Cause* (London: Allen & Unwin, 1968), 30.
89. Anthony Beevor, T*he Spanish Civil War*, 127; Ronald Radosh, "The Spanish Civil War and the Intellectuals," *Quadrant*, June 1987, pp. 41–47, 40; Wyden, 192.
90. Thomas, 551 n. 1. Cf. Leo Palacio, *1936: La Maldonne Espanola* (Paris: Editions Privat, 1988), 51.
91. Henri Dupré, *La Legion Tricolore en Espagne (1936–1939)* (Paris: Editions de la Ligue Française [Mouvement Social Européen], 28 November 1942), 13. This book is recommended as a source of information on the André Marty Battalion of French volunteers in James W. Cortada, ed., *Dictionary of the Spanish Civil War 1936–1939* (Westport: Greenwood, 1982), 30.
92. Leo Palacio, 51 and 65.
93. Milt Felsen, *The Anti-Warrior: A Memoir* (Iowa City: University of Iowa Press, 1989), 56.

94. The masterwork on the relationships between the Republic and the anarchists is Burnett Bolloten, *The Spanish Civil War: Revolution and Counterrevolution* (Chapel Hill: University of North Carolina Press, 1991).
95. Sulpice Dewez, *Gloire aux volontaires internationaux* (Madrid: Dianh, 1937), 24.
96. Among them Seigismundo Casado, *The Last Days of Madrid,* trans. R. Croft-Cooke (London: Peter Arnold, 1939), 100.
97. Krammer, 67.
98. José Manuel Martinez Bande, *Communist Intervention in the Spanish Civil War* (Madrid: Spanish Information Service, 1966), 150. See Claude Bowers, *My Mission to Spain* (London: Gollancz, 1954), 316; Colodny (1958), 186–187; Louis Fischer, *Men and Politics* (New York: Duell, Sloan and Pearce, 1941), 381; and *Las Brigades Internacionales* (Madrid: Oficina Informativa Española, 1948), 81.
99. John Sommerfield, *Volunteer for Spain* (New York: Knopf, 1937), 146.
100. In 1936, some members of the French press reported not a single Spaniard in the Republican army defending Madrid; see David Pike, *Conjecture, Propaganda, and Deceit and the Spanish Civil War* (No city given: California Institute of International Studies, 1968), 73.
101. Gerassi, 172.
102. Richardson, 82–84.
103. Carr, *The Comintern and the Spanish Civil War,* 27.
104. Orwell, *Homage to Catalonia,* 240.
105. Ramón Salas Larrazabel, *Historia del Ejército Popular de la República* (Madrid: Editora Nacional, 1973), 3: 2108.
106. Manuel Azñar, *Historia Militar de la Guerra de España* (Madrid: Editorial Nacional, 1060).
107. Arturo Barea, *The Clash* (London: Faber and Faber, 1946), 195.
108. Thomas, 480–481.
109. Mitchell, 82.
110. Richardson, 87.
111. Wyden, 212.
112. Richardson, 84.
113. Ibid., 89.
114. Herbert Matthews, *The Education of a Correspondent* (New York: Harcourt, 1946), 141.
115. Wintringham, 254.

CHAPTER 8

Political Dying

Summoned to the eternal field.

Edwin Rolfe

1. Who were they?

With all the publicity surrounding them, the volunteers became extremely self-conscious. Who were they? Why were they here? Many of them had been asking these questions. These are questions they asked themselves, which have also been asked in these pages. At the end of the day, Edwin Rolfe wrote:

> Who were these young Americans? What impelled them to leave the shores of a peaceful land to plunge into the horror of modern war? To answer these questions fully, one would need the biography of each American volunteer.[1]

The same question appeared in British veteran William Rust's book, asking why the International Brigaders volunteered:

> It would be a fruitful study to analyze the motives of each volunteer and the exact reasons which led him at a given moment to offer his services, for such a study would, without a shadow of doubt, furnish a glorious page in the history of humanity.[2]

For good or ill, examining and analyzing the biographies of 32,000 men would be impossible. Though knowing a great deal more than we do about the International Brigaders would be instructive, this would most probably not change the general characterization of their social identity or motivation. Even knowing all there was to know of their identity and motivation, even knowing each of their biographies would not answer all the questions.

To know what happened and why does not delineate its meaning, a question that cannot be settled on the evidence yet is too important to be ignored. It is too simple to conclude, as Communists supporting the Republic and Nationalists opposing it have done, that the men of the International Brigades were of a cloth, each an ideologue. Portraying them all as ardent Communists is like assuming that all Union soldiers were abolitionists and that all Confederates were proponents of slavery in the American Civil War.

That thousands of men did go as volunteers, none of them having any kind of duty (real or imagined), prompts Delperrie de Bayac to call them heroes.[3] Perhaps it was a kind of heroism, like a knight setting off to find a dragon to slay. Don Quixote was a clown for slaying dragons of the mind where others saw none; but the dragon of fascism the International Brigaders saw was real enough. If the beast was not yet resident in Spain, their aim was to keep it that way. Where they failed was in the perception of themselves as dragon-slayers.

2. Right is Might

Testimonials to the justice of the cause for which the International Brigades fought were issued with numbing regularity by the International Brigades' publicists and the Comintern. Proof of the justice of the cause was offered from all quarters. Consider this instance from Upton Sinclair's *roman-à-clef* that traces the course of an American volunteer: "Men do not fight machineguns with clubs and reaping hooks, women do not defend barricades with kitchen knives, unless there is a long history of suffering behind them."[4] Note the thesis that fierce fighters are just fighters. That the ferocity might only prove that Spaniards hated each other is not considered.

Antoine de Saint-Exupéry saw the ferocity that moved Upton Sinclair, but drew a different conclusion. He put it like this:

> When they [ordinary people] read in their provincial newspaper the story of Basil Zaharoff [a great financier], master of the world, they transpose it into their own language. They recognize in him the nurseryman, or the pharmacist.

If we are told of great scoundrels, we may come to think that even those around us, who have a little more than we do, are also scoundrels. Why else do they have more? So, Saint-Exupéry continues:

> When they shoot the pharmacist, in a way they are shooting Basil

Zaharoff. The one who does not understand is the pharmacist.[5]

There are always victims but there are seldom villains.

More interesting is the frequency with which the men themselves avow the thesis that their cause will triumph because it is right, or put differently, that right is might. Not only did the noble end justify the hideous means of war; the noble end itself would ensure the final victory. So noble was the cause that even avowed pacifists could take up arms.[6] But then selfstyled pacifists have usually been ready to fight the endless war-to-end-war, and some convinced themselves and others that this was Spain's meaning. Abhorring the slaughter of the Great War, many had declared for pacifism only to embrace "romantic war-mongering," as George Orwell called it.[7] Orwell charged these pacifist war-mongers with hypocrisy, as he himself has been charged by French volunteer and novelist Claude Simon, who has objected to the contrived character of important parts of *Homage to Catalonia*.[8] All too often, both the men in the ranks and their officers assumed that the correct ideological analysis of the material foundation of society led directly to victory in a kind of historical materialist version of a *Monopoly* game. One International commander, a man known as Victor Copíc, was quoted as saying, "the Americans fought so well because they understood the issues so well."[9] Fighting well requires the right interpretation, a just cause. A corollary to the right-is-might thesis is that fighting well is possible only if one's cause is just; the corollary is that a wrong cause is a weak one.

This delusion pervades Stephen Spender's autobiographical *World Within World*, where Spender reports that he convinced his homosexual boyfriend, Jimmy Younger, to become a Communist, after which Jimmy volunteered for the International Brigades.[10] Did Jimmy think that volunteering for Spain would win him Spender's affection? Spender later visited Spain on a propaganda tour as a guest of the Comintern, and came across his friend Jimmy. Once they were alone, Jimmy begged Spender to get him out of Spain. Jimmy said he would do "anything so long as he left Spain." Spender reports that he talked Jimmy out of this idea. Is this a case of loving the cause more than the friend? Later Jimmy dutifully sent Spender a note to thank him for his advice. Jimmy's name does not appear again in Spender's book; the fate of spear carriers like Jimmy is obscure. Spender's famous and rewarding recantation of communism in *The God that Failed* omits this episode.

Spender's autobiography later recounts an interview with a British journalist who had first covered the war from the Nationalist side and later from the Republican side, comparing the two. Spender asked him "What's the difference between the two sides?" The journalist replied, "None." This very wise answer was not enough for Spender who insisted on more. Finally the journalist said, the Franco salute was an open hand and the Republican salute a closed fist. War's logic is more powerful than any ideology.

It was common at the time for Republican propaganda to emphasize atrocities alleged to have been committed by Nationalists. These allegations are routinely repeated in books about the International Brigades.[11] What is omitted is any mention of the atrocities committed by Republicans, or the misdeeds committed by the International Brigaders.

This juncture may be the place to broach another subject even more taboo than desertions from the International Brigades. International Brigaders shot prisoners; and at least one commissar with the International Brigades admits that American International Brigaders shot prisoners.[12] If volunteers from remote American towns shot prisoners, it is likely that angry volunteers driven into exile by demon fascism did, too, on a larger scale and more often. It has also been admitted that Spaniards serving with the International Brigades shot prisoners.[13]

The complete military innocence of so many of the International Brigaders made it easy for them to believe the right-is-might thesis. Sandor Voros reported that he had believed all the glowing reports in the *Daily Worker*, the Communist newspaper in New York City, of the successes of the Lincoln Battalion in battle . . . until he went to Spain.[14] A veteran of the Great War might have been more skeptical. There was a formula: "Marx + courage = success."[15] Jason Gurney saw this clearly in retrospect.[16] The importance attached to anti-fascism was so overwhelming that it defied expression. One International said that they were "going up to fight and die for the only things in the world that are worth fighting and dying for," things that are evidently too sacred for the naming since they are not specified.[17] To know the justice of one's case was apparently thought sufficient to make untrained men into soldiers, and that they were untrained is beyond doubt.[18] One writer claimed that the International Brigades formed one of the finest forces of troops the world had ever seen. This was because "every one of them knew for what he was fighting," and this knowledge made him "willing to die for it if necessary."[19] It was not because of their splendid training or modern equipment. Another man said after the debacle at Jarama: "Not one [of the fallen International Brigaders] would have regretted dying as he did."[20] That a propagandist would say this is one thing, that a soldier would say it is a completely different matter. If it is true that the

International Brigaders died without regrets, obeying mad orders, unable to read tracer bullets, and blind to fields of fire, then they would be among the few soldiers ever to have done so. After all, that great hero Achilles regretted his warrior's death.[21] If the fallen sparrows knew no regrets, then they were more than heroes and gods, and this they were not. No one has a life without regrets; and no one has a death without regrets, as certain as anything can be on this side of paradise.

Returning to the right-is-might thesis, if the enemy's cause is unjust he will not fight well. A letter attributed to a volunteer in a propaganda book in 1937 confidently declared that the Italian troops allied to the Nationalists fought only for material gain and so fought only reluctantly. In contrast, the International Brigaders and the Republicans fought for a just cause and consequently were courageous.[22] The proposition was reiterated nearly 50 years later by volunteer Rosario Pistone in 1986.[23] A photographic account of the Lincolns in 1989 confirmed it.[24]

Forgotten is the extraordinary Nationalist defense of the Alcazar military academy on the hill in the center of the small city of Toledo early in the war.[25] The irony is, as George Orwell observed at the time, that

> The photographs of groups of the defenders [of the Alcazar] bring home one of the most pathetic aspects of civil war. They are so like groups of Government militiamen that if they were changed around no one would know the difference.[26]

War is the greatest equalizer. In Gurney's formula of "Marx + courage = victory," the cause makes the man. In this context, recall the Poles who decided not to take cover in battle but to stand like free men, waiting to slay the oppressors like rabbits.[27] It is not clear whether any of these upright men survived. Similarly, French volunteer David Diamant asked readers in 1979 to believe that the slaughter of International Brigaders proved their courage.[28]

Even shell shock was related to the just cause. One commissar, Steve Nelson, said:

> Where soldiers don't have any real interest in the war they're fighting, shell shock can and must exist as a scientific fact. But in this army—in our army—it is different. Our boys know what they're fighting for. They're here because they want to be here.[29]

Nelson's statement is undoubtedly sincere, although these sentiments might have been cynically exploited by publicists. What is in doubt is the veracity of the statement.

These doubts become all the more important when one realizes that Nelson's shell shock diagnosis has been accepted by other disinterested observers. The social psychologist John Dollard conducted interviews with American veterans of Spain as the U.S. Army prepared itself for the future World War II. When Dollard heard his subjects repeating variants of Nelson's diagnosis, he accepted it without a word of qualification or criticism.[30] In his popular history of the Canadian battalion, written in 1969, Victor Hoar concurs with Dollard that "without question, the volunteer whose identification with what one might call 'war aims' remained steadfast was more likely to be a better soldier than the mercenary or adventurer," a judgment delivered unencumbered by either evidence or argument.[31] Along the line from adventurer to zealot lie many points, some of which are more congenial to the International Brigades' sparrows than either extreme.

If the International Brigades were to be a model of moral commitment to the just cause for the watching world, starting with the Spanish, they also foolishly imagined this commitment sufficed to make them good soldiers. High ideals do not make a man into a warrior. International Brigaders grimly learned that the paid professionals of the rebel army knew much of war.[32] The cause does not make the soldier, as the soldier does not make the cause. The meaning and value of each is determined by its own calculus. Whatever an individual may say before or after combat about motivation, under fire there is a different counting. To understand soldiers involves looking at what they do as well as listening to what they say that they do, as Albert Einstein said of physicists.[33] Consider again the passage from Harold Smith quoted at the outset of these pages. He described his own experience under fire at Brunete using the third person:

> The unanswerable logic that had brought him across the sea to Spain did not appear at this moment. The slogans . . . were not on his lips . . .. There was no conscious decision but he knew he would not turn back. His decision had been made before.[34]

He pressed on with his mind a blank, as most minds are in battle.

Aristotle begins his discussion of the virtue courage with the example of death in battle being the most noble death. As the most noble death, battle would offer the most perfect instance of courage. Aristotle's battle death would be noble in defense of an existing polity, not in pursuit of a dream polity. Many Republicans might have met this criterion, but not many International Brigaders, considering the catalogue of motivations presented earlier. The exiles fought for real polities, but those from the new world did not. Aristotle does not assume that all fighting for the defense of a polity is just, only that it is likely to be just. Where the polis itself is corrupt, fighting would be unjust; thus each side in the Spanish Civil War accused the other. To appreciate courage, for Aristotle, requires a further look beyond the cause and the polity to what we value and what we fear.

The just cause is not the only place in which the warrior or those who watch the warrior find value. The cause is too abstract and remote to remain a source of value to hungry, nauseated, diseased, and frightened men hour after hour, day after day, week after week, month after month. Here, as so often, George Orwell puts it best:

> The consciousness of being in the right can bolster up morale, though this affects the civilian population more than the troops. (People forget that a soldier anywhere near the front line is usually too hungry or frightened, or cold, or above all, too tired to bother about the political origins of the war.) But the laws of nature are not suspended for a "red" army any more than for a "white" one. A louse is a louse and a bomb is a bomb, even though the cause you are fighting for happens to be just.[35]

As the letters of soldiers always are, the letters of Australian volunteer Lloyd Edmonds brim with references to food, not justice.[36] Motivation requires something concrete—the others around the soldier, the others who depend on him and on whom he depends. Jef Last, a Dutchman, said, "a military unit . . . is also a community of friends . . . for which I lived" and fought.[37] William Herrick's novel *Hermanos!* implicitly developed this fraternity thesis. Another volunteer from Belgium, Nick Gillain, argued that the International Brigaders fought as well as they did, because they loved their leader at the time, Colonel Putz, not because they were quickened by the abstract cause of proletarian unity against dreaded fascism. Gillain promoted no illusions about how well they fought.

> Croyezvous que la chose eut êté possible avec un autre chef? Ce n'est pas amour de "la patrie proletarienne," de la "grande cause des miséraux," ni par idéal politique que les Internationaux ont répris de défaillance. Non, c'est à cause de Putz, afin de ne pas le laisse seul que les volontaires sont repartis au combat.[38] (Do you believe that this was possible with another leader? It is not love of the 'proletarian cause,' of the 'great cause of the impoverished,' nor for a political ideal that the Internationals have remained unflinching. No, it is because of Putz, so as not to leave him alone that the volunteers rejoined combat.)

At the sword's edge, the leader inspired affection and courage in his men, as leaders are supposed to do and many succeed in doing, no matter what the cause. Though this observation may seem simple, Gillain occupies an important place in the demonology of the defenders of the faith of the International Brigades. This is the very same Nick Gillain from Chapter Three where he described himself as an adventurer—better sunny Spain than cloudy Brussels. His lack of serious commitment to the cause made him suspect. Was he a member of Dupré's La Légion Tricolore? Leo Palacio and Alexander Szurek are sure that he was. If so, Dupré missed an opportunity because Gillain was not placed in any important office. Palacio and Szurek allege that Gillain joined the Waffen SS during World War II. They do so to discredit his testimony in general, yet on the facing page Palacio, like Gillain, praises Colonel Putz, a veteran of the Great War who died in Spain.[39] Restless and rootless men may seek action more than a cause.

Saint-Exupéry went to Spain during the civil war, he said, "for an answer to another question: How does it happen that men are sometimes willing to die?" The answer he discovered is more complex and subtler than a just cause. The action of joining arms was the result of a collision of events, some general and some personal. It was a decision that Saint-Exupéry's interlocutors could not articulate.[40]

At one of his own moments of truth, Steve Nelson knew all of this and more, despite his diagnosis of shell shock. A day in the campaign came when the American unit that Nelson commanded was bloodied, exhausted, and dissipated, and yet there came another call to a distant sector of the battlefield to secure the line again, suffering another forced march so that on arrival more of their number could suffer hideous wounds or die. Bearing these orders back to his exhausted and dispirited men, Nelson did not speak by all accounts, including his own, of the glory of the noble cause, nor did he dwell on the demonic evils of the Fascist enemy. He did what every effective officer has always done; spoke instead of the need to hold the line, not for the cause, but to save themselves and their comrades who would otherwise be lost. He spoke to the men of themselves and of other men like themselves. He did not order them to action or invoke the higher purpose. Rather, he strove to bring out the most that these men had to give. Throughout his tenure, Nelson did not make speeches but rather took care of his subordinates' needs and led them by moral example as they were supposed to lead the Spanish.[41] The abstraction may recruit for war, but to make a person fight something more is needed, particularly leadership and fraternity. Note that when the U.S. Army thoroughly investigated combat motivation in World War II the just cause did not rank highly.[42]

The belief in the power of the cause has intellectual roots in the teaching of Niccolò Machiavelli, that sagacious and experienced observer, who argued that mercenaries were not to be trusted because they fought for gain. Worse, he thought, they would not readily risk their lives. He preferred a civic militia and devoted much of his political career to the creation of such a force.[43] The mercenaries Machiavelli despised were nothing but the professional soldiers of his day, men who had every desire to live, if necessary, to fight again another day. Machiavelli, who repeatedly claimed to be a realist, whose claim has largely been accepted by each new generation of readers of *The Prince*, recommended an amateur militia whose members would throw their bodies on the sword rather than surrender the homeland. The amateur volunteers of the International Brigades would have pleased Machiavelli in their zeal.

3. The Fraternity of Fear

Much more highly ranked than the cause in that World War II research was the fraternity of fear among fellow combatants. Men seem to fight more for someone than against the enemy. While one team of American army psychiatrists seemingly agreed with Nelson when they stressed the motivating power of clear war aims, their own evidence returns time and again to show that "the soldier fights for his buddies."[44] They also emphasized the importance of leadership by example.[45] Throughout this body of research, which can only be mentioned here and nothing more, the most frequently volunteered remark from respondents is "I feel closer to him [a fellow fighter] than to my own brother."[46] Combat forms an intense blood brotherhood that few siblings can rival. When one international volunteer asked: "Why do we go on?" the answer within himself was this fraternity of dependence.[47]

This fraternity can even extend to the enemy, for who else but the enemy really knows what it is like? Who else but the enemy endures the same conditions? In this vein, George Orwell described his experience as a sniper in the trenches outside Huesca:

> A man presumably carrying a message to an officer, jumped out of the trench and ran along the top of the parapet in full view. He was half-dressed and was holding up his trousers with both hands as he ran ... I did not shoot partly because of that detail about the trousers. I had come here to shoot at "Fascists"; but a man who is holding up his trousers isn't a "Fascist," he is a fellow-creature, similar to yourself, and you don't feel like shooting at him.[48]

Laws of war exist in the state of nature.

In Spain, Alvah Bessie confessed that he and his brother had not been as close as he and his blood brothers were.[49] For the

International Brigaders, and doubtless for many others as well, Jef Last summed up his fraternity as the "invisible threads" of comradeship.[50] For him, these threads amounted to "socialism in action." The same sentiment underlies Hywel Francis's description of the Welsh volunteers as an "army of comrades,"[51] suggesting the argument that the common experiences of the working class produce an ethics of mutuality.[52] But as William James argued long ago, following Georg Hegel, nothing is morally equivalent to war.[53] Last and Francis are wrong to think that these feelings of fear and fraternity are the unique provenance of socialism in action. It is more a matter of being "socialism *of* action"; action engenders society, which is the product of the experience and not the ideology.

The International Brigaders had to learn the laws of nature in the state of war—through their skins. The skin is vulnerable, and often the lessons were fatal. Once the battle is joined, then war's logic supersedes the justice of the cause. There are always two wars:[54] that watched by civilians and that experienced by soldiers. The civilian perspective does not change, but with the experience of war, the soldiers' perspective does. War has its own dynamic, far more powerful than any set of beliefs an individual brings to it. Once started, war is virtually autonomous, and war invariably exceeds expectations. Furthermore, in doing what has to be done, combatants do noble and horrible acts beyond their own comprehension, acts that forever change the human world. Like the demon god it is, war feeds off itself. Both its fear and fraternity are realities for adventurers, mercenaries, sparrows, and zealots alike. The mercenary may have little else in his life than what Gurney called "the military ethos."[55] Years later one volunteer, Jack Jones, said: "I've had experiences of all kinds, but the happiest days of my life were spent in Spain. For the first time I recognized the dignity, the goodness and the bravery of ordinary people."[56] This experience in the nature of war knows no uniform. Inevitably, the enemy has a cause, too, and much more importantly, a share of exemplary leaders under fire and frightened men who grow together under the thunder and lightning of war, and so the struggle goes on and on.[57] If the publicist promoted a fictitious, sham fraternity among the nationalities gathered to the cause, as George Orwell argued, the fraternity of fear within the small unit on the firing line was not any the less real.[58] In World War II American war correspondent Ernie Pyle described the experience of the foot soldier's war as "the camaraderie of misery" as the circle of survivors steadily decreases.[59] War is the universal means of production that reduces each worker to both a cog and a commodity, always the same in eternity's sunset.

So many ironies are apparent. The rallying cry of the Spanish Republic, taken up by many International Brigaders, was La Pasionaria's famous declamation "No Pasarán!" (They won't pass!). This phrase became a slogan because to an audience of the 1930s, it resonated the French vow at Verdun in the dark days of the Great War "Ils ne passeront pas!" (They shall not pass!). At the crucible of Verdun, the materially superior German enemy was defeated; so too the materially superior enemy would be defeated in Spain. These famous words at Verdun were attributed to General Pétain who, in a few short years, would preside over the regime at Vichy that surrendered Spanish Republicans and International Brigaders to the Gestapo.

Not only were the volunteers of the International Brigades wrong to think that right made might, but they were also wrong to think, as they seem to have done, that a soldier's courage is fearlessness. The combination of the just cause and fearless courage could be nothing but heroism. So opined a 21-year-old American volunteer writing in a propaganda work that "the deeds of heroism which we perform in the name of Anti-Fascism amaze the soldiers who were in the last war."[60] Walking unknowingly into interlocking machine gun fire, digging straight trench lines to invite enfilading fire, bunching together to advance in an open field, not deigning to take cover—would these be cited as instances of fearless courage? They would amaze soldiers who had survived the Great War.

Ignorance is not courage, and courage is not fearlessness. Someone who feels no fear can exhibit no courage. When that veteran spear carrier, Socrates, discussed courage with the generals Laches and Nicias, they agreed that courage consists in knowing what things are to be feared and fearing them as is their due.[61] Bravery controls fear but does not eradicate it. A man without fear is a fool. A courageous individual acts despite fear. A fearless person takes needless risks and, what is worse, imposes needless risks on others. Death is a thing greatly feared, but that fear may be controlled by a greater fear of things other than death.[62] The pages of history are replete with the examples of women and men who have suffered death rather than betray others; fear for others allowed control of their own fear of death.

Soldiers react to fear itself, the fear of shame. For the sake of argument, marginality and ideology brought the foreign volunteers to Spain, but making them warriors required the combination of fear and fraternity. This social pressure and support of comrades glued the International Brigaders together, not the cant and catechism of the cause. As for the universal soldier, there were many days when each of the International Brigaders would have run away, as those who deserted did, had it not been for the others, for the shame of having their flight witnessed, and for the suffering imposed on others who depended on each bearing a part.[63] This socialism of action made possible the courage of the volunteers, not the justice of the cause. The men were noble whatever the cause. There is an analogy. Marcel Proust argued that love reveals the lover, not the beloved,

> that when we are in love with a woman we simply project into her a state of our own soul, that the important thing is therefore, not the worth of the woman but the depth of the state; and that the emotions which a young girl of no kind ofdistinction arouses in us can enable us to bring to the surface of our consciousness some of the most intimate parts of our being, more personal, more remote, more essential. . . .[64]

The beauty of love lies within the lover, not the beloved. The lover sees something in the beloved that no one else sees, least of all the beloved. Is the same not true of the International Brigaders? Whatever the merits of the cause, this inner dimension remains. In this sense, they are "true soldiers," transcending their time and place. With greatest respect, I dissent from Orwell's conclusion that the foreign volunteers of the International Brigades "made good infantry."[65] Suffice it to make them heroes, as Negrín said, heroes for their endurance, heroes for each other, heroes for pulling one another to safety, but not heroes for killing Fascists.

Establishing themselves as true soldiers meets the third justification for the International Brigades. In being models of moral commitment to the inattentive Spaniards, the International Brigaders proved their own moral worth to their compatriots back home and, harder still, proved their moral worth to themselves. Randolfo Pacciardi said that he went to Spain to prove to the people in Italy that fascism could be fought.[66] Perhaps he wanted to prove that Italians, in particular, could and should fight fascism, a lesson worth the teaching as well the learning and remembering. Pacciardi and his comrades were not the first to enter (someone else's) war to prove something to those at home. Sarpedon from far Lycia went to Troy as ally to Hector to prove to the Lycians that he was a noble warrior, worthy of their honor.[67] Is this reasoning so very different from Pacciardi's?

The history of the Spanish Civil War always ends in the same way; the Republic, like Troy, was defeated. The Spanish Republic was outnumbered in men, guns, and planes, as Paul Preston has lamented.[68] Preston implies that the Nationalist strategy of seeking to gain and use numerical advantage was perfidious. A more chivalrous approach, Preston implies, would have seen an equal contest. In reality, the rebels defeated the Republic by superior diplomatic and military strategies through which they gradually amassed their numerical superiority, as soldiers always hope their leaders will do. How did Thomas Hobbes put it in the seventeenth century? Only an incompetent leader needs brave followers. Another of the myths of the Spanish Civil War is that it all came easily for Franco.[69] According to this myth, virtually the entire army swung instantly to the rebels, the rebel side had from the outset one united purpose, and the powerful allies immediately poured in men and material on request with no questions asked. Nothing could be further from the truth, though such details lie well beyond the purposes at hand. These myths are propounded to enlarge the heroic nature of the Republic's resistance, but that resistance and the part played by the International Brigades needs no enlargement.

In 1939 when the Republic was toppled, some of the last International Brigaders, those who had not been repatriated under League of Nations supervision, crossed into France with Republican soldiers, national art treasures, and civilian refugees in a carnival of flight. The International Brigaders, seven thousand in one estimate, were interned in barbed wire concentration camps, built to house German prisoners-of-war in the Great War, many on the windswept sand at Gurs.[70] The schizophrenia of Gurs bespoke the times. On the one hand, the vanquished were imprisoned behind barbed wire with little food, water, or clothing, and no shelter or medicine. Meanwhile, the casinos along the cliffs were full of the wealthy, dancing the tango and drinking martinis.[71] The floundering French government did not know what to do with these unbidden guests so they were kept there. They could not be trusted with weapons, and there they remained when the war came. Conditions in the Republican camps were bad enough to drive some to suicide and for others to die of disease.[72] There they remained when France capitulated rather than endure. After 1940, Vichy authorities allowed the Gestapo free rein in searching Gurs and throughout France for the enemies of the Reich, anti-Fascists who had fled Spain.[73] At about the same time, the Vichy regime of Pétain also turned over to German authorities thousands of other German and Austrian expatriates who had served in the French Foreign Legion and fought the Germans in 1940 after having been proudly paraded in Paris in 1939. The former Legionnaires were organized into suicide regiments to act as cannon fodder for Erwin Rommel's Afrika Corps.

Mexico offered to receive veterans from the International Brigades; but the offer provoked domestic opposition, and in the end, the Mexican government trimmed its sails. Significant segments of Mexican opinion viewed the International Brigaders as Red Soldiers, and in the interest of accepting Spanish Republican refugees the offer to International Brigaders was muted. In this way, once again, the International Brigaders served the interest of the Spanish Republic. Those International Brigaders who had acquired Spanish citizenship, however, found entry into Mexico possible, thanks to the blind eye of officialdom.[74]

4. Conclusion

Summoning men to the eternal field, to use Edwin Rolfe's image of death for the International Brigaders, has never been difficult. Strangers rush into burning buildings to pull strangers to safety. Family, friend, and station each have and have always had their martyrs and heroes. Religion and philosophy have also had their saints and martyrs. But surely Michael Walzer's observation is right: the most persistently successful claimant on human life, after religion, is politics.[75] Political dying is, of course, irrational and even incomprehensible to the psychological and ethical egoism of Thomas Hobbes's legacy that now sets limits to so much philosophical thinking. According to egoism, nothing surpasses the importance of the self to the self; thus, no person can ever sacrifice herself or himself in the interests of others. Such seeming sacrifices are explained away, that is, the person who made the sacrifice did not realize the price to be exacted; or if the sacrifice was willingly made, choice means no sacrifice, assuming—wrongly—that people do only what they want, and to do is to choose and to choose is to will.[76] The crew of a sinking ship may decide to lighten the load by throwing the collected works of Picasso (a supporter of Republican Spain) over the side, or a victim may commit a terrible crime in the hope of gaining the freedom of a child held hostage. Both are volitional acts in Aristotle's meaning, but neither is what the individual wants to do.[77] Different degrees and different kinds of volition mean that in little ways on most days, all of us do things we would rather not do.

Political dying is as common as it is poorly understood and all the more important for being ineffable. The ordinary citizen who becomes soldier, the foreigner who becomes soldier, is not the calculating egoist beloved of philosophers, as economists once courted the rational being. At a time when society places a premium on the study of the experiences of ordinary persons, what more common and profound experience visits the ordinary person than war? A sacrifice willingly made is no less a sacrifice, as a charity willingly given is no less a charity. Convincing men to die for politics becomes easy where men convince themselves. If the poles of the moral justification of war to a soldier who fights are marked by defense of the community, *à la* Jean-Jacques Rousseau, and the preservation of individuals, including the soldiers, *pace* Hobbes, the International Brigades elude classification. Perhaps the truth of the International Brigaders touches not the reaches of political theory but rather the analogy to religion. War mimics religion in that only these two social institutions possess the capacity to bestow meaning on death. In the words of Max Weber: "the warrior experiences a consecrated meaning of death that is very nearly unique. The army standing in a field is the community in microcosm, literally a community unto death."[78]

For one reason or another, the marginal men of the International Brigades, being a part of no community, made their own communities, not in the proletarian brotherhood of the International Brigades as a single whole but in secondary groups with a common language at the level of fighting units. The socialism of action engendered the opportunity to belong. The result for the sparrows was too often the fall, but at least they, like the volunteers in the underground war of the French resistance that Jean-Paul Sartre called "La République du silence," could enjoy the ultimate freedom to choose meaning for their own deaths and lives, an achievement that most of them sought.[79] Even if they had known the death and injury that awaited, they would have gone. Great was their need for a place to go. Little wonder that these few months spent in Spain marked survivors for the rest of their lives. At the sword's edge, a lifetime may be lived or lost in a second. The International Brigaders show a fine moral example for all their deficiencies as a military model, exemplifying moral qualities that made their real military contributions possible and also ensured a high human price for those contributions. Maybe this recognition moved Negrín to speak to the International Brigades or drove La Pasionaria to the heights of her oratory when the International Brigades disbanded, somehow compensating for the official silence that greeted their arrival. Whether fools or heroes, the International Brigaders were not knaves like the privileged Kim Philbys of their generation who happily sacrificed others to their cause.[80]

Above all, what the men of the International Brigades did was political, not in the limited, modern sense of ruling and being ruled, but in the more profound and ancient sense of creating something out of nothing. In response to a morally incoherent world they created enduring political meaning. Hannah Arendt is the chief exponent of this deeper conception of politics in our time. A Jew who escaped from Germany, she was briefly interned at Gurs while the International Brigaders were there. Unlike them, she had connections and managed to make her way to the United States where in the 1950s she composed her great books. Though she had in mind Greek heroes like Achilles and Sarpedon, her words may also interpret the deeds of the International Brigaders. In an essay on freedom she wrote that "the essence of politics . . . is not to rule over others or to achieve instrumental objectives, but rather to join with others in collective deeds that win immortal remembrance." She continued:

> A worldly reality, tangible in words which can be heard, in deeds which can be seen, and in events which are talked about, remembered, and turned into stories before they are finally incorporated into the great storybook of human history. Whatever occurs in this space of appearance is political by definition.[81]

Surely by this criterion the men of the International Brigades succeeded beyond all measure. They spawned a literature, much of which has the character of myth. Behind the famous few, nameless men of the International Brigades became like the nameless men at Troy who stood behind Achilles, Sarpedon, Hector, and the others, with this difference that none was there at the order of a sovereign, that each had made up his own mind, and that each had to keep choosing to stay there.

Consider a contrast. Before the battle of Agincourt in Shakespeare's *Henry V*, the men in the ranks discuss the war. A common soldier, John Bates, explains to the disguised King Henry that if the cause is wrong, "our obedience to the king wipes the crime out of us." Other common soldiers around the camp fire agree with this thesis of sole sovereign responsibility. The men of the International Brigades would not, because they each made up their own minds and consciences. Their personal declarations of war meant that they willingly entered a state of nature, which was a state of war far more terrible than Thomas Hobbes imagined. While in that state of war, they created a community among themselves, a community based on their common experience in Spain. That community endured after Spain, to judge by the efforts of International Brigade veterans to keep alive the memory of their efforts.

In a national war, rituals remove the soldier from the society and other rituals later restore survivors to the society.[82] (The absence of these rituals, made politically impossible by the extra-constitutional nature of the Vietnam War, partly stimulated anti-war sentiment and later embittered many veterans of that conflict.) One aspect is that these rituals insulate individual soldiers from the responsibility to consider the justice of the cause, as Henry's men said. The flags, uniforms, parades, presentations, and the like—these answer any doubts at the outset and later restore veterans. "True soldiers," like the International Brigaders, learned the difference between soldier and civilian by living in filth, amid disease, and seeing friends destroyed. Not until World War II did civilians learn this difference.

Near the beginning of that terrible Greek civil war described by Thucydides, the Corcyraeans pleaded with the Athenians to take their part against Corinth. In their plea, the Corcyraeans conceded that they had no claim on the Athenians, that Athens owed Corcyraea nothing. But, they argued, the Corcyraean request provided Athens with the opportunity to do a noble act—to enter the war voluntarily and on the side of the weaker. If Athens so acted, the Corcyraeans claimed, the world would admire its nobility.

Is this not what the men of the International Brigades did, taking the perceived weaker side? The exercise of their individual sovereign choice distinguishes the members of the International Brigades, not the justice of their cause. They created meaning for themselves, where the act becomes an end in itself that needs no just cause for explanation, though without belief in a just cause, the action would never have been initiated. The Trojan War, hardly a just war for its cause, became noble in its conduct. The experience itself remains in the end, not the cause, to compel those who write and read about the International Brigades.

In his novel, *La Peste,* Albert Camus causes Rambert, an International Brigade veteran, to declare to Dr. Rieux that his experiences in Spain taught him a lesson: "Maintenant je sais que l'homme est capable de grandes actions. Mais s'il n'est pas capable d'un grand sentiment, il ne m'intéresse pas" (Now I know that man is capable of great actions. But if he is not capable of great sensibility, he does not interest me).[83] Heroism no longer moves Rambert for it often brings death and he prefers life. In Oran where the story takes place, the plague does not respect anyone's preferences. Niccolò Machiavelli taught that necessity requires action, which the foreign volunteers in the International Brigades understood in their morally incoherent world.

Much about war has been written in these pages for the subject is worth exploring. An agnostic can see that the world is a better place, a richer place, for cathedrals, as a pacifist can see the nobility in war without advocating it. Republican general Vincente Rójo observed that the Spanish Civil War has ended in deed but not in word.[84] The surviving International Brigaders have not come to terms with their own experience but "want recognition," according to one, "that what we went to do in Spain . . . was . . . the right thing to do."[85]

Juan Negrín's prophecy—that a tribute would be paid to these men by their own countries—has not been fulfilled with a few desultory exceptions, more a product of the Cold War than respect for the International Brigaders, like the East Germany issue of a commemorative postage stamp in 1969 and the Polish erection of a small monument in their honor. In Spain itself, the extraordinary monument at *El Valle de los Caidos* (The Valley of the Fallen), built to Franco's specifications, now ostensibly honors *all* who fell in the Spanish Civil War. Much of the back-breaking work at this site was done by Republican prisoners of war, including Internationals. But the plaques above the two sacred crypts where the remains are kept, open only to family members, still declare that those who lie there died for their country *and* for God. Neither dedication would apply to the International Brigaders. Judging from reports of visits to Spain by International Brigade veterans, *El Valle de los Caidos* does not figure in their itineraries.[86] A contrast might be the Cathedral in Washington, D. C., where plaques ennobling Ulysses S. Grant and Robert E. Lee are affixed to facing walls. Or the National Park at Civil War battlefields where opposing officers and men who died are honored side by side. In 1982, King Juan Carlos, in a gesture of reconciliation, dedicated another memorial in the city of Madrid, making no reference to its foreigner saviors of 1936.

Veteran Laurie Lee recalls seeing index cards in boxes recording the names of many of the British volunteers when he visited William Rust, after leaving Spain. He later wrote that "there must have been five or six hundred of them. Many—more than half—were marked 'killed in action' or 'missing', at such fronts as Brunete, Guadalajara, the Ebro." Lee thought that

> here were the names of dead heroes, piled into little cardboard boxes, never to be inscribed later in official Halls of Remembrance. Without recognition, often ridiculed . . ..[87]

Lee's observation remains pertinent today. If the end of the Cold War means that the propaganda value of the International Brigaders is now gone, the men in the ranks will be forgotten even faster.

Vae Victis.

ENDNOTES

1. Edwin Rolfe, *The Lincoln Battalion* (New York: Random House, 1939), 9.
2. William Rust, *Britons in Spain* (New York: International, 1939), 6.
3. Jacques Delperrie de Bayac, *Les Brigades Internationales* (Paris: Fayard, 1968), 366.
4. Upton Sinclair, *No Pasarán* (London: Werner Lawrie, 1937), 114.

5. Antoine de Saint-Exupéry, *Wind, Sand and Stars* (New York: Harcourt, 1940), 198.
6. See Esmond Romilly, *Boadilla* (London: Hamish Hamilton, 1937) 33; Rust, 18; John Sommerfield, *Volunteer in Spain* (New York: Knopf, 1937) 153; and also Carl Geiser, *Prisoners of the Good Fight* (Westport: Lawrence Hill, 1988), 247.
7. Orwell, *Homage to Catalonia*, 226. Erridge who goes to fight in Spain is a pacifist in the novel *Casanova's Chinese Restaurant* (London: Heinemann, 1960) by Anthony Powell, 64–65.
8. Claude Simon, "Interview with Claude Simon: Autobiography, the Novel, and Politics," *Review of Contemporary Fiction*, 5 (1984) 1, pp. 8–9. It is assumed that the character "O" in Simon's novel *The Georgics* (London: Calder, 1989) is meant to invoke Orwell. Simon served in the Spanish Civil War, and his accounts of it are very similar to Orwell's, apart from the punctuation. See also his *La Palace* (Paris: Editions de Minuit, 1962). Orwell's descriptive accuracy was also questioned more generally in Bernard Crick, *George Orwell: A Life* (London: Secker and Warburg, 1980). For other anti-Orwell remarks, see the works of American veterans Milt Felsen, *The Anti-Warrior: A Memoir* (Iowa City: University of Iowa Press, 1989), 124 and Gerassi, 144.
9. Copíc is quoted in Joseph North, *Men in the Ranks* (New York: Friends of the Abraham Lincoln Brigade, 1939), 7. As a matter of fact, the Americans did not fight well and hated Copíc; see Cecil Eby, *Between the Bullet and the Lie* (New York: Holt, Rinehart, and Winston, 1969), 61 ff. Philosophers also over-value the just cause; see Douglas Walton, *Courage: A Philosophical Investigation* (Berkeley: University of California Press, 1986).
10. Stephen Spender, *World Within World* (London: Faber & Faber, 1951), 212–225.
11. Two examples suffice, Massino Mangilli-Climpson, *Men of Heart of Red, White and Green* (New York: Vantage, 1985), 36 and William L. Katz and Marc Crawford, *The Lincoln Brigade: A Picture History* (New York: Athenaeum, 1989), 3.
12. Carl Geiser, *Prisoners of the Good Fight: The Spanish Civil War 1936–1939* (Westport: Lawrence Hill, 1988), 30.
13. Francisco Pérez López, *The Dark and Bloody Ground* (Boston: Little Brown, 1970), 25.
14. Sandor Voros, *American Commissar* (Philadelphia: Chilton, 1961), 270.
15. Inevitably, Karl Marx himself was not left to rest in peace but rather conscripted when some of his newspaper articles were assembled and re-issued with an anonymous preface drawing an analogy between the Spain of 1854 and 1936. See Karl Marx and Frederich Engels, *Revolution in Spain* (London: Lawrence and Wishart, 1939), 13.
16. Jason Gurney, *Crusade in Spain* (London: Faber and Faber, 1974), 111.
17. Alvah Bessie, *Men in Battle* (New York: Scribner's, 1939), 292.
18. See the admission in "Une année de lutte et de gloire des Brigades internationales," *L'humanité*, 17 October 1937, p. 4.
19. Geoffrey Cox, *The Defense of Madrid* (London: Gollancz, 1937), 169.
20. Sommerfield, 107 and cf. Bessie, 292.
21. Achilles regrets in the *Odyssey* in book XI, line 489.
22. So says a letter attributed to Robert Taylor, dated 25 February 1937 in Marcel Acier, ed., *From Spanish Trenches* (New York: Modern Age, 1937), 151.
23. Gerrassi, 163.
24. William L. Katz and Marc Crawford, *The Lincoln Brigade: A Picture History* (New Athenaeum, 1989), 21.
25. Cecil Eby, *The Siege of the Alcazar* (London: Bodley Head, 1966).
26. Orwell, Review of John Sommerfield's *Volunteer in Spain, Collected Essays, Journalism, and Letters*, 1 (1920–1940) (Harmondsworth: Penguin, 1971): 322.
27. Gustav Regler, *The Great Crusade*, trans. W. Chambers and B. Mussey (New York: Longmans, 1940), 129–130.

28. Diamant, 60.
29. Steve Nelson, *The Volunteers*, 305.
30. John Dollard, *Fear in Battle*, 56–57.
31. Victor Hoar, *The MacKenzie-Papineau Battalion* (Toronto: Copp Clark, 1969), 26.
32. Gurney, 111.
33. Albert Einstein, *Comment Je Vois Le Monde*, trans. M. Solovine (Paris: Flammarion, 1958), 146.
34. Harold Smith, "Action at Brunete," *The Heart of Spain*, ed. Alvah Bessie (New York: Veterans of the Abraham Lincoln Brigade, 1952), 187.
35. Orwell, *Homage*, 226.
36. Edmonds, *Letters from Spain*, 123, 135, 146, and 180. Food figures prominently in memoirs, too, e.g., Milt Felsen, *Anti-Warrior: A Memoir* (Iowa City: University of Iowa, 1989), 96.
37 Jef Last, *The Spanish Tragedy*, trans. D. Hallet (London: Routledge, 1939), 183.
38. Nick Gillain, *Le Mercenaire* (Paris: Fayard, 1938), 107–108.
39. Leo Palacio, *1936: La Maldonne d'Espange* (Paris: Editions Privat, 1986), 51–52 and 98. The same charges are pressed against the long-dead Gillain by Polish International Brigade veteran Alexander Szurek in his *The Shattered Dream* (New York: Columbia University Press, 1989), 124.
40. Antoine de Saint-Exupéry, *Wind, Sand and Stars* (New York: Harcourt, 1940), 225.
41. On Nelson's leadership see Robert Rosenstone, *Crusade of the Left* (New York: Pegasus, 1969), 155, or Herrick, *Hermanos!* (London: Weidenfeld and Nicolson, 1969), 296.
42. The idealistic reason of "What we are fighting for" garnered affirmations from 1–2 percent of respondents; see Samuel A. Stouffer et al., *The American Soldier: Combat and its Aftermath* (Princeton: Princeton University Press, 1949), 1: 100.
43. Niccolò Machiavelli, *The Art of War* (Indianapolis: Bobbs-Merrill, 1965 [1521]).
44. Roy R. Grinker and John Spiegel, *War Neuroses* (Philadelphia: Blakiston, 1945), 67, 118, and 14. A number of other such wartime investigations are reviewed in Stanley J. Rachman, *Fear and Courage* (San Francisco: Freeman, 1978), 66–72. Historian John A. Lynn sees the same primary group cohesion in *The Bayonets of the Republic: Motivation and Tactics in the Army of Revolutionary France 1791–1794* (Urbana: University of Illinois Press, 1986).
45. Grinker and Spiegel, *Men under Stress* (Philadelphia: Blakiston, 1945), 46–47.
46. Ibid., 25.
47. Herrick, 263.
48. Orwell, 41. Stories recounting exactly the same restraint when presented with an enemy answering the call of nature can be found in many other war memoirs.
49. Bessie, 187, and Rolfe, 228.
50. Last, 148.
51. Hywel Francis, *Miners Against Fascism: Wales and the Spanish Civil War* (London: Lawrence and Wishart, 1984), 230.
52. David Montgomery, *The Fall of the House of Labor: The Workplace, The State, and American Labor Activism, 1865–1925* (Cambridge: Cambridge University Press, 1988).
53. William James, "The Moral Equivalent of War," *International Conciliation* (New York: American Association for International Conciliation, 1911), 18.
54. This thesis is from Gerald Lindeman, *Embattled Courage* (New York: Free Press, 1987), 1 ff.
55. Gurney, 111.
56. Jack Jones in Judith Cook, 10.
57. For the perspective of an English volunteer for the Nationalists, see Peter Kemp, *Mine Were of Trouble* (London: Cassell, 1957), 148, and also his dinner with Esmond Romilly in France while each was on leave from his chosen side, 187.

Another solitary individual who served the Nationalist cause is described in Judith Keene, "An Antipodean Bridegroom of Death: An Australian volunteer with Franco's Forces," *Journal of the Royal Australian Historical Society*, 70 (1985) 4, pp. 251–270; or at another level see *Ciano: Diary 1937–1938*, trans. A. Mayer (London: Methuen, 1948), 26.

58. Regler, *The Owl of Minerva*, trans. N. Denny (New York: Farrar and Strauss, 1959), 283.
59. Lee Miller, *The Story of Ernie Pyle* (New York: Viking, 1950), 400.
60. See the letter attributed to Charles O'Flaherty in Acier, 140. Cf. Arthur Landis, *The Abraham Lincoln Brigade* (New York: The Citadel Press, 1967), 85 and 427, or Sinclair, 236.
61. Plato, *The Laches.*
62. Aristotle, *The Ethics*, Book 3, 1115b.
63. Last, 173.
64. Marcel Proust, *Within a Budding Grove*, S. Moncrief, trans. (New York: Vintage, 1970 [1924]), 299.
65. Orwell, *Homage to Catalonia*, 241.
66. Randolfo Pacciardi, *Il Battaglione Garibaldi* (Lugano: Nuove Edizioni di Capolago, 1938), 23.
67. *Iliad*, Book 12, lines 310–330.
68. Preston, *The Spanish Civil War*, 7 and 160.
69. Marjorie A. Valleau, *The Spanish Civil War in American and European Films* (Ann Arbor: University Microfilms Research Press, 1982), 2.
70. John H. Simpson, *Refugees: A Review of the Situation Since September 1938* (London: Royal Institute of International Affairs, June 1939), 114.
71. Judith Keene, "A Spanish Springtime: Aileen Palmer and the Spanish Civil War," *Labour History*, (May 1987) 52, p. 86.
72. Nancy Macdonald, *Homage to the Spanish Exiles: Voices from the Spanish Civil War* (New York: Insight, 1987), 98 and 281.
73. David W. Pike, *Vae Victis! Los Republicanos Españoles Refugiados en Francia 1939–1944* (Paris: Ruédo Iberico, 1969), 107 n. 103.
74. Lois Smith, *Mexico and the Spanish Republicans* (Berkeley: University of California Press, 1955), 183–220.
75. Michael Walzer, "The Obligation to Die for the State," *Obligations* (Cambridge: Harvard University Press, 1970), 77.
76. See Moritz Schlick, *Problems of Ethics*, trans. D. Rynin, (New York: Dover, 1961 [1939]), 41–42. For a critique see Richard T. Garner and Bernard Rosen, *Moral Philosophy* (New York: Macmillan, 1967), 36–54.
77. Aristotle, *The Ethics*, Book 3, 1110a 10–30.
78. Max Weber, "Religious Rejections of the World and Their Directions," *From Max Weber*, ed. H. Gerth and C. W. Mills (New York: Oxford University Press, 1946), 335.
79. Jean-Paul Sartre, "La République du Silence," *Situations III*, 2nd ed. (Paris: Gallimard, 1949), 12–14.
80. See Kim Philby, *My Silent War* (London: Granada, 1973 [1964]), 120 and 143.
81. Hannah Arendt, *The Human Condition* (Chicago: University of Chicago Press, 1958), 154.
82. Eric J. Leed, *No Man's Land: Combat and Identity in World War I* (Cambridge: Cambridge University Press, 1979), 1–39.
83. Albert Camus, *La Peste* (Paris: Gallimard, 1961), 179.
84. Vincente Rójo, *España Heroica* (Barcelona: Editorial Ariel, 1975 [1942]), 14.
85. Wayne Gooding, "45 Canadians Returning to the Spanish Battlefields," *Toronto Globe and Mail*, 24 August 1979, p. 12. More recently, Charles Miranda, "Spanish War Memorial Fund Reaches $3000," *Canberra Times*, 16 November 1992, p. 16.
86. "Brigadistas Internacionales Homenajeados en España," *El Pais* (International Edition), 20 October 1986, p. 14. Cf. Francisco Basterra, "Miembros de la

Brigada Lincoln Commemoran el 50o Aniversario de la Guerra de España," *El Pais* (International Edition), 20 October 1986, p. 15. The myth that the Lincolns formed a brigade is now set in Spanish.

87. Laurie Lee, *A Moment of War* (London: Viking, 1991), 174.

Chapter 9

To Endure

The International Brigaders, among the few soldiers since the rise of nation-states to go to war on their own initiative without the aid and comfort of their patrimony, suffered ignominy and alienation. Unlike other returned soldiers, the International Brigaders received no tribute from a grateful state or nation. Those who survived Spain could steel themselves to this neglect, but for those who died, neglect threatened final extinction from the minds of others. The International Brigaders themselves have honored their own dead by remembering them and by inspiring others in this task. Consequently, one of the most striking features of books by the International Brigaders, and those inspired by them, has been the lists of names reproduced.[1] These lists record for posterity the names of some of those who served, including the fallen, but so many names must have been lost.

Moreover, display between the covers of a book is not the public monument that an obelisk or a military cemetery is. Though even today the search for war criminals from World War II can be front-page news, recognition of the International Brigades seems as unlikely as ever. Negrín's prophecy has not been fulfilled and probably never will be, because the moral lesson that the International Brigaders' war teaches has not been absorbed. Right is not might, as Albert Camus noted, but nobility is endurance.[2]

Disbanded, the International Brigades became immortal. They

were individuals who transcended the confusion and complexity of a morally incoherent world. Their journey to the cutting edge of the political world created a myth. While that myth is an important phenomenon in its own right, it also hides a more common but nonetheless more profound reality experienced by the men in the ranks: that right is not might, that the socialism of action is all that remains. Yet, according to the criteria of Hannah Arendt, the men in the ranks were antique heroes for trying to re-create the political world.

Perhaps in a small way they were like the famous men praised in *Ecclesiasticus:*

All of these were honored in their generations
and were the glory of their times.
There be of them that have left a name behind them,
that their praises might be reported.
And some there be which have no memorial,
who are perished as though they had never been.
And are become as though they had never been born
and their children after them.
But these were merciful men
whose good works hath not been forgotten.
With their seed shall continually remain
a good inheritance.
And their children are within the covenant.
Their seed standeth fast,
And their children for their sakes.
Their seed shall remain for ever,
And their glory shall not be blotted out.
Their bodies are buried in peace,
But their name liveth for evermore.

Ecclesiasticus, xliv

ENDNOTES

1. Recent examples by volunteers William Beeching, *Canadian Volunteers: Spain, 1936–1939* (Regina: Canadian Plains Research Center, 1989), pp. x-xxix and James Yates, *Mississippi to Madrid* (Seattle: Open Hand, 1989), 176–177.
2. Camus is quoted in Allen Guttmann, *The Wound in the Heart* (Glencoe: The Free Press, 1962), p. x.

Bibliography

ANONYMOUS. "The International Brigades," *Spain*, 2, 1 January 1938, 22.
AARONS, SAM. "Reminiscences of the Spanish Civil War," *Australian Left Review*, March 1973, 39, pp. 24–29.
ACIER, MARCEL, ed. *From Spanish Trenches.* New York: Modern Age Books, 1937.
Adelante! Pasaremos! Cologne: Verlag Internationale Solidarität, 1976.
AGUILERA DURAN, LUÍS. *Orígenes de las Brigadas Internacionales.* Madrid: Editora Nacional, 1974.
ALBA, VICTOR. *Histoire des Républiques Espagnoles.* Vincennes: Nord-Sud, 1948.
ALCOFAR NASSAES, JOSÉ LUÍS. *Spansky: Los Extranjeros Que Lucharon en la Guerra Civil Espanola.* Barcelona: Dopesa, 1973.
ALEXANDER, BILL. *British Volunteers for Liberty.* London: Lawrence and Wishart, 1982.
ALMOND, GABRIEL. *The Appeals of Communism.* Princeton: Princeton University Press, 1954.
ALPERT, MICHAEL. *El Ejército Repúblicano en la Guerra Civil.* Barcelona: Ruédo Iberico, 1977.
ALVAREZ, MANUEL. *The Tall Soldier: My 40 year Search for the Man Who Saved My Life.* Toronto: Virgo, 1990.
ALVAREZ DEL VAYO, J. *Freedom's Battle.* London: Heinemann, 1940.
AMERICAN INSTITUTE OF PUBLIC OPINION. "Surveys 1938–1939," *Public Opinion Quarterly*, 3, 1939, 4, pp. 581–607.
"Americans have died fighting for Democracy in Spain," *Life*, 4, 1937, pp. 14–28.
ARENDT, HANNAH. *The Human Condition.* Chicago: University of Chicago Press, 1958.
ARISTOTLE. *The Ethics*, Book 3.
"Arthur Koestler . . . .," *The Australian*, 5 March 1983, p.10.
Australians and the Spanish Civil War. Melbourne: Red Pen Publications, 1986.
AZÑAR, MANUEL. *Historia Militar de la Guerra de España.* Madrid: Editorial Nacionel, 1969.
Bajo la Bandera de la España Republicana: Recuerdan los Voluntarios Sovieticos Participantes en la Guerra Nacional-Revolucionaria en España. Moscow: Progresso, n.d.

BARCO TERUEL, ENRIQUE. *Valle de Jarama (Brigada Internacional).* Barcelona: Ediciones Marte, 1969.

BAREA, ARTURO. *The Clash.* London: Faber and Faber, 1946.

BAUMAN, GEROLD GINO F. *Extranjeros en la Guerra Civil Española.* Lima: no publisher given, 1979.

BEDDOES, DICK. "Remembering the Mac-Paps," *Toronto Globe and Mail,* 10 January 1980, p. 8.

BEECHING, WILLIAM. *Canadian Volunteers: Spain 1936–39.* Regina: Canadian Plains Research Center, 1989.

———. "Fighting the Fascists in Spain," *Toronto Star,* 18 November 1989, p. M15.

BEEVOR, ANTHONY. *The Spanish Civil War.* London: Orbis, 1982.

Ben Leider: American Hero. New York: Ben Leider Memorial Fund, n.d.

BESSIE, ALVAH. *Men in Battle.* New York: Scribner's, 1939.

———. *Songs of the Spanish Civil War.* New York: Folkways, 1961.

———, ed. *The Heart of Spain.* New York: Veterans of the Abraham Lincoln Brigade, 1952.

BLINKHORN, MARTIN. "Darkness and Light," *History Today,* 37, February 1987, pp. 54–55.

BLYTHE, HENRY. *Spain over Briton.* London: Routledge, 1937.

BOLÍN, LUIS. *Spain: The Vital Years.* London: Cassell, 1967.

BOLLOTEN, BURNETT. *The Spanish Civil War: Revolution and Counterrevolution.* Chapel Hill: University of North Carolina Press, 1991.

The Book of the XV Brigade. Madrid: Commissariat of War, 1938.

BOWERS, CLAUDE. *My Mission to Spain.* London: Gollancz, 1954.

BRENAN, GERALD. *Spanish Labyrinth.* Cambridge: Cambridge University Press, 1010.

BROME, VINCENT. *The International Brigades.* New York: Morrow, 1966.

BROUÉ, PIERRE and TÉMINE, EMILE. *La Revolution et la Guerre d'Espagne.* Paris: Les Editions du Minuit, 1961.

BROUÉ, PIERRE, FRASER, RONALD, and VILAR, PIERRE. *Methologic Historica de la Guerra y Revolucion España.* Barcelona: Editorial Fontamara, 1980.

BURNS, JAMES, M. *John Kennedy.* New York: Harcourt, 1960.

BUTLER, RUPERT. *The Black Angels: A History of the Waffen SS.* New York: St. Martins, 1979.

CAMPBELL, JOSEPH. *The Hero with a Thousand Faces.* London: Abacus, 1948.

CAMUS, ALBERT. *La Peste.* Paris: Gallimard, 1961.

CANDELA, ANTONIO. *Adventures of an Innocent in the Spanish Civil War.* Cornwall: United Writers, 1989.

CARR, E. H. *The Comintern and the Spanish Civil War.* London: Macmillan, 1984.

———. *Images of the Spanish Civil War.* London: Allen & Unwin, 1986.

CASADO, SEIGISMUNDO. *The Last Days of Madrid,* R. Croft-Cooke, trans. London: Peter Arnold, 1939.

CASTELLS PEIG, ANDREU. *Las Brigadas Internacionales de la Guerra de España.* Barcelona: Editorial Ariel, 1974.

CATTELL, DAVID. *Communism and the Spanish Civil War.* New York: Russell and Russell, 1955.

CEBRIAN, JUAN LUÍS. "La Memoria Historica," *El Pais,* International Edition, 21 July 1986.

Ciano: Diary 1937–1938, A. Mayer, trans. London: Methuen, 1948.

CIERVA Y DE HOCES, RICARDO DE LA. *Historia Ilustrada de la Guerra Civil Española.* Barcelona: Ediciones Danue, 1970.

———. *Leyenda y Tragedia de las Brigadas Internacionales.* Madrid: Editorial Prensa Española, 1973.

CLAUSEWITZ, CARL VON. *On War.* Princeton: Princeton University Press, 1976 [1832].

CLOVERDALE, JOHN F. *Italian Intervention in the Spanish Civil War.* Princeton: Princeton University Press, 1975.

COLODNY, ROBERT. *El Asedio de Madrid*, J. Tomas de Salas, trans. Paris: Ruedo Iberico, 1970.

———. *The Struggle for Madrid.* New York: Paine-Whitman, 1958.

COOK, JUDITH. *Apprentices of Freedom.* London: Quartet, 1979.

CORKILL, D. and RAWNSLEY, S., eds. *The Road to Spain: Anti-Fascists at War, 1936-1939.* Dumfermline: Borderline, 1981.

COPEMAN, FRED. *Reason and Revolt.* London: Blandford Press, n.d.

CORTADA, JAMES W., ed. *A City at War.* Wilmington: Scholarly Resources, 1985.

———., ed. *Historical Dictionary of the Spanish Civil War.* Westport: Greenwood, 1981.

COWLES, VIRGINIA. *Looking for Trouble.* London: Hamilton, 1941.

COX, GEOFFREY. *The Defence of Madrid.* London: Gollancz, 1937.

CRICK, BERNARD. *George Orwell: A Life.* London: Secker and Warburg, 1980.

CROME, LEN. "Document: Walter (1937–1947): A Soldier in Spain," *History Workshop Journal*, 9, Spring 1980, pp. 116–128.

CUNNIGHAM, VALENTINE. "Preface," *Spanish Front: Writers on the Civil War.* Oxford: Oxford University Press, 1986.

CUTHBERTSON, GILBERT M. *Political Myth and Epic.* East Lansing: Michigan State University Press, 1975.

DELPERRIE DE BAYAC, JACQUES. *Les Brigades Internationales.* Paris: Fayard, 1968.

DE WET, OLOFF. *The Patrol is Ended.* New York: Doubleday, 1938.

DEWEZ, SULPICE. *Gloire aux Volontaires Internationaux.* Madrid: Dianh, 1937.

DIAMANT, DAVID. *Combattants Juifs das L'Armée Républicaine Espagnole, 1936–1939.* Paris: Editions Renouveau, 1979.

DIMITROV, GEORG. *Une Anée de Lutte Héroïque du Peuple Espanol.* Paris: Bureau d'Editions, 1937.

DOLLARD, JOHN. *Fear in Battle.* New Haven: Institute of Human Relations, Yale University, 1943.

DUPRÉ, HENRI. *La Legion Tricolore en Espagne (1936–1939).* Paris: Editions de la Ligue Française (Mouvement Social Européen), 1942.

DUPUY, R.E. and T.N. *The Encyclopedia of Military History.* Rev. ed. New York: Harper and Row, 1970.

EBY, CECIL. *Between the Bullet and the Lie.* New York: Holt Rinehart and Winston, 1969.

———. "The Real Robert Jordan," *American Literature*, 38, 1966, 3, pp. 380–396.

———. *The Siege of the Alcazar.* London: Bodley Head, 1966.

EDMONDS, LLOYD. *Letters from Spain.* Sydney: Allen & Unwin, 1985.

EHRENBERG, ILYA. *Memoirs: 1921–1941.* New York: Grosset & Dunlap, 1963.

EINSTEIN, ALBERT. *Comment Je Vois Le Monde*, M. Solovine, trans. Paris: Flammarion, 1958.

ELLIS, JOHN. *The Sharp End of the War.* London: David and Charles, 1980.

ELLWOOD, SHEELAGH. "Spanish Notes," *Times Literary Supplement*, 9–15 October 1987, p. 1108.

ELSTOB, PETER. *Spanish Prisoner.* London: Macmillan, 1939.

L'épopée de L'espagne. Paris: Amicale des anciens volontaires français en Espagne républicaine, 1957.

EVANIER, DAVID. "How Sammy Klarfeld Became a Vacillating Element in Spain," *Journal of Contemporary Studies*, Summer/Fall 1985, pp. 89–106.

FAGEN, PATRICIA. *Exiles and Citizens.* Austin: University of Texas Press, 1973.

FARIAS, VICTOR. *Heidegger and Nazism.* Philadelphia: Temple University Press, 1989 [1987].

FELSEN, MILT. *The Anti-Warrior: A Memoir.* Iowa City: University of Iowa Press, 1989.

FERNANDEZ, ALBERTO. "Judios en la Guerra de España," *Tiempo de Historia* (Madrid), September 1975, pp. 4–15.

FISCHER, LOUIS. *Men and Politics.* New York: Duell, Sloan and Pearce, 1941.

———. "Worshippers from Afar," *The God that Failed*, R. H. Grossman, ed. New York: Harper & Row, 1949.

FRANCIS, HYWEL. *Miners Against Fascism: Wales and the Spanish Civil War.* London: Lawrence and Wishart, 1984.

———. "Welsh Miners and the Spanish Civil War," *Journal of Contemporary History,* 5, 1970, 3, pp. 177–191.

FRASER, RONALD. *The Blood of Spain.* New York: Pantheon, 1979.

GALEY, J. H. "Bridegrooms of Death," *Journal of Contemporary History,* 4, 1969, 2, pp. 47–69.

GALLUP, GEORGE H. *The Gallup Poll,* 1, 1935–1948, New York: Random House, 1972.

GARCÍA, JUAN. "The International Brigades in Spain, 1937–1938" (in Russian), *Voprosy Istorii,* 1956, 7, pp. 33–48.

GARNER, RICHARD T. and ROSEN, BERNARD. *Moral Philosophy.* New York: Macmillan, 1967.

GARRATT, G. T. *Mussolini's Roman Empire.* Harmondsworth: Penguin, 1938.

GATES, JOHN. *The Story of an American Commissar.* New York: Nelson, 1958.

GEISER, CARL. *Prisoners of the Good Fight: The Spanish Civil War 1936–1939.* Westport: Lawrence Hill, 1988.

GERASSI, JOHN. *The Premature Anti-Fascists: North American Volunteers in the Spanish Civil War 1936–1939.* New York: Praeger, 1986.

GILLAIN, NICK. *Le Mercenaire.* Paris: Libraire Arthème Fayard, 1938.

GISCLON, JEAN. *La Désillusion: Espagne, 1936.* Paris: Editions France-Empire, 1986.

GOLDSTON, ROBERT. *The Civil War in Spain.* London: Phoenix, 1966.

GOODING, WAYNE. "45 Canadians Returning to Spanish Battlefields," *Toronto Globe and Mail,* 24 August 1979, p. 12.

GORNICK, VIVAN. *The Romance of American Communism.* New York: Basic, 1977.

GREAT BRITAIN, HOME OFFICE. *Communist Papers,* Command 2682. London: His Majesty's Stationary Office, 1926.

GREGORY, WALTER. *The Shallow Grave.* London: Gollancz, 1986.

GRINKER, ROY and SPIEGEL, JOHN. *Men under Stress.* Philadelphia: Blakiston, 1945.

———. *War Neuroses.* Philadelphia: Blakiston, 1945.

Guerra Y Revolucion en España 1936–1939. Moscow: Editions Progreso, 1966.

GURNEY, JASON. *Crusade in Spain.* London: Faber and Faber, 1974.

GUTTMANN, ALLEN. *The Wound in the Heart.* Glencoe: The Free Press, 1962.

HEGGEN, THOMAS. *Mr. Roberts.* Boston: Houghton Mifflin, 1946.

Hello Canada. Toronto: Friends of the Mackenzie-Papineau Battalion, n.d.

HEMINGWAY, ERNEST. *For Whom the Bell Tolls.* New York: Scribner's, 1940.

HERRICK, WILLIAM. *Hermanos!* London: Weidenfeld and Nicholson, 1969.

"HISPANICUS." *Foreign Intervention in Spain.* London: United Editorial, n.d.

HOAR, VICTOR. *The Mackenzie-Papineau Battalion.* Toronto: Copp Clark, 1969.

HOBBES, THOMAS. *The Leviathan.*

HOLLANDER, PAUL. *Political Pilgrims.* Oxford: Oxford University Press, 1981.

HOMBERGER, ERIC. *American Writers and Radical Politics.* London: Macmillan, 1987.

HOMER. *Iliad,* Book 21.

———. *ODYSSEY,* Book 11.

HOOVER, J. EDGAR. *The Masters of Deceit.* New York: Pocket Books, 1959.

HUGHES, DOROTHY B. *The Fallen Sparrow.* New York: Carroll & Graf, 1988 [1942].

Interbrigadisten. Berlin: Social Science Faculty, Friederich Engels Military Academy, 1966.

JACKSON, GABRIEL. *The Spanish Republic and the Civil War.* Princeton: Princeton University Press, 1965.

JACKSON, JULIAN. *The Popular Front in France: Defending Democracy, 1934–1938.* Cambridge: Cambridge University Press, 1989.

JAKOBSON, MAX. *The Diplomacy of the Winter War.* Cambridge: Harvard University Press, 1961.

JAMES, WILLIAM. "The Moral Equivalent of War," *International Conciliation.* New York: American Association for International Conciliation, 1911, pp. 9–20.

JANSON, MARC. "International Class Solidarity or Foreign Intervention?

Internationalists and Latvian Rifles in the Russian Revolution and the Civil War," *International Review of Social History*, 31, 1986, 1, pp. 68–79.

JOHNSTON, VERLE. *The International Brigades in the Spanish Civil War 1936–1939*. Rev. ed. Stanford: Hoover Institute Library, 1958 [1952].

———. *The Legion of Babel*. Philadelphia: University of Pennsylvania Press, 1967.

KANTOROWICZ, ALFRED. *Spanische Tagebuch*. Berlin: Aufbau-Verlag, 1948.

KATZ, WILLIAM L. and CRAWFORD, MARC. *The Lincoln Brigade: A Picture History*. New York: Atheneum, 1989.

KEEGAN, JOHN. *The Face of Battle*. New York: Viking, 1976.

KEENE, JUDITH. "An Antipodean Bridegroom of Death: An Australian volunteer with Franco's Forces," *Journal of the Royal Australian Historical Society*, 70, 1985, 4, pp. 251–270.

———. *The Last Mile to Huesca: An Australian Nurse in the Spanish Civil War*. Sydney: University of New South Wales Press, 1988.

———. "A Spanish Springtime: Aileen Palmer and the Spanish Civil War," *Labour History*, May 1986, 52, pp. 75–87.

KEMP, PETER. *Mine Were of Trouble*. London: Cassell, 1957.

KEMPTON, MURRAY. *Part of our Time*. New York: Dell, 1955.

KISCH, RICHARD. *They Shall Not Pass*. London: Wayland, 1974.

KLEHR, HARVEY. *Communist Cadre*. Stanford: Hoover Institute Press, 1978.

KLENFIELD, GERALD and TAMBS, LEWIS. *Hitler's Spanish Legion*. Carbondale: Southern Illinois University Press, 1974.

KNIGHTLY, PHILLIP. *The Second Oldest Profession: The Spy as Patriot, Bureaucrat, Fantasist, and Whore*. London: Pan, 1986.

KOEHL, ROBERT LEWIS. *The Black Corps: The Structure and Power Struggles of the Nazi SS*. Madison: University of Wisconsin Press, 1983.

KRAMMER, ARNOLD. "Germans Against Hitler," *Journal of Contemporary History*, 4, 1969, 2, pp. 65–82.

KRIVITSKY, W.G. *I Was Stalin's Agent*. London: Hamilton, 1939.

LAMOUR, PHILLIPE and CAYETTE, ANDRÉ. *Sauvons la France en Espagne*. Paris: Baudinière, 1937.

LANDIS, ARTHUR. *The Abraham Lincoln Brigade*. New York: The Citadel Press, 1967.

LARDNER, RING, JR. *The Lardners*. New York: Harper and Row, 1976.

Las Brigadas Internacionales. Madrid: Oficina Informativa Española, 1948.

LAST, JEF. *The Spanish Tragedy*, D. Hallett, trans. London: Routledge, 1939 [1938].

LAWSON, DON. *The Abraham Lincoln Brigade: Americans fighting Fascism in the Spanish Civil War*. New York: Crowell, 1989.

LEAGUE OF NATIONS. *Official Journal, Special Supplement, Number 183*, Records of the Assembly, 19th Session, 21 September 1938.

LEE, LAURIE. *A Moment of War*. London: Viking, 1991.

LEED, ERIC J. *No Man's Land: Combat and Identity in World War I*. Cambridge: Cambridge University Press, 1979.

Letters from Spain. New York: Friends of the Abraham Lincoln Brigade, 1937.

LINDEMAN, GERALD. *Embattled Courage*. New York: Free Press, 1987.

LIZÓN GADEA, ADOLFO. *Brigadas Internacionales en España*. Madrid: Editora Nacional, 1940.

LONDON, ARTHUR. *Espagne*. Paris: Français Réunis, 1955.

LYN, JOHN A. *The Bayonets of the Republic: Motivation and Tactics in the Army of Revolutionary France 1791–1794*. Urbana: University of Illinois Press, 1986.

MACDONALD, NANCY. *Homage to the Spanish Exiles: Voices from the Spanish Civil War*. New York: Insight, 1987.

MCNAIR, JOHN. *Spanish Diary*. Manchester: International Labor Party, n.d.

MACHIAVELLI, NICCOLÒ. *The Art of War*. Indianapolis: Bobbs-Merrill, 1965 [1521].

MAIDANIK, K. L. *Ispanskii Proletariat v Natsionalno-Revoliusioni Voine*. Moscow: Academy of Sciences, 1960.

MALRAUX, ANDRÉ. *L'Espoir*. Paris: Gallimard, 1937.

MANGILLI-CLIMPSON, MASSIMO. *Men of Heart of Red, White and Green.* New York: Vantage, 1985.

MARTINEZ BANDE, JOSÉ MANUEL. *Communist Intervention in the Spanish Civil War.* Madrid: Spanish Information Service, 1966.

MARX, KARL and ENGELS, FREDERICK. *Revolution in Spain.* London: Lawrence and Wishart, 1939.

MARX MEMORIAL LIBRARY. *Catalogue of the International Brigade Memorial Archive.* London: Marx Memorial Library, 1990.

MATTHEWS, HERBERT. *The Education of a Correspondent.* New York: Harcourt, 1946.

———. *Two Wars and More to Come.* New York: Carrick and Evans, 1938.

———. *The Yoke and the Arrow.* New York: Braziller, 1957.

MERRIMAN, MARION and LERUDE, WARREN. *American Commander in Spain: Robert Hale Merriman and the Abraham Lincoln Brigade.* Reno: University of Nevada Press, 1986.

MILLER, LEE. *The Story of Ernie Pyle.* New York: Viking, 1950.

MITCHELL, DAVID. *The Spanish Civil War.* London: Granada, 1982.

MONTGOMERY, DAVID. *The Fall of the House of Labor: The Workplace, the State, and American Labor Activism, 1865–1925.* Cambridge: Cambridge University Press, 1988.

MORGAN, JANE. *Conflict and Order: The Police and Labour Disputes in England and Wales, 1900–1939.* Oxford: Oxford University Press, 1989.

MULGAN, JOHN. *Man Alone.* Auckland: Longman, 1939.

NELSON, STEVE. *The Volunteers.* New York: Masses and Mainstream, 1953.

NELSON, S., BARRETT, J.R., and RUCK, R. *Steve Nelson: American Radical.* Pittsburgh: University of Pittsburgh Press, 1981.

NENNI, PIETRO. *Espagne.* Milan: Edizioni del Gallo, 1958.

NORTH, JOSEPH. *Men in the Ranks.* New York: Friends of the Abraham Lincoln Brigades, 1939.

NOTHCOMB, PAUL. *Belges dans les tranchées d'Espagne.* Brussels: Amicale des combattants d'Espagne, 1938.

ORWELL, GEORGE. *Homage to Catalonia.* London: Secker and Warburg, 1959.

———. Review of John Sommerfield's *Volunteer in Spain, Collected Essays, Journalism, and Letters,* 1: 1920–1940. Harmondsworth: Penguin, 1971 [1939], p. 322.

———. *The Road to Wigan Pier.* Harmondsworth: Penguin, 1982 [1937].

PACCIARDI, RANDOLFO. *Il Battaglione Garibaldi.* Lugano: Nuove Edizioni di Capolago, 1938.

PALACIO, LEO. *1936: La Maldonne Espagnole: Où la Guerre d'Espagne comme Répétition Générale du Deuxième Conflit Mondial.* Paris: Editions Privat, 1986.

PALMER, NELLIE, et al. *Australians in Spain.* Rev. ed. Sydney: Current Books, 1948.

PARRY, HUGH JONES. "The Spanish Civil War: A Study in American Public Opinion, Propaganda, and Pressure Groups." Unpublished thesis, University of Southern California, 1949.

PAYNE, STANLEY G. *The Franco Regime, 1936–1975.* Madison: University of Wisconsin Press, 1987.

———. *Politics and the Military in Modern Spain.* Stanford: Stanford University Press, 1967.

———. *The Spanish Revolution.* London: Weidenfeld, 1970.

PENCHIENATI, CARLO. *Brigate Internazionali in Spagne: Delitti della "Cheka" Communista.* Milan: Echi del Secolo, 1950.

PÉREZ LÓPEZ, FRANCISCO. *Dark and Bloody Ground: A Guerrilla Diary of the Spanish Civil War,* Joseph D. Harris, trans. Boston: Little Brown, 1970.

PESCE, GIOVANNI. *And No Quarter: An Italian Partisan in World War II.* Athens: Ohio University Press, 1972.

PHILBY, KIM. *My Silent War.* London: Granada, 1973 [1964].

PIKE, DAVID W. *Conjecture, Propaganda, and Deceit and the Spanish Civil War: The International Crisis over Spain, 1936–1939, As Seen in the French Press.* No place given: California Institute of International Studies, 1968.

PIKE, DAVID W. *Les Français et La Guerre d'Espagne.* Paris: Presses Universitaires de France, 1975.

———. *Vae Victis! Los Republicanos Españoles Refugiados en Francia 1939–1944.* Paris: Ruédo Iberico, 1969.

PLATO *The Laches.*

POWELL, ANTHONY. *Casanova's Chinese Restaurant.* London: Heinemann, 1960.

PRAGO, ALBERT. "Jews in the International Brigades in Spain," *Jewish Currents,* February 1979, pp. 15–21 and March 1979, pp. 6–9 and 24–27.

PRESTON, PAUL. *The Spanish Civil War,* 1936–1939. London: Weidenfeld and Nicholson, 1986.

PRITTIE, TERRACE. *Willy Brandt.* London: Weidenfeld and Nicholson, 1974.

PROUST, MARCEL. *Within a Budding Grove,* S. Moncrief, trans. New York: Vintage, 1970 [1924].

RACHMAN, STANLEY J. *Fear and Courage.* San Francisco: Freeman, 1978.

REGLER, GUSTAV. *The Great Crusade,* W. Chambers and B. Mussey, trans. New York: Longmans, 1940.

———. *The Owl of Minerva,* N. Denny, trans. New York: Farrar and Strauss, 1959.

RENN, LUDWIG. *Der Spanische Krieg.* Berlin: AufbauVerlag, 1955.

RICHARDSON, R. DAN. *Comintern Army: the International Brigades and the Spanish Civil War.* Lexington: University Press of Kentucky, 1982.

ROBINSON, A. *Los Orígines de la España de Franco.* Barcelona: Exito, 1978 [1971].

RÓJO LLUCH, VINCENTE. *España Heroica.* 3rd ed. Barcelona: Ariel, 1975 [1942].

ROLFE, EDWIN. *The Lincoln Battalion.* New York: Random House, 1939.

ROMILLY, ESMOND. *Boadilla.* London: Hamish Hamilton, 1937.

ROSENSTONE, ROBERT. *Crusade of the Left.* New York: Pegasus, 1969.

ROSSELLI, CARLO. *Oggi in Spagna, Domani in Italia.* Turin: Einaudi, 1967 [1938].

RUNCIMAN, STEVEN. *A History of the Crusades.* Cambridge: Cambridge University Press, 1957.

RUST, WILLIAM. *Britons in Spain.* New York: International, 1939.

SAINT-EXUPÉRY, ANTOINE DE. *Wind, Sand and Stars,* Lewis Galaniere, trans. New York: Harcourt, 1940.

SALAS LARRAZABAL, RAMÓN. *Historia del Ejército Popular de la República.* Madrid: Editora Nacional, 1973.

SARTRE, JEAN-PAUL. "La République du Silence," *Situations III.* 2nd ed. Paris: Gallimard, 1949.

SCHLATTER, R., ed. *Hobbes's Thucydides.* New Brunswick: Rutgers University Press, 1975 [1651].

SCHLEIMANN, J. "The Life and Work of Willi Müzenberg," *Survey,* April 1965, 55: 78–79.

SCHLESINGER, ARTHUR. *New York Times, Book Review,* 6 February 1983, p. 3.

SCHLICK, MORTIZ. Problems of Ethics, D. Rynin, trans. New York: Dover, 1961 [1939].

SIMEON VIDARTE, JUAN. *Todos Fuimos Culpables: Testimonio de un Socialista Español.* Barcelona: Ediciones Grijalbo, 1978.

SIMON, CLAUDE. *The Georgics.* London: Calder, 1989.

———. "Interview with Claude Simon: Autobiography, the Novel, and Politics," *Review of Contemporary Fiction,* 5, 1984, 1, pp. 4–13.

———. *La Palace.* Paris: Editions de Minuit, 1962.

SIMPSON, JOHN HOPE. *Refugees: A Review of the Situation Since September 1938.* London: Royal Institute of International Affairs, June 1939.

SINCLAIR, UPTON. *No Pasarán!* London: Werner Lawrie, 1937.

SIQUEIROS, DAVID ALFARO. *Me Llamaban el Coronelazo.* Mexico: Biografias Gandes, 1977.

SMITH, HAROLD. "Action at Brunete," Alvah Bessie, ed. *The Heart of Spain.* New York: Veterans of the Abraham Lincoln Brigade, 1952.

SMITH, LOIS E. *Mexico and the Spanish Republicans.* Berkeley: University of California Press, 1955.

SMOLER, FREDERIC. "The Secret of the Soldiers Who Didn't Shoot," *American Heritage*, 40, 1989, 2, pp. 37–45.

SOMMERFIELD, JOHN. *Volunteer in Spain.* New York: Knopf, 1937.

SOREL, GEORGES. *Reflections on Violence*, T. Hulme and J. Roth, trans. New York: Collier, 1950 [1906].

SOUTHWORTH, HERBERT. *Guernica! Guernica!* Berkeley: University of California Press, 1977.

"Spain," *Economist*, 10 October 1936, pp. 62–63.

SPIEGEL, HERBERT. "Psychiatric Observations in the Tunisian Campaign," *American Journal of Orthopsychiatry*, 14, 1944, p. 381.

SPRIANO, PAOLO. *Storia del Partito Communiste Italiano.* Turin: G. Einaudi, 1970.

STANSKY, PETER and ABRAHAMS WILLIAM. *Journey to the Frontier.* London: Constable, 1966.

STARÓBIN, JOSEPH. *The Life and Death of an American Hero: The Story of Dave Doran.* New York: New Age, 1938.

STERN, LOUIS. *Beyond Death and Exile.* Cambridge: Harvard University Press, 1979.

STEWART, CAMERON. "Summoned to the Eternal Field: An Inquiry into the Development and Composition of the Abraham Lincoln Brigade in the Spanish Civil War, 1936-1939." Unpublished PhD dissertation, Claremont Graduate School, 1972.

STORE, HENRI. *De Retour d'Espagna.* Paris: Jeunesse de France, 1938.

STOUFFER, SAMUEL A., et al. *The American Soldier: Combat and its Aftermath.* Princeton: Princeton University Press, 1949.

SYMONS, JULIAN. *The Thirties: A Dream Revolved.* London: Cresset, 1975 [1960].

SZINDA, GUSTAV. *Die XI Brigade.* Berlin: Verlag des Ministeriums für National Verteidigung, 1950.

SZUREK, ALEXANDER. *The Shattered Dream*, Jacques and Hilda Grunblatt, trans. New York: Columbia University Press, 1989.

TAMAMES, RAMON et al. *La Guerra Civil Española: Una Reflexion Moral 50 años despures.* Barcelona: Editorial Paneta, 1986.

THOMAS, HUGH. *La Guerra Civil Española, 1936–1939.* Barcelona: Ediciones Exito, 1978.

———. *The Spanish Civil War.* 3rd ed. Harmondsworth: Penguin, 1977.

THOREZ, MAURICE. *Fils du Peuple.* Paris: Editions Sociales, 1960.

THUCYDIDES. *The Peloponnesian War*, Book 3, Ch. 81–82.

TISA, JOHN. *Recalling the Good Fight.* South Hadley: Bergin & Garvey, 1985.

TOGLIATTI, PALMIRO. *Le Parti Communiste Italien*, R. Paris, trans. Paris: Maspero, 1961.

TORRIENTE-BRAU, PABLO DE LA. *En España, Peleando con los Milicianos.* Mexico: Editorial Grijalbo, 1972.

TRILLING, LIONEL. *The Middle of the Journey.* New York: Viking, 1947.

TUDOR, HENRY. *Political Myth.* London: Macmillan, 1971.

TUNON DE LARA, MANUEL. *La Guerra Civil Española.* Barcelona: Editorial Labor, 1985.

ULAM, ADAM. *Expansion and Coexistence.* 2nd ed. New York: Praeger, 1975.

U.S. CONGRESS, 83rd Congress, Senate, Committee on the Judiciary, Sub-Committee to Investigate the Administration of the Internal Security Act, *Hearings on Interlocking Subversion in Government Departments*, 1st Session, 1953.

VALLEAU, MARJORIE A. *The Spanish Civil War in American and European Films.* Ann Arbor: University Microfilm Research Press, 1982.

VALTIN, JAN. *Out of the Night.* London: Heinemann, 1941.

VEGA GONZALEZ, ROBERTO. *Cadetes Méxicanos en la Guerra de España.* Mexico: Compania General de Ediciones, 1954.

VERRIER, ANTHONY. *Through the Looking Glass.* London: Cape, 1983.

VOROS, SANDOR. *American Commissar.* Philadelphia: Chilton & Co., 1961.

Vrijwilligers voor de Vriheid: Belgische Anti-Fasicsten in de Spanse Burgeroolag. Amersfoort: Kritak, 1978.

WALZER, MICHAEL. "The Obligation to Die for the State," *Obligations*. Cambridge: Harvard University Press, 1970.
WATSON, KEITH S. *Single to Spain*. New York: Dutton, 1937.
"WAYFARER." *The International Brigade*. Sussex: Ditching Press, n.d.
WEBER, MAX. "Religious Rejections of the World and Their Directions," *From Max Weber*, H. Gerth and C.W. Mills, eds. New York: Oxford University Press, 1946.
WEINSTEIN, IRVING. *The Cruel Years*. London: Bailey Bros., 1974.
WEINTRAUB, STANLEY. *The Last Great Cause*. London: Allen and Unwin, 1968.
WINTRINGHAM, TOM. *English Captain*. London: Faber and Faber, 1939.
"Withdrawal of Non-Spanish Combatants from Spain," *Official Journal of the League of Nations*, 104th Session of the Council, January 1939, p. 132.
WOLIN, RICHARD. *The Politics of Being: The Political Thought of Martin Heidegger*. New York: Columbia University Press, 1990.
WOOD, NEAL. *Communism and British Intellectuals*. London: Gollancz, 1959.
WYDEN, PETER. *The Passionate War*. New York: Simon & Schuster, 1983.
YATES, JAMES. *Mississippi to Madrid: Memoir of a Black American in the Abraham Lincoln Brigade*. Seattle: Open Hand, 1989.
YDEWALLE, CHARLES D'. *An Interlude in Spain*. London: Readers Union, 1946.
ZSCHKKE, HELMUT. *Die Schweize und der spanische Bürgerkreig*. Zürich: Limmat, 1976.

Name Index

Subject Index

www.ingramcontent.com/pod-product-compliance
Lightning Source LLC
Chambersburg PA
CBHW080926100426
42812CB00007B/2380

9780871692122